南無本師釋迦牟尼佛

NAMO FUNDAMENTAL TEACHER SHAKYAMUNI BUDDHA

佛像：國立故宮博物院藏品　Buddha image, National Palace Museum Archives

萬佛聖城日誦儀規

SAGELY CITY OF 10,000 BUDDHAS
DALLY RECITATION HANDBOOK

萬佛聖城日誦儀規

The Daily Recitation Handbook in Sagely City Of Ten Thousand Buddhas

Published and translated by:

Buddhist Text Translation Society

1777 Murchison Drive,

Burlingame, CA 94010-4504

http:\\www.drba.org

First Printing: 1980   Second Printing: 1982

Third Printing: 1985   Fourth Printing: 1989

Fifth Printing: 1991   Sixth Printing: 2001

Seventh Printing: 2002

07 06 05 04 03 02   10 9 8 7 6 5 4 3

ISBN 0-88139-857-8

Printed in Taiwan, R.O.C.

六大條款：

不爭、不貪、不求、
不自私、不自利、不妄語。

三大宗旨：

凍死不攀緣，餓死不化緣，窮死不求緣，
隨緣不變，不變隨緣，抱定我們三大宗旨。
捨命為佛事，造命為本事，正命為僧事，
即事明理，明理即事，推行祖師一脈心傳。

The Six Ideals:

No fighting, no greed, no seeking, no selfishness,
no pursuing personal advantage, and no lying.

The Three Great Principles:

Freezing, we do not scheme.

Starving, we do not beg.

Dying of poverty, we ask for nothing.

According with conditions, we do not change.

Not changing, we accord with conditions.

We adhere firmly to our three great principles.

We renounce our lives to do the Buddha's work.

We take the responsibility to mold our own destinies.

We rectify our lives to fulfill the Sanghan's role.

Encountering specific matters, we understand the principles.

Understanding the principles, we apply them in specific matters.

We carry on the single pulse of the Patriarchs' mind-transmission.

TABLE OF CONTENTS
目次

PREFACE

THE ESSENTIALS OF MORNING AND EVENING RECITATION

From limitless time until now, we have carried with us the seeds of karma. Karma brings its corresponding retribution. In the *Earth Store Sutra* the Buddha explains, "I see that every single movement or stirring of thought on the part of living beings of Jambudvipa is an offense." From such seeds, more seeds are produced, and from karma more karma is accumulated. If we don't rely on meditation and recitation ceremonies, how can we hope to eradicate such offenses? This is especially true for those who have set forth from the home-life and entered the Way, who neither serve the government nor assume other livelihoods, but who solely rely on the offerings of donors. If those people do not apply effort in cultivating the Way, then it will be difficult for them to digest the offerings made by faithful donors. The Great Dhyana Master Jan Jou said, "If one doesn't accomplish the Way in this very life, then one will have to repay the debts accrued by wearing horns and fur in the future."

Moreover, Morning Recitation and Evening Recitation are performed not only for the sake of benefiting oneself, but also for the sake of enabling living beings throughout the Dharma Realm to attain Anuttarasamyaksambodhi (Unsurpassed, Proper, Equal, and Right Enlightenment). How can we overlook such an important matter?

As participants in recitation ceremonies, we should carry our bodies erect and never be casual. We should sound each syllable of every recitation passage, our minds concentrated and unmoving, from the beginning to the end of the entire recitation. Then the Three Karmas (of body, speech, and mind) and the Three Stoppings (the stopping that leads to the meshing with True Substance; the stopping of expedients according with conditions; and the stopping of the two extremes) will be in harmony. If we can maintain an attitude of respect in our physical demeanors, if we recite with clear and crisp voices, and if we formulate in our minds the contemplations in keeping with the passages as we recite them, then the Three Karmas will mesh with the Three Contemplations (of emptiness, falseness, and the Middle). The Three Stoppings and Three Contemplations

will then become like a mirror reflecting the myriad
images, and our minds and the Sages' mind can come
together in an intertwining response, just as when
water is poured into water, and empty space unites
with empty space, so that our merit fills the Dharma Realm, and our measures become equal to the void.

MORNING RECITATION

Cultivators should first study the recitation
ceremonies to comprehend their deeper intent. That
facilitates our contemplating while reciting and
upholding. We should familiarize ourselves with
the liturgy. Otherwise, in the face of the various
states that could arise during recitation, our
minds would become scattered and we would not suc-
ceed in reaching a proper state of contemplation.

In the early morning, when the myriad states
have not arisen, when our minds are quiet and tranquil, we should awaken and get dressed and immediately commence the recitation of the *Shurangama
Mantra of the Buddha's Summit*. This mantra serves to
regulate the five desires before they have had time
to arise so that our minds quickly penetrate and
directly reveal the wonderful nature of the Treasury
of the Thus Come One as it truly is. As it is said,
"Still and unmoving, there is a response and a
spontaneous penetration."

Next we go on to recite the *Great Compassion Mantra,* which has the ability to cleanse the mind of
filth. After enlightening to the compassion of mutual identity with all things, we recite the *Ten
Small Mantras*: we turn the Dharma Wheel with the *As-
You-Will Wheel King Dharani.* The *Disaster-Eradicating Auspicious Spirit Mantra* prevents calamities and brings
good fortune. That is followed with the *Meritorious
Virtue Jeweled Mountain Mantra.* Auspiciousness in our
minds, we dwell on the Mountain of the Dharma-nature
and obtain the jewel of meritorious virtue. The
Jwun Ti Spirit Mantra completely dispels the obstructions regarding phenomena, so that the Dharma-nature
can be revealed in its fullness. Next, we intone
the *Sagely Resolute Light King Dharani of Limitless Life
Mantra,* to entreat the Thus Come One Light King to
bestow wisdom-life upon us. Our wisdom-lives having come forth, we go on to intone the *Medicine Master
True Words for Anointing the Crown of the Head,* which further enhances our wisdom so that it becomes like
crystal encompassing a jeweled moon within. At

this point, light pours forth, anointing the crowns
of our heads. With the recitation of the *Gwan Yin
Efficacious Response True Words*, we mesh with Gwan Yin's
efficacious ear-organ and the entire Dharma Realm,
and the magical responses are boundless. The *True
Words of Seven Buddhas for Eradicating Offenses* roots out at
their very source the beginningless karma that im-
pedes the brilliant light of our wisdom and that
prevents it from shining forth. The *Mantra for Rebirth
in the Pure Land* affects our karma, which is originally
pure, as we request Amita Buddha to anoint our
heads as certification that we will be reborn in
the Pure Land. The last of the *Ten Small Mantras*,
the *Good Goddess Mantra*, culminates the sublime contemplations described above.

Together those mantras serve to quicken the
wonderful functioning of the Dharma-nature and the
fulfillment of our wishes. However, we should know
that although we may enter a wonderful state of
contemplation by reciting those mantras, they must
be recited with a single-minded concentration in
order for the contemplations to be actualized.

Further, to prevent us from becoming attached
to those states of contemplation, the *Heart of Prajna
Paramita Sutra* is recited. That Sutra points directly
to the mind's substance in its fundamental emptiness, by proclaiming that ultimately there is no
wisdom that can be obtained; even the mark of emptiness itself is empty. Thus, the state of wisdom is
revealed in its entirety--not one; not many. The
two extremes are eliminated and the Three Contemplations are perfectly fused.

Those twelve mantras of the Secret School and
one Sutra of the Apparent Teaching share a mutual
identity and are mutually encompassing.

As a means to attain actual certification, we
next recite the Buddha's name. In the recitation
of one Buddha's name, the names of all Buddhas are
implied, because of the mutual inclusion of the one
with the many and the perfect fusion between self
and others.

Next the *Ten Great Vows of Universal Worthy Bodhisattva* are recited. As we recite, we should contemplate that these great vows are our own vows,
and that they must direct our every thought, word,
and deed throughout all time. Universal Worthy
Bodhisattva's explanation of the *Ten Great Vows* in
Chapter 40 of the *FLOWER ADORNMENT SUTRA* should be studied so that we may become familiar with the vows'
meaning and scope.

Morning Recitation is concluded with the Three
Refuges, as we return the merit generated from
reciting the mantras and Sutra of the Secret and
Apparent Teachings to the Triple Jewel of our own
natures. We don't seek refuge by relying on any-
thing external to our own natures. The great, all-
encompassing Dharma-door of the One Mind is completely manifested. In this way, everything that
we encounter belongs to the Treasury of the Thus
Come One.

* * * *

EVENING RECITATION

When evening comes, we should gather in
the myriad virtues and dedicate them to the Pure
Land. This is known as "creating merit at the
beginning and returning the virtue at the end."
And so one begins the recitation with the Amitabha
Sutra. This Sutra causes us to awaken to the sublime
primary and dependent rewards of the Land of Ultimate Bliss. We are exhorted to practice the Dharma
of reciting the Buddha's name, as it is the proper
cause for living beings to beget loathing for the
extreme filth of the Saha world and aspire toward
the utter purity of the Pure Land. With the Rebirth Mantra we beseech Amita Buddha to anoint the
crowns of our heads, to pull out the fundamental
cause of our karmic obstacles, and to guarantee
that we will certainly be reborn in his land.
If the practitioner's mind is admixed with
defilement, his obstacles are not easily eradicated,
and so we rely on the Eighty-eight Buddhas Repentance
Ceremony, with its verses of Universal Worthy Bodhisattva, to expand upon the Ten Kings of Vows recited
earlier in the day. With those recitations, both
relative truths and Absolute Truth are perfectly
fused and the Sea-seal Samadhi is realized.
Both the Amitabha Sutra and the Eighty-eight
Buddhas Repentance Ceremony are followed with the Meng
Mountain Offering, bringing vast benefit to beings
of the lower realms, and the Prajna Paramita
Heart Sutra is recited to affect their understanding that both offenses and blessings have no host
and that people and dharmas are empty, so that they
may come to realize the True Reality of all dharmas.
Once again, the Rebirth Mantra is recited, as we
rely upon Amita Buddha to release light to anoint
the crowns of our heads and protect us. We

pray that the six paths transform into the Pure
Land, and that all sentient creatures immediately
be certified to the Ten Grounds.

Next, we recite the Buddha's name as we
transfer merit and seek actual certification.
We conclude with the *Three Refuges*. All goodness
gained throughout the day, from beginning to end,
is returned to the Triple Jewel of our own natures,
and we vow that the living beings throughout the
Dharma Realm will all bring forth the unsurpassed
resolve and together perfect the Wisdom of all
Modes.

—by National Master Yu Lin (died 1676)
of the Ching Dynasty

序言

　　吾人從有生以來，即有業種，由業由窮。舉心動念，無非是罪，六道障緣，流入那。況緇流不耕不織，唯賴檀施。趙州大師：若有念止明契，纖如等量。業能出三界，然能交道法界。口要與音相應，三業與聲相感，可謂功薄。身要端肅不移，則三業無惰。心能作觀，如鏡鑑象，則三業無惰。地藏經云：以業禮懺，託事王侯，功則難消。信道披毛戴角還。種禪不道不了，今生招報，匪道不日。

　　凡念誦者，身要端肅不移，則三業與聲相感，可謂功薄。口要與音相應，然能交道法界。意要注身隨文作觀，如鏡鑑象，我心與聖心，以空合空。此則能三遺。若能三遺水，徹至意止不投空矣。貫合，誦相爽，三毫水虛空矣。

早課綸貫

　　行人先究全課文義貫通，以便誦雜之心顯而。否則萬境未動，嚴頂楞嚴。純熟，直。定心於晨早，念佛心精通溜，不動感。故於晨早即起，速期性。所謂寂然不動，感而。整衣即萌，如真如性。復當想於真，難成。觀想怙五欲妙，治五藏妙。行起觀，觀心。持起心隙，咒，如來藏。持心隙，咒如來。

遂通也。加持大悲神咒，滌諸心垢。如意寶輪王咒，心垢既淨，悟同體之大悲，轉如意之法輪。消災吉祥咒，災消吉至，法輪更得自在。功德寶山咒，吉既心現，居法性山獲功德寶。準提咒，猶恐法性難顯，深消理障，方使果遂。決定光明王咒，得果遂已，即求光明王如來之智壽。藥師灌頂咒，智壽已發，更如琉璃內含寶月，流光灌頂。觀音靈感咒，深契觀音法界耳根靈感無窮，如月照而且寂寂而且照。七佛滅罪咒，猶恐本業朦朧，智月難明，須滅無始業根。往生咒，根本業淨，希彌陀灌頂，如證淨土。善女天咒，總上妙觀，共成法性妙用，所願果遂。然諸密咒，既入妙觀，故加般若心經，直指心體本空，無觀境可得，空相亦空，智境歷然，非一非異，二邊絕待，三觀圓融。

　　以上十二密咒，及一顯經，互該互攝。以此功德，總申回向三寶龍天，普及四恩三有，八難三途，國泰民安，檀增福慧，三門清淨，十地頓超，故結回向偈，然後念佛，以求實證。當知念一佛則諸佛咸趣一佛。一多互攝，自他相融。末以三皈,全收上諸顯密功德,結成自性三寶,不假外皈,全顯一心大總相法門.爾則何遇非如來藏哉.

暮課綸貫

若於暮時,應總攝眾善,歸趣淨土。故於暮境,特勸娑婆希果依正,即我必求,乃入前蒙主陀,即結歸同圓伽藍等,消歸自心。

之妙厭離往生咒根本非,不為菩提重,禮重設福蒙有證,消除罪障。正欲眾生淨業障障心,今發普賢印心三昧,誦往生咒,變為淨土,以取上諸天。

歸德依正全除業雜障心,得同根普賢三昧,誦心經,般若實相,六道回向,有諸眾生,一一無獻諸天,以安正道。

於始悟正,極樂因邦,拔人行,云我眾始通融冥,了頂然後,始當時祝三寶。

極樂正因,取我往生。雖然文與懺,二濟雙灌地,從寶始當時祝三寶禦。

造彌陀經,使名號欣取往生。發願法界無融幽冥,了頂然從寶始當時祝三寶。

可謂念專之彌陀,決懺至八願,山人舒證三皈三性種神。

造陀經持極陀決懺,廣法光十皈,地,擁護。

JEWELED CENSER PRAISE
寶鼎讚

寶 bau 鼎 ding 熱 re

名 ming 香 syang

普 pu 徧 byan

十 shr

方 fang

虔 chyan 誠 cheng 奉 feng

獻 syan 法 fa 中 jung

王 wang

端 dwan 為 wei 民 ming 主 ju

1

祝ju 萬wan 歲swei

地di 久jyou 天tyan

長jang 端dwan 為wei

世shr 界jye 祝ju 和he

平ping 地di

久jyou 天tyan 長jang

南na 無mwo 香syang 雲yun 蓋gai

菩pu 薩sa

1.2

摩mwo 訶he

3.

薩sa 訶he 薩sa

MORNING RECITATION
朝 時 課 誦
Jau shr ke sung

*(On the first and fifteenth of each lunar month, begin with
the JEWELED CENSOR PRAISE, page 1)* 朔望時則先唱寶鼎讚/頁

SHURANGAMA MANTRA
楞 嚴 咒
Leng yan jou

NAMO SHURANGAMA ASSEMBLY OF BUDDHAS AND BODHISATTVAS. (3x)

南 無 楞 嚴 會 上 佛 菩 薩 (三稱)

Na mwo leng yan hwei shang fwo pu sa (3x)

O DEEP AND WONDROUS DHARANI UNMOVING HONORED ONE

妙 湛 總 持 不 動 尊

Myau jan dzung chr bu dung dzwun

SUPREME SHURANGAMA APPEARS MOST RARELY IN THE WORLD.

首 楞 嚴 王 世 希 有

Shou leng yan wang shr syi you

EXTINGUISHING DELUDED THOUGHTS FROM COUNTLESS KALPAS
PAST.

銷 我 億 劫 顛 倒 想

Syau wo yi jye dyan dau syang

I NEEDN'T PASS THROUGH AEONS TILL THE DHARMA BODY'S GAINED.

不 歷 僧 祇 獲 法 身

Bu li seng chi hwo fa shen

I WISH TO NOW ATTAIN THE WAY: AND AS THE DHARMA KING.

願 今 得 果 成 寶 王

Ywan jin de gwo cheng bau wang

I'LL THEN RETURN TO RESCUE BEINGS MORE THAN GANGES'
SANDS.

還 度 如 是 恒 沙 眾

Hwan du ru shr heng sha jung

3

THIS DEEP RESOLVE I OFFER TO THE MYRIAD BUDDHAS' LANDS,

将此深心奉塵刹

Jyang tsz shen syin feng chen cha

AND THUS ENDEAVOR TO REPAY THE BUDDHA'S BOUNDLESS GRACE.

是則名為報佛恩

Shr dze ming wei bau fwo en

I NOW REQUEST THE BHAGAVAN TO CERTIFY MY QUEST:

伏請世尊為證明

Fu ching shr dzwun wei jeng ming

TO ENTER FIRST THE EVIL WORLD--THE FIVE TURBIDITIES;

五濁惡世誓先入

Wu jwo e shr shr syan ru

IF YET A SINGLE BEING'S NOT ACCOMPLISHED BUDDHAHOOD

如一眾生未成佛

Ru yi jung sheng wei cheng fwo

ACCORDINGLY I ALSO MUST RENOUNCE NIRVANA'S BLISS.

終不於此取泥洹

Jung bu yu tsz chyu ni hwan

O GREAT IN COURAGE, GREAT IN POWER, GREAT COMPASSIONATE ONE!

大雄大力大慈悲

Da syung da li da tsz bei

I PRAY WOULD NOW UNCOVER AND DISPEL MY SUBT'LEST DOUBTS.

希更審除微細惑

Syi geng shen chu wei syi hwei

THUS CAUSE ME QUICKLY TO ATTAIN SUPREME ENLIGHTENMENT,

令我早登無上覺

Ling wo dzau deng wu shang jyau

AND SIT WITHIN THE BODHIMANDAS OF THE TENFOLD REALMS

4

於十方界坐道場
Yu shr fang jye dzwo dau chang

AND EVEN COULD THE NATURE OF SHUNYATA MELT AWAY
舜若多性可銷亡
Shwun rau dwo sying ke syau wang

MY VAJRA-LIKE SUPREME RESOLVE WOULD STILL REMAIN UNMOVED.
爍迦羅心無動轉
Shwo jya la syin wu dung jwan

NA MO ETERNALLY ABIDING BUDDHAS OF THE TEN DIRECTIONS.
南無常住十方佛◎
Na mwo chang ju shr fang fwo

NA MO ETERNALLY ABIDING DHARMA OF THE TEN DIRECTIONS.
南無常住十方法
Na mwo chang ju shr fang fa

NA MO ETERNALLY ABIDING SANGHA OF THE TEN DIRECTIONS.
南無常住十方僧
Na mwo chang ju shr fang seng

NAMO SHAKYAMUNI BUDDHA.
南無釋迦牟尼佛
Na mwo shr jya mu ni fwo

NA MO SUPREME SHURANGAMA OF THE BUD DHA'S SUMMIT.
南無佛頂首楞嚴
Na mwo fwo ding shou leng yan

NA MO GWAN SHR YIN BODHISATTVA.
南無觀世音菩薩
Na mwo gwan shr yin pu sa

NAMO VAJRA TREASURY BODHISATTVA
南無金剛藏菩薩
Na mwo jin gang dzang pu sa

5

AT THAT TIME THE WORLD HONORED ONE FROM THE FLESH MOUND
AT THE CROWN OF HIS HEAD RELEASED A HUNDRED-JEWELLED
LIGHT AND A THOUSAND PETALLED RARE LOTUS AROSE FROM THE
MIDST OF THE LIGHT.

爾時世尊. 從肉髻中. 涌百寶光.
光中涌出. 千葉寶蓮.

Er shr shr dzwun, tsung rou ji jung, yung bai bau gwang,
gwang jung yung chu, chyan ye bau lyan,

SEATED WITHIN THE PRECIOUS FLOWER WAS A TRANSFORMATION
BODY OF THE THUS COME ONE, WHOSE CROWN IN TURN EMITTED TEN
RAYS OF THE HUNDRED-JEWELLED EFFULGENCE.

有化如來. 坐寶華中. 頂放十道.
百寶光明.

You hwa ru lai, dzwo bau hwa jung, ding fang shr dau, bai
bau gwang ming,

ALL THE MYRIAD LIGHTS SHONE 'ROUND ABOUT, EVERYWHERE
REVEALING SECRET TRACE VAJRA SPIRITS, MANY AS THE SANDS OF
TEN GANGES RIVERS. EACH HOLDING ALOFT A MOUNTAIN AND
WIELDING A PESTLE, THEY PERVADED THE REALM OF EMPTY SPACE.

一一光明. 皆徧示現. 十恒河沙.
金剛密迹. 擎山持杵. 徧虛空界.

Yi yi gwang ming, jye byan shr syan, shr heng he sha, jin
gang mi ji, ching shan chr chu, byan syu kung jye.

THE GREAT ASSEMBLY GAZED UPWARD AT ONCE FILLED WITH FEAR
AND ADMIRATION. SEEKING THE BUDDHA'S KIND PROTECTION
THEY SINGLE-MINDEDLY LISTENED

大眾仰觀. 畏愛兼抱. 求佛哀祐.
一心聽佛.

Da jung yang gwan, wei ai jyan bau, chyou fwo ai you, yi
syin ting fwo,

AS, STREAMING LIGHT AT THE BUD DHA'S INVISIBLE CROWN
THE TRANSFORMATION THUS COME ONE PROCLAIMED THE SPIRITUAL
MAN TRA:☉

無見頂相. 放光如來. 宣說神咒.

Wu jyan ding syang, fang gwang ru lai, sywan shwo shen jou:

6

I.   （第一會）

1) NA MWO SA DAN TWO 南無薩怛他

2) SU CHYE DWO YE 蘇伽多耶

3) E LA HE DI 阿羅訶帝

4) SAN MYAU SAN PU TWO SYE 三藐三菩陀寫

5) NA MWO SA DAN TWO 南無薩怛他

6) FWO TWO JYU JR SHAI NI SHAN 佛陀俱胝瑟尼釤

7) NA MWO SA PE 南無薩婆

8) BWO TWO BWO DI 勃陀勃地

9) SA DWO PI BI 薩跢鞞弊

10) NA MWO SA DWO NAN 南無薩多南

11) SAN MYAU SAN PU TWO 三藐三菩陀

12) JYU JR NAN 俱知南

13) SWO SHE LA PE JYA 娑舍囉婆迦

14) SENG CHYE NAN 僧伽喃

15) NA MWO LU JI E LWO HAN 南無盧雞阿羅漢
   DWO NAN 跢喃

16) NA MWO SU LU DWO BWO 南無蘇盧多波
   NWO NAN 那喃

17) NA MWO SWO JYE LI TWO 南無娑羯唎陀
   CHYE MI NAN 伽彌喃

18) NA MWO LU JI SAN MYAU 南無盧雞三藐
   CHYE DWO NAN 伽跢喃

7

19)	SAN MYAU CHYE BE LA	三貌伽波囉
20)	DI BWO DWO NWO NAN	底波多那喃
21)	NA MWO TI PE LI SHAI NAN	南無提婆離瑟報
22)	NA MWO SYI TWO YE	南無悉陀耶
23)	PI DI YE	毗地耶
24)	TWO LA LI SHAI NAN	陀囉離瑟報
25)	SHE PWO NU	舍波奴
26)	JYE LA HE	揭囉訶
27)	SWO HE SWO LA MWO TWO NAN	娑訶娑囉摩他喃
28)	NA MWO BA LA HE MWO NI	南無跋囉訶摩尼
29)	NA MWO YIN TWO LA YE	南無因陀囉耶
30)	NA MWO PE CHYE PE DI	南無婆伽婆帝
31)	LU TWO LA YE	盧陀囉耶
32)	WU MWO BWO DI	烏摩般帝
33)	SWO SYI YE YE	娑醯夜耶
34)	NA MWO PE CHYE PE DI	南無婆伽婆帝
35)	NWO LA YE	那囉野
36)	NA YE	拏耶
37)	PAN JE MWO HE SAN MWO	槃遮摩訶三慕
	TWO LA	陀囉
38)	NA MWO SYI JYE LI DWO YE	南無悉羯唎多耶
39)	NA MWO PE CHYE PE DI	南無婆伽婆帝
40)	MWO HE JYA LA YE	摩訶迦羅耶
41)	DI LI BWO LA NA	地唎般剌那

8

42)	CHYE LA PI TWO LA	伽囉毗陀囉
43)	BWO NA JYA LA YE	波拏迦囉耶
44)	E DI MU DI	阿地目帝
45)	SHR MWO SHE NWO NI	尸摩舍那泥
46)	PE SYI NI	婆悉泥
47)	MWO DAN LI CHYE NA	摩怛唎伽拏
48)	NA MWO SYI JYE LI DWO YE	南無悉羯唎多耶
49)	NA MWO PE CHYE PE DI	南無婆伽婆帝
50)	DWO TWO CHYE DWO JYU LA YE	多他伽跢俱囉耶
51)	NA MWO BE TOU MWO JYU LA YE	南無般頭摩俱囉耶
52)	NA MWO BA SHE LA JYU LA YE	南無跋闍囉俱囉耶
53)	NA MWO MWO NI JYU LA YE	南無摩尼俱囉耶
54)	NA MWO CHYE SHE JYU LA YE	南無伽闍俱囉耶
55)	NA MWO PE CHYE PE DI	南無婆伽婆帝
56)	DI LI CHA	帝唎茶
57)	SHU LA SYI NA	輸囉西那
58)	BWO LA HE LA NA LA SHE YE	波囉訶囉拏囉闍耶
59)	DWO TWO CHYE DWO YE	跢他伽多耶
60)	NA MWO PE CHYE PE DI	南無婆伽婆帝
61)	NA MWO E MI DWO PE YE	南無阿彌多婆耶
62)	DWO TWO CHYE DWO YE	跢他伽多耶

63)	E LA HE DI	阿囉訶帝
64)	SAN MYAU SAN PU TWO YE	三藐三菩陀耶
65)	NA MWO PE CHYE PE DI	南無婆伽婆帝
66)	E CHU PI YE	阿芻鞞耶
67)	DWO TWO CHYE DWO YE	跢他伽多耶
68)	E LA HE DI	阿囉訶帝
69)	SAN MYAU SAN PU TWO YE	三藐三菩陀耶
70)	NA MWO PE CHYE PE DI	南無婆伽婆帝
71)	BI SHA SHE YE	鞞沙闍耶
72)	JYU LU FEI JU LI YE	俱盧吠拄喇耶
73)	BWO LA PE LA SHE YE	般囉婆囉闍耶
74)	DWO TWO CHYE DWO YE	跢他伽多耶
75)	NA MWO PE CHYE PE DI	南無婆伽婆帝
76)	SAN BU SHR BI DWO	三補師毖多
77)	SA LYAN NAI LA LA SHE YE	薩憐捺囉剌闍耶
78)	DWO TWO CHYE DWO YE	跢他伽多耶
79)	E LA HE DI	阿囉訶帝
80)	SAN MYAU SAN PU TWO YE	三藐三菩陀耶
81)	NA MWO PE CHYE PE DI	南無婆伽婆帝
82)	SHE JI YE MU NWO YE	舍雞野母那曳
83)	DWO TWO CHYE DWO YE	跢他伽多耶
84)	E LA HE DI	阿囉訶帝
85)	SAN MYAU SAN PU TWO YE	三藐三菩陀耶
86)	NA MWO PE CHYE PE DI	南無婆伽婆帝

87)	LA DAN NA JI DU LA	剌怛那雞都囉
	SHE YE	闍耶
88)	DWO TWO CHYE DWO YE	跢他伽多耶
89)	E LA HE DI	阿囉訶帝
90)	SAN MYAU SAN PU TWO YE	三藐三菩陀耶
91)	DI PYAU	帝瓢
92)	NA MWO SA JYE LI DWO	南無薩羯唎多
93)	YI TAN PE CHYE PE DWO	翳曇婆伽婆多
94)	SA DAN TWO CHYE DU	薩怛他伽都
	SHAI NI SHAN	瑟尼釤
95)	SA DAN DWO BWO DA LAN	薩怛多般怛囕
96)	NA MWO E PE LA SHR DAN	南無阿婆囉視耽
97)	BWO LA DI	般囉帝
98)	YANG CHI LA	揚岐囉
99)	SA LA PE	薩囉婆
100)	BWO DWO JYE LA HE	部多揭囉訶
101)	NI JYE LA HE	尼羯囉訶
102)	JYE JYA LA HE NI	揭迦囉訶尼
103)	BA LA BI DI YE	跋囉毖地耶
104)	CHR TWO NI	叱陀你
105)	E JYE LA	阿迦囉
106)	MI LI JU	密唎柱
107)	BWO LI DAN LA YE	般唎怛囉耶
108)	NING JYE LI	儜揭唎

11

109)	SA LA PE	薩囉婆
110)	PAN TWO NWO	槃陀那
111)	MU CHA NI	目叉尼
112)	SA LA PE	薩囉婆
113)	TU SHAI JA	突瑟吒
114)	TU SYI FA	突悉乏
115)	BWO NA NI	般那你
116)	FA LA NI	伐囉尼
117)	JE DU LA	赭都囉
118)	SHR DI NAN	失帝南
119)	JYE LA HE	羯囉訶
120)	SWO HE SA LA RAU SHE	娑訶薩囉若闍
121)	PI DWO BENG SWO NA JYE LI	毗多崩娑那羯唎
122)	E SHAI JA BING SHE DI NAN	阿瑟吒冰舍帝南
123)	NA CHA CHA DAN LA RAU SHE	那叉剎怛囉若闍
124)	BWO LA SA TWO NA JYE LI	波囉薩陀那羯唎
125)	E SHAI JA NAN	阿瑟吒南
126)	MWO HE JYE LA HE RAU SHE	摩訶羯囉訶若闍
127)	PI DWO BENG SA NA JYE LI	毗多崩薩那羯唎
128)	SA PE SHE DU LU	薩婆舍都嚧
129)	NI PE LA RAU SHE	你婆囉若闍
130)	HU LAN TU SYI FA	呼藍突悉乏
131)	NAN JE NA SHE NI	難遮那舍尼
132)	PE SHA SHE	毖沙舍

133)	SYI DAN LA	悉怛囉
134)	E JI NI	阿吉尼
135)	WU TWO JYA LA RAU SHE	烏陀迦囉若闍
136)	E BWO LA SHR DWO JYU LA	阿般囉視多具囉
137)	MWO HE BWO LA JAN CHR	摩訶般囉戰持
138)	MWO HE DYE DWO	摩訶疊多
139)	MWO HE DI SHE	摩訶帝闍
140)	MWO HE SHWEI DWO SHE PE LA	摩訶稅多闍婆囉
141)	MWO HE BA LA PAN TWO LA	摩訶跋囉槃陀囉
142)	PE SYI NI	婆悉你
143)	E LI YE DWO LA	阿唎耶多囉
144)	PI LI JYU JR	毗唎俱知
145)	SHR PE PI SHE YE	誓婆毗闍耶
146)	BA SHE LA MWO LI DI	跋闍囉摩禮底
147)	PI SHE LU DWO	毗舍嚧多
148)	BWO TENG WANG JYA	勃騰罔迦
149)	BA SHE LA JR HE NWO E JE	跋闍囉制喝那阿遮
150)	MWO LA JR PE	摩囉制婆
151)	BWO LA JR DWO	般囉質多
152)	BA SHE LA SHAN CHR	跋闍囉擅持
153)	PI SHE LA JE	毗舍囉遮
154)	SHAN DWO SHE	扇多舍
155)	PI TI PE	鞞提婆
156)	BU SHR DWO	補視多

13

157)	SU MWO LU BWO	蘇摩嚧波
158)	MWO HE SHWEI DWO	摩訶稅多
159)	E LI YE DWO LA	阿唎耶多囉
160)	MWO HE PE LA E BWO LA	摩訶婆囉阿般囉
161)	BA SHE LA SHANG JYE LA JR PE	跋闍囉商揭囉制婆
162)	BA SHE LA JYU MWO LI	跋闍囉俱摩唎
163)	JYU LAN TWO LI	俱藍陀唎
164)	BA SHE LA HE SA DWO JE	跋闍囉喝薩多遮
165)	PI DI YE	毗地耶
166)	CHYAN JE NWO	乾遮那
167)	MWO LI JYA	摩唎迦
168)	KU SU MU	㖤蘇母
169)	PE JYE LA DWO NWO	婆羯囉跢那
170)	PI LU JE NA	鞞嚧遮那
171)	JYU LI YE	俱唎耶
172)	YE LA TU	夜囉菟
173)	SHAI NI SHAN	瑟尼釤
174)	PI JE LAN PE MWO NI JE	毗折藍婆摩尼遮
175)	BA SHE LA JYA NA JYA BWO LA PE	跋闍囉迦那迦波囉婆
176)	LU SHE NA	嚧闍那
177)	BA SHE LA DWUN JR JE	跋闍囉頓稚遮
178)	SHWEI DWO JE	稅多遮

179)	JYA MWO LA	迦摩囉
180)	CHA CHE SHR	剎奢尸
181)	BWO LA PE	波囉婆
182)	YI DI YI DI	翳帝夷帝
183)	MU TWO LA	母陀囉
184)	JYE NA	羯拏
185)	SWO PI LA CHAN	娑鞞囉懺
186)	JYWE FAN DU	掘梵都
187)	YIN TU NA MWO MWO SYE	印兔那麼麼寫
II.		(第二會)
188)	WU SYIN	烏䤙
189)	LI SHAI JYE NA	唎瑟揭拏
190)	BWO LA SHE SYI DWO	般剌舍悉多
191)	SA DAN TWO	薩怛他
192)	CHYE DU SHAI NI SHAN	伽都瑟尼釤
193)	HU SYIN DU LU YUNG	虎䤙都嚧雍
194)	JAN PE NA	瞻婆那
195)	HU SYIN DU LU YUNG	虎䤙都嚧雍
196)	SYI DAN PE NA	悉耽婆那
197)	HU SYIN DU LU YUNG	虎䤙都嚧雍
198)	BWO LA SHAI DI YE	波羅瑟地耶
199)	SAN BWO CHA	三般叉
200)	NA JYE LA	拏羯囉
201)	HU SYIN DU LU YUNG	虎䤙都嚧雍

202)	SA PE YAU CHA	薩婆藥叉
203)	HE LA CHA SWO	喝囉刹娑
204)	JYE LA HE RAU SHE	揭囉訶若闍
205)	PI TENG BENG SA NA JYE LA	毗騰崩薩那羯囉
206)	HU SYIN DU LU YUNG	虎𤲚都嚧雍
207)	JE DU LA	者都囉
208)	SHR DI NAN	尸底南
209)	JYE LA HE	揭囉訶
210)	SWO HE SA LA NAN	娑訶薩囉南
211)	PI TENG BENG SA NA LA	毗騰崩薩那囉
212)	HU SYIN DU LU YUNG	虎𤲚都嚧雍
213)	LA CHA	囉叉
214)	PE CHYE FAN	婆伽梵
215)	SA DAN TWO	薩怛他
216)	CHYE DU SHAI NI SHAN	伽都瑟尼釤
217)	BWO LA DYAN	波囉點
218)	SHE JI LI	闍吉喇
219)	MWO HE SWO HE SA LA	摩訶娑訶薩囉
220)	BWO SHU SWO HE SA LA	勃樹娑訶薩囉
221)	SHR LI SHA	室喇沙
222)	JYU JR SWO HE SA NI	俱知娑訶薩泥
223)	DI LI E BI TI SHR PE LI DWO	帝隸阿弊提視婆喇多
224)	JA JA YING JYA	吒吒罌迦
225)	MWO HE BA SHE LU TWO LA	摩訶跋闍嚧陀囉

16

226)	DI LI PU PE NA	帝唎菩婆那
227)	MAN CHA LA	曼茶囉
228)	WU SYIN	烏鈝
229)	SWO SYI DI	莎悉帝
230)	BWO PE DU	薄婆都
231)	MWO MWO	麼麼
232)	YIN TWO NA MWO MWO SYE	印兔那麼麼寫
III.		(第三會)
233)	LA SHR PE YE	囉闍婆夜
234)	JU LA BA YE	主囉跋夜
235)	E CHI NI PE YE	阿祇尼婆夜
236)	WU TWO JYA PE YE	烏陀迦婆夜
237)	PI SHA PE YE	毗沙婆夜
238)	SHE SA DWO LA PE YE	舍薩多囉婆夜
239)	PE LA JAU JYE LA PE YE	婆囉斫羯囉婆夜
240)	TU SHAI CHA PE YE	突瑟叉婆夜
241)	E SHE NI PE YE	阿舍你婆夜
242)	E JYA LA	阿迦囉
243)	MI LI JU PE YE	密唎柱婆夜
244)	TWO LA NI BU MI JYAN	陀囉尼部彌劍
245)	BWO CHYE BWO TWO PE YE	波伽波陀婆夜
246)	WU LA JYA PE DWO PE YE	烏囉迦婆多婆夜
247)	LA SHE TAN CHA PE YE	剌闍壇茶婆夜
248)	NWO CHYE PE YE	那伽婆夜

17

249)	PI TYAU DAN PE YE	毗條怛婆夜
250)	SU BWO LA NA PE YE	蘇波囉拏婆夜
251)	YAU CHA JYE LA HE	藥叉揭囉訶
252)	LA CHA SZ JYE LA HE	囉叉私揭囉訶
253)	BI LI DWO JYE LA HE	畢唎多揭囉訶
254)	PI SHE JE JYE LA HE	毗舍遮揭囉訶
255)	BU DWO JYE LA HE	部多揭囉訶
256)	JYOU PAN CHA JYE LA HE	鳩槃茶揭囉訶
257)	BU DAN NA JYE LA HE	補丹那揭囉訶
258)	JYA JA BU DAN NA JYE LA HE	迦吒補丹那揭囉訶
259)	SYI CHAN DU JYE LA HE	悉乾度揭囉訶
260)	E BWO SYI MWO LA JYE LA HE	阿播悉摩囉揭囉訶
261)	WU TAN MWO TWO JYE LA HE	烏檀摩陀揭囉訶
262)	CHE YE JYE LA HE	車夜揭囉訶
263)	SYI LI PE DI JYE LA HE	醯唎婆帝揭囉訶
264)	SHE DWO HE LI NAN	社多訶唎南
265)	JYE PE HE LI NAN	揭婆訶唎南
266)	LU DI LA HE LI NAN	嚧地囉訶唎南
267)	MANG SWO HE LI NAN	忙娑訶唎南
268)	MI TWO HE LI NAN	謎陀訶唎南
269)	MWO SHE HE LI NAN	摩闍訶唎南

18

270)	SHE DWO HE LI NYU	闍多訶唎女
271)	SHR BI DWO HE LI NAN	視比多訶唎南
272)	PI DWO HE LI NAN	毗多訶唎南
273)	PE DWO HE LI NAN	婆多訶唎南
274)	E SHU JE HE LI NYU	阿輸遮訶唎女
275)	JR DWO HE LI NYU	賀多訶唎女
276)	DI SHAN SA PI SHAN ◎	帝釤薩鞞釤◎
277)	SA PE JYE LA HE NAN	薩婆揭囉訶南
278)	PI TWO YE SHE	毗陀耶闍
279)	CHEN TWO YE MI	瞋陀夜彌
280)	JI LA YE MI	雞囉夜彌
281)	BWO LI BA LA JE JYA	波唎跋囉者迦
282)	CHI LI DAN	訖唎擔
283)	PI TWO YE SHE	毗陀夜闍
284)	CHEN TWO YE MI	瞋陀夜彌
285)	JI LA YE MI	雞囉夜彌
286)	CHA YAN NI	茶演尼
287)	CHI LI DAN	訖唎擔
288)	PI TWO YE SHE	毗陀夜闍
289)	CHEN TWO YE MI	瞋陀夜彌
290)	JI LA YE MI	雞囉夜彌
291)	MWO HE BWO SU BWO DAN YE	摩訶般輸般怛夜
292)	LU TWO LA	嚧陀囉
293)	CHI LI DAN	訖唎擔

294)	PI TWO YE SHE	毗陀夜闍
295)	CHEN TWO YE MI	瞋陀夜彌
296)	JI LA YE MI	雞囉夜彌
297)	NWO LA YE NA	那囉夜拏
298)	CHI LI DAN	訖唎擔
299)	PI TWO YE SHE	毗陀夜闍
300)	CHEN TWO YE MI	瞋陀夜彌
301)	JI LA YE MI	雞囉夜彌
302)	DAN TWO CHYE LU CHA SYI	怛埵伽嚧茶西
303)	CHI LI DAN	訖唎擔
304)	PI TWO YE SHE	毗陀夜闍
305)	CHEN TWO YE MI	瞋陀夜彌
306)	JI LA YE MI	雞囉夜彌
307)	MWO HE JYA LA	摩訶迦囉
308)	MWO DAN LI CHYE NA	摩怛唎伽拏
309)	CHI LI DAN	訖唎擔
310)	PI TWO YE SHE	毗陀夜闍
311)	CHEN TWO YE MI	瞋陀夜彌
312)	JI LA YE MI	雞囉夜彌
313)	JYA BWO LI JYA	迦波唎迦
314)	CHI LI DAN	訖唎擔
315)	PI TWO YE SHE	毗陀夜闍
316)	CHEN TWO YE MI	瞋陀夜彌
317)	JI LA YE MI	雞囉夜彌

318)	SHE YE JYE LA	闍耶羯囉
319)	MWO DU JYE LA	摩度羯囉
320)	SA PE LA TWO SWO DA NA	薩婆囉他娑達那
321)	CHI LI DAN	訖唎擔
322)	PI TWO YE SHE	毗陀夜闍
323)	CHEN TWO YE MI	瞋陀夜彌
324)	JI LA YE MI	雞囉夜彌
325)	JE DU LA	赭咄囉
326)	PE CHI NI	婆耆你
327)	CHI LI DAN	訖唎擔
328)	PI TWO YE SHE	毗陀夜闍
329)	CHEN TWO YE MI	瞋陀夜彌
330)	JI LA YE MI	雞囉夜彌
331)	PI LI YANG CHI LI JR	毗唎羊訖唎知
332)	NAN TWO JI SHA LA	難陀雞沙囉
333)	CHYE NA BWO DI	伽拏般帝
334)	SWO SYI YE	索醯夜
335)	CHI LI DAN	訖唎擔
336)	PI TWO YE SHE	毗陀夜闍
337)	CHEN TWO YE MI	瞋陀夜彌
338)	JI LA YE MI	雞囉夜彌
339)	NA JYE NA SHE LA PE NA	那揭那舍囉婆拏
340)	CHI LI DAN	訖唎擔
341)	PI TWO YE SHE	毗陀夜闍

21

342)	CHEN TWO YE MI	瞋陀夜彌
343)	JI LA YE MI	雞囉夜彌
344)	E LWO HAN	阿羅漢
345)	CHI LI DAN	訖唎擔
346)	PI TWO YE SHE	毗陀夜闍
347)	CHEN TWO YE MI	瞋陀夜彌
348)	JI LA YE MI	雞囉夜彌
349)	PI DWO LA CHYE	毗多囉伽
350)	CHI LI DAN	訖唎擔
351)	PI TWO YE SHE	毗陀夜闍
352)	CHEN TWO YE MI	瞋陀夜彌
353)	JI LA YE MI	雞囉夜彌
354)	BA SHE LA BWO NI	跋闍囉波你
355)	JYU SYI YE JYU SYI YE	具醯夜具醯夜
356)	JYA DI BWO DI	迦地般帝
357)	CHI LI DAN	訖唎擔
358)	PI TWO YE SHE	毗陀夜闍
359)	CHEN TWO YE MI	瞋陀夜彌
360)	JI LA YE MI˘	雞囉夜彌
361)	LA CHA WANG	囉叉罔
362)	PE CHYE FAN	婆伽梵
363)	YIN TU NA MWO MWO SYE	印兔那麼麼寫
IV.		（第四會）
364)	PE CHYE FAN	婆伽梵

22

365)	SA DAN DWO BWO DA LA	薩怛多般怛囉
366)	NA MWO TSWEI DU DI	南無粹都帝
367)	E SYI DWO NA LA LA JYA	阿悉多那囉剌迦
368)	BWO LA PE	波囉婆
369)	SYI PU JA	悉普吒
370)	PI JYA SA DAN DWO BE DI LI	毗迦薩怛多鉢帝唎
371)	SHR FWO LA SHR FWO LA	什佛囉什佛囉
372)	TWO LA TWO LA	陀囉陀囉
373)	PIN TWO LA PIN TWO LA	頻陀囉頻陀囉
374)	CHEN TWO CHEN TWO	瞋陀瞋陀
375)	HU SYIN HU SYIN	虎斛虎斛
376)	PAN JA PAN JA PAN JA PAN JA PAN JA	泮吒泮吒泮吒泮吒泮吒
377)	SWO HE	娑訶
378)	SYI SYI PAN	醢醢泮
379)	E MU JYA YE PAN	阿牟迦耶泮
380)	E BWO LA TI HE DWO PAN	阿波囉提訶多泮
381)	PE LA BWO LA TWO PAN	婆囉波囉陀泮
382)	E SU LA	阿素囉
383)	PI TWO LA	毗陀囉
384)	BWO JYA PAN	波迦泮
385)	SA PE TI PI BI PAN	薩婆提鞞弊泮
386)	SA PE NA CHYE BI PAN	薩婆那伽弊泮

23

387)	SA PE YAU CHA BI PAN	薩婆藥叉弊泮
388)	SA PE CHYAN TA PE BI PAN	薩婆乾闥婆弊泮
389)	SA PE BU DAN NA BI PAN	薩婆補丹那弊泮
390)	JYA JA BU DAN NA BI PAN	迦吒補丹那弊泮
391)	SA PE TU LANG JR DI BI PAN	薩婆突狼枳帝弊泮
392)	SA PE TU SZ BI LI	薩婆突澀比犛
393)	CHI SHAI DI BI PAN	訖瑟帝弊泮
394)	SA PE SHR PE LI BI PAN	薩婆什婆犛弊泮
395)	SA PE E BWO SYI MWO LI BI PAN	薩婆阿播悉摩犛弊泮
396)	SA PE SHE LA PE NA BI PAN	薩婆舍囉婆拏弊泮
397)	SA PE DI DI JI BI PAN	薩婆地帝雞弊泮
398)	SA PE DAN MWO TWO JI BI PAN	薩婆怛摩陀繼弊泮
399)	SA PE PI TWO YE	薩婆毗陀耶
400)	LA SHR JE LI BI PAN	囉誓遮犛弊泮
401)	SHE YE JYE LA	闍夜羯囉
402)	MWO DU JYE LA	摩度羯囉
403)	SA PE LA TWO SWO TWO JI BI PAN	薩婆囉他娑陀雞弊泮
404)	PI DI YE	毗地夜
405)	JE LI BI PAN	遮喇弊泮

406)	JE DU LA	者都囉
407)	FU CHI NI BI PAN	縛者你弊泮
408)	BA SHE LA	跋闍囉
409)	JYU MWO LI	俱摩唎
410)	PI TWO YE	毗陀夜
411)	LA SHR BI PAN	囉誓弊泮
412)	MWO HE BWO LA DING YANG	摩訶波囉丁羊
413)	YI CHI LI BI PAN	义者唎弊泮
414)	BA SHE LA SHANG JYE LA YE	跋闍囉商羯囉夜
415)	BWO LA JANG CHI LA SHE YE PAN	波囉丈耆囉闍耶泮
416)	MWO HE JYA LA YE	摩訶迦囉夜
417)	MWO HE MWO DAN LI JYA NA	摩訶末怛唎迦拏
418)	NA MWO SWO JYE LI DWO YE PAN	南無娑羯唎多夜泮
419)	BI SHAI NA BEI YE PAN	毖瑟拏婢曳泮
420)	BWO LA HE MWO NI YE PAN	勃囉訶牟尼曳泮
421)	E CHI NI YE PAN	阿耆尼曳泮
422)	MWO HE JYE LI YE PAN	摩訶羯唎曳泮
423)	JYE LA TAN CHR YE PAN	羯囉檀持曳泮
424)	MYE DAN LI YE PAN	蔑怛唎曳泮
425)	LAU DAN LI YE PAN	嘮怛唎曳泮
426)	JE WEN CHA YE PAN	遮文茶曳泮

25

427)	JYE LWO LA DAN LI YE PAN	羯邏囉怛喇 曳泮
428)	JYA BWO LI YE PAN	迦般喇曳泮
429)	E DI MU JR DWO	阿地目質多
430)	JYA SHR MWO SHE NWO	迦尸摩舍那
431)	PE SZ NI YE PAN	婆私你曳泮
432)	YAN JI JR	演吉質
433)	SA TWO PE SYE	薩埵婆寫
434)	MWO MWO YIN TU NA MWO MWO SYE	麼麼印兔那 麼麼寫
V.		(第五會)
435)	TU SHAI JA JR DWO	突瑟吒質多
436)	E MWO DAN LI JR DWO	阿末怛喇質多
437)	WU SHE HE LA	烏闍訶囉
438)	CHYE PE HE LA	伽婆訶囉
439)	LU DI LA HE LA	嚧地囉訶囉
440)	PE SWO HE LA	婆娑訶囉
441)	MWO SHE HE LA	摩闍訶囉
442)	SHE DWO HE LA	闍多訶囉
443)	SHR BI DWO HE LA	視毖多訶囉
444)	BA LYAU YE HE LA	跋畧夜訶囉
445)	CHYAN TWO HE LA	乾陀訶囉
446)	BU SHR BWO HE LA	布史波訶囉
447)	PWO LA HE LA	頗囉訶囉

26

448)	PE SYE HE LA	婆寫訶囉
449)	BE BWO JR DWO	般波質多
450)	TU SHAI JA JR DWO	突瑟吒質多
451)	LAU TWO LA JR DWO	嘮陀囉質多
452)	YAU CHA JYE LA HE	藥叉揭囉訶
453)	LA CHA SWO JYE LA HE	囉剎婆揭囉訶
454)	BI LI DWO JYE LA HE	閉隸多揭囉訶
455)	PI SHE JE JYE LA HE	毗舍遮揭囉訶
456)	BU DWO JYE LA HE	部多揭囉訶
457)	JYOU PAN CHA JYE LA HE	鳩槃茶揭囉訶
458)	SYI CHYAN TWO JYE LA HE	悉乾陀揭囉訶
459)	WU DAN MWO TWO JYE LA HE	烏怛摩陀揭囉訶
460)	CHE YE JYE LA HE	車夜揭囉訶
461)	E BWO SA MWO LA JYE LA HE	阿播薩摩囉揭囉訶
462)	JAI CHYWE GE	宅祛革
463)	CHA CHI NI JYE LA HE	茶耆尼揭囉訶
464)	LI FWO DI JYE LA HE	喇佛帝揭囉訶
465)	SHE MI JYA JYE LA HE	闍彌迦揭囉訶
466)	SHE JYU NI JYE LA HE	舍俱尼揭囉訶
467)	MU TWO LA	姥陀囉
468)	NA DI JYA JYE LA HE	難地迦揭囉訶
469)	E LAN PE JYE LA HE	阿藍婆揭囉訶
470)	CHYAN DU BWO NI JYE LA HE	乾度波尼揭囉訶

471)	SHR FWO LA	什伐囉
472)	YIN JYA SYI JYA	堙迦醯迦
473)	JWEI DI YAU JYA	墜帝藥迦
474)	DAN LI DI YAU JYA	怛隸帝藥迦
475)	JE TU TWO JYA	者突託迦
476)	NI TI SHR FA LA	昵提什伐囉
477)	BI SHAN MWO SHR FA LA	毖鈐摩什伐囉
478)	BWO DI JYA	薄底迦
479)	BI DI JYA	鼻底迦
480)	SHR LI SHAI MI JYA	室隸瑟密迦
481)	SWO NI BWO DI JYA	娑你般帝迦
482)	SA PE SHR FA LA	薩婆什伐囉
483)	SHR LU JI DI	室嚧吉帝
484)	MWO TWO PI DA LU JR JYAN	末陀鞞達嚧制劍
485)	E CHI LU CHYAN	阿綺嚧鉗
486)	MU CHYWE LU CHYAN	目佉嚧鉗
487)	JYE LI TU LU CHYAN	羯唎突嚧鉗
488)	JYA LA HE	揭囉訶
489)	JYE LAN JYE NA SHU LAN	揭藍羯拏輸藍
490)	DAN DWO SHU LAN	憚多輸藍
491)	CHI LI YE SHU LAN	迄唎夜輸藍
492)	MWO MWO SHU LAN	末麼輸藍
493)	BA LI SHR PE SHU LAN	跋唎室婆輸藍
494)	BI LI SHAI JA SHU LAN	毖栗瑟吒輸藍

28

495)	WU TWO LA SHU LAN	烏 陀 囉 輸 藍
496)	JYE JR SHU LAN	羯 知 輸 藍
497)	BA SYI DI SHU LAN	跋 悉 帝 輸 藍
498)	WU LU SHU LAN	鄔 嚧 輸 藍
499)	CHANG CHYE SHU LAN	常 伽 輸 藍
500)	HE SYI DWO SHU LAN	喝 悉 多 輸 藍
501)	BA TWO SHU LAN	跋 陀 輸 藍
502)	SWO FANG ANG CHYE	娑 房 盎 伽
503)	BWO LA JANG CHYE SHU LAN	般 囉 丈 伽 輸 藍
504)	BU DWO BI DWO CHA	部 多 毖 跢 茶
505)	CHA CHI NI	茶 耆 尼
506)	SHR PE LA	什 婆 囉
507)	TWO TU LU JYA	陀 突 嚧 迦
508)	JYAN DU LU JI JR	建 咄 嚧 吉 知
509)	PE LU DWO PI	婆 路 多 毗
510)	SA BWO LU	薩 般 嚧
511)	HE LING CHYE	訶 凌 伽
512)	SHU SHA DAN LA	輸 沙 怛 囉
513)	SWO NA JYE LA	娑 那 羯 囉
514)	PI SHA YU JYA	毗 沙 喻 迦
515)	E CHI NI	阿 耆 尼
516)	WU TWO JYA	烏 陀 迦
517)	MWO LA PI LA	末 囉 鞞 囉
518)	JYAN DWO LA	建 跢 囉

29

519)	E JYA LA	阿迦囉
520)	MI LI DU	密唎咄
521)	DA LYAN BU JYA	怛斂部迦
522)	DI LI LA JA	地栗剌吒
523)	BI LI SHAI JR JYA	毖唎瑟質迦
524)	SA PE NA JYU LA	薩婆那俱囉
525)	SZ YIN CHYE BI ◎	肆引伽弊◎
526)	JYE LA LI YAU CHA	揭囉唎藥叉
527)	DAN LA CHU	怛囉芻
528)	MWO LA SHR	末囉視
529)	FEI DI SHAN	吠帝釤
530)	SWO PI SHAN	娑鞞釤
531)	SYI DAN DWO BWO DA LA	悉怛多鉢怛囉
532)	MWO HE BA SHE LU	摩訶跋闍嚧
533)	SHAI NI SHAN	瑟尼釤
534)	MWO HE BWO LAI JANG CHI LAN	摩訶般賴丈耆藍
535)	YE BWO TU TWO	夜波突陀
536)	SHE YU SHE NWO	舍喻闍那
537)	BYAN DA LI NA	辮怛隸拏
538)	PI TWO YE	毗陀耶
539)	PAN TAN JYA LU MI	槃曇迦嚧彌
540)	DI SHU	帝殊
541)	PAN TAN JYA LU MI	槃曇迦嚧彌
542)	BWO LA PI TWO	般囉毗陀

543) PAN TAN JYA LU MI 槃曇迦嚧彌

544) DA JR TWO 跢姪他

545) NAN ◎ 唵◎

546) E NA LI 阿那棣

547) PI SHE TI 毗舍提

548) PI LA 鞞囉

549) BA SHE LA 跋闍囉

550) TWO LI 陀唎

551) PAN TWO PAN TWO NI 槃陀槃陀你

552) BA SHE LA BANG NI PAN 跋闍囉謗尼泮

553) HU SYIN DU LU YUNG PAN 虎䤵都嚧甕泮

554) SWO PE HE 莎婆訶

31

GREAT COMPASSION MANTRA
大悲咒
Da bei jou

1) NA MWO HE LA DA NWO DWO 南無喝囉怛那哆

LA YE YE ◎ 囉夜耶◎

2) NA MWO E LI YE 南無阿唎耶

3) PWO LU JYE DI SHAU BWO LA YE 婆盧羯帝爍鉢囉耶

4) PU TI SA TWO PE YE 菩提薩埵婆耶

5) MWO HE SA TWO PE YE 摩訶薩埵婆耶

6) MWO HE JYA LU NI JYA YE 摩訶迦盧尼迦耶

7) NAN 唵

8) SA PAN LA FA YE 薩皤囉罰曳

9) SWO DA NWO DA SYE 數怛那怛寫

10) NA MWO SYI JI LI TWO YI 南無悉吉㗚埵伊

MENG E LI YE 蒙阿唎耶

11) PE LU JI DI SHR FWO LA 婆盧吉帝室佛囉

LENG TWO PE 楞馱婆

12) NA MWO NWO LA JIN CHR 南無那囉謹墀

13) SYI LI MWO HE PAN DWO 醯唎摩訶皤哆

SA MYE 沙咩

14) SA PE E TWO DOU SHU PENG 薩婆阿他豆輸朋

15) E SHR YUN 阿逝孕

16) SA PE SA DWO NA MWO PE SA DWO 薩婆薩哆那摩婆薩多

17) NA MWO PE CHYE 那摩婆伽

18) MWO FA TE DOU 摩罰特豆

32

19) DA JR TWO　　　　　　　　怛姪他

20) NAN　　　　　　　　　　　唵

21) E PE LU SYI　　　　　　　阿婆盧醯

22) LU JYA DI　　　　　　　　盧迦帝

23) JYA LA DI　　　　　　　　迦羅帝

24) YI SYI LI　　　　　　　　夷醯唎

25) **MWO** HE PU TI SA TWO　　摩訶菩提薩埵

26) SA PE SA PE　　　　　　　薩婆薩婆

27) MWO LA MWO LA　　　　　摩囉摩囉

28) MWO SYI MWO SYI LI TWO YUN　摩醯摩醯唎馱孕

29) JYU LU JYU LU JYE MENG　俱盧俱盧羯蒙

30) DU LU DU LU FA SHE YE DI　度盧度盧罰闍耶帝

31) MWO HE FA SHE YE DI　　摩訶罰闍耶帝

32) TWO LA TWO LA　　　　　陀囉陀囉

33) DI LI NI　　　　　　　　地唎尼

34) SHR FWO LA YE　　　　　室佛囉耶

35) JE LA JE LA　　　　　　遮囉遮囉

36) MWO MWO FA MWO LA　　麼麼罰摩囉

37) MU DI LI　　　　　　　　穆帝隸

38) YI SYI YI SYI　　　　　伊醯伊醯

39) SHR NWO SHR NWO　　　室那室那

40) E LA SHEN FWO LA SHE LI　阿囉嘇佛囉舍利

41) FA SHA FA SHEN　　　　罰娑罰嘇

42) FWO LA SHE YE　　　　　佛囉舍耶

33

43) HU LU HU LU MWO LA	呼盧 呼盧 摩囉
44) HU LU HU LU SYI LI	呼盧 呼盧 醯利
45) SWO LA SWO LA	娑囉 娑囉
46) SYI LI SYI LI	悉唎 悉唎
47) SU LU SU LU	蘇嚧 蘇嚧
48) PU TI YE PU TI YE	菩提夜 菩提夜
49) PU TWO YE PU TWO YE	菩馱夜 菩馱夜
50) MI DI LI YE	彌帝利夜
51) NWO LA JIN CHR	那囉謹墀
52) DI LI SHAI NI NWO	地利瑟尼那
53) PE YE MWO NWO	婆夜摩那
54) SWO PE HE	娑婆訶
55) SYI TWO YE	悉陀夜
56) SWO PE HE	娑婆訶
57) MWO HE SYI TWO YE	摩訶悉陀夜
58) SWO PE HE	娑婆訶
59) SYI TWO YU YI	悉陀喻藝
60) SHR PAN LA YE	室皤囉耶
61) SWO PE HE	娑婆訶
62) NWO LA JIN CHR	那囉謹墀
63) SWO PE HE	娑婆訶
64) MWO LA NWO LA	摩囉那囉
65) SWO PE HE	娑婆訶
66) SYI LU SENG E MU CHYWE YE	悉囉僧阿穆佉耶

67) SWO PE HE	婆婆詞
68) SWO PE MWO HE E SYI TWO YE	婆婆摩訶阿悉陀夜
69) SWO PE HE	婆婆詞
70) JE JI LA E SYI TWO YE	者吉囉阿悉陀夜
71) SWO PE HE	婆婆詞
72) BWO TWO MWO JYE SYI TWO YE	波陀摩羯悉陀夜
73) SWO PE HE	婆婆詞
74) NWO LA JIN CHR PAN CHYE LA YE	那囉謹墀皤伽囉耶
75) SWO PE HE	婆婆詞
76) MWO PE LI SHENG JYE LA YE	摩婆利勝羯囉夜
77) SWO PE HE	婆婆詞
78) NA MWO HE LA DA NWO DWO LA YE YE	南無喝囉怛那哆囉夜耶
79) NA MWO E LI YE	南無阿利耶
80) PWO LU JI DI	婆嚧吉帝
81) SHAU PAN LA YE	爍皤囉夜
82) SWO PE HE	婆婆詞
83) NAN	唵
84) SYI DYAN DU	悉殿都
85) MAN DWO LA	漫多囉
86) BA TWO YE	跋陀耶
87) SWO PE HE	婆婆詞

TEN SMALL MANTRAS
十小咒

AS-YOU-WILL JEWEL WHEEL KING DHARANI 如意寶輪王陀羅尼

1) NA MWO FWO TWO YE ◎   南無佛馱耶◎

2) NA MWO DA MWO YE   南無達摩耶

3) NA MWO SENG CHYE YE   南無僧伽耶

4) NA MWO GWAN DZ DZAI PU SA   南無觀自在菩薩

    MWO HE SA   摩訶薩

5) JYU DA BEI SYIN JE   具大悲心者

6) DA JR TWO   怛姪他

7) NAN   唵

8) JAU JYE LA FA DI   斫羯囉伐底

9) JEN DWO MWO NI   震多末尼

10) MWO HE BWO DENG MI   摩訶鉢蹬迷

11) LU LU LU LU   嚕嚕嚕嚕

12) DI SHAI JA   底瑟吒

13) SHAU LA E JYE LI   篅囉阿羯利

14) SHA YE HUNG   沙夜吽

15) PAN SWO HE   癹莎訶

16) NAN   唵

17) BWO TA MWO   鉢蹋摩

18) JEN DWO MWO NI   震多末尼

19) SHAU LA HUNG   篅攞吽

20) NAN   唵

21) BA LA TWO   跋喇陀

22) BWO TAN MI HUNG　　　鉢亶謎吽

DISASTER ERADICATING AUSPICIOUS SPIRIT MANTRA
消災吉祥神咒

1) NA MWO SAN MAN DWO　　　曩謨三滿哆
   MU TWO NAN　　　　　　　母馱喃
2) E BWO LA DI　　　　　　　阿鉢囉底
3) HE DWO SHE　　　　　　　賀多舍
4) SWO NANG NAN　　　　　　娑曩喃
5) DA JR TWO　　　　　　　　怛姪他
6) NAN　　　　　　　　　　　唵
7) CHYWE CHYWE　　　　　　佉佉
8) CHYWE SYI　　　　　　　佉呬
9) CHYWE SYI　　　　　　　佉呬
10) HUNG HUNG　　　　　　　吽吽
11) RU WA LA　　　　　　　入嚩囉
12) RU WA LA　　　　　　　入嚩囉
13) BWO LA RU WA LA　　　　鉢囉入嚩囉
14) BWO LA RU WA LA　　　　鉢囉入嚩囉
15) DI SAI CHA　　　　　　　底瑟姹
16) DI SAI CHA　　　　　　　底瑟姹
17) SHAI JR LI　　　　　　　瑟致哩
18) SHAI JR LI　　　　　　　瑟致哩
19) SWO PAN JA　　　　　　　娑發吒

20) SWO PAN JA　　娑 鈸 吒

21) SHAN DI JYA　　扇 底 迦

22) SHR LI YE　　室 哩 曳

23) SWO WA HE　　娑 嚩 訶

MERITORIOUS VIRTUE JEWELLED MOUNTAIN SPIRIT MANTRA
功德寶山神咒

1) NA MWO FWO TWO YE　　南 無 佛 馱 耶

2) NA MWO DA MWO YE　　南 無 達 摩 耶

3) NA MWO SENG CHYE YE　　南 無 僧 伽 耶

4) NAN　　唵

5) SYI DI HU LU LU　　悉 帝 護 嚕 嚕

6) SYI DU LU　　悉 都 嚕

7) JR LI PE　　只 利 婆

8) JI LI PE　　吉 利 婆

9) SYI DA LI　　悉 達 哩

10) BU LU LI　　布 嚕 哩

11) SA WA HE　　沙 嚩 訶

JWUN TI SPIRIT MANTRA　　準提神咒

JI SHOU GWEI YI SU SYI DI◎　　稽首皈依蘇悉帝◎

TOU MYAN DING LI CHI JYU JR　　頭面頂禮七俱胝

WO JIN CHENG DZAN DA JWUN TI　　我今稱讚大準提

WEI YWAN TSZ BEI CHWEI JYA HU　　唯願慈悲垂加護

38

1) NA MWO SA DWO NAN　　南無颯哆喃

2) SAN MYAU SAN PU TWO　　三藐三菩陀

3) JYU JR NAN　　俱胝喃

4) DA JR TWO　　怛姪他

5) NAN　　唵

6) JE LI JU LI　　折戾主戾

7) JWUN TI　　準提

8) SWO PE HE　　娑婆訶

THE RESOLUTE LIGHT KING DHARANI OF HOLY LIMITLESS LIFE
聖無量壽決定光明王陀羅尼

1) NAN　　唵

2) NAI MWO PAN GE WA DI　　捺摩巴葛瓦帝

3) YA BA LA MI DA　　阿巴囉密沓

4) YA YOU LI YA NA　　阿優哩阿納

5) SU BI NI　　蘇必你

6) SHR JR DA　　實執沓

7) DYE DZWO LA DZAI YE　　牒左囉宰也

8) DA TA GE DA YE　　怛塔哿達也

9) E LA HE DI　　阿囉訶帝

10) SAN YAU SAN PU DA YE　　三藥三不達也

11) DA NI YE TA　　怛你也塔

12) NAN　　唵

13) SA LI BA　　薩哩巴

14) SENG SZ GE LI　　桑斯葛哩

15) BA LI SU TA   叭 哩 述 沓

16) DA LA MA DI   達 囉 馬 帝

17) GE GE NAI   哿 哿 捺

18) SANG MA WU GE DI   桑 馬 兀 哿 帝

19) SWO BA WA   莎 巴 瓦

20) BI SU DI   比 述 帝

21) MA HE NAI YE   馬 喝 捺 也

22) BA LI WA LI SWO HE   叭 哩 瓦 哩 婆 喝

MEDICINE MASTER'S TRUE WORDS FOR ANOINTING THE CROWN

藥師灌頂真言

1) NA MWO BWO CHYE FA DI   南 無 薄 伽 伐 帝

2) BI SHA SHE   鞞 殺 社

3) JYU LU BI LYOU LI   窶 嚕 薜 琉 璃

4) BWO LA PWO   鉢 喇 婆

5) HE LA SHE YE   喝 囉 闍 也

6) DA TWO JYE DWO YE   怛 他 揭 多 也

7) E LA HE DI   阿 囉 喝 帝

8) SAN MYAU SAN PU TWO YE   三 藐 三 勃 陀 耶

9) DA JR TWO   怛 姪 他

10) NAN   唵

11) BI SHA SHR   鞞 殺 逝

12) BI SHA SHR   鞞 殺 逝

13) BI SHA SHE   鞞 殺 社

14) SAN MWO JYE DI SWO HE   三 没 揭 帝 莎 訶

GWAN YIN'S EFFICACIOUS RESPONSE TRUE WORDS
觀音靈感真言

1) NAN   唵

2) MA NI BA MI HUNG   嘛 呢 叭 彌 吽

3) MA HA NI YA NA   嘛 曷 倪 牙 納

4) JI DAU TWO BA DA   積 都 特 巴 達

5) JI TWO SYE NA   積 特 此 納

6) WEI DA LI GE   微 達 哩 葛

7) SA ER WA ER TA   薩 而 斡 而 塔

8) BU LI SYI TA GE   卜 哩 悉 塔 葛

9) NA BU LA NA   納 補 囉 納

10) NA BU LI   納 卜 哩

11) DYOU TE BA NA   丢 忒 班 納

12) NA MWO LU JI   㖃 嘛 嚧 吉

13) SHWO LA YE   説 囉 耶

14) SWO HE   莎 訶

THE TRUE WORDS OF SEVEN BUDDHAS FOR ERADICATING OFFENSES
七佛滅罪真言

1) LI PE LI PE DI   離 婆 離 婆 帝

2) CHYOU HE CHYOU HE DI   求 訶 求 訶 帝

3) TWO LA NI DI   陀 羅 尼 帝

4) NI HE LA DI   尼 阿 囉 帝

5) PI LI NI DI   毗 黎 你 帝

6) MWO HE CHYE DI   摩 訶 伽 帝

7) JEN LIN CHYAN DI　真陵乾帝

8) SWO PE HE　莎婆訶

SPIRIT MANTRA FOR REBIRTH IN THE PURE LAND
往生淨土神咒

1) NA MWO E MI DWO PE YE◎　南無阿彌多婆夜◎

2) DWO TWO CHYE DWO YE　哆他伽多夜

3) DWO DI YE TWO　哆地夜他

4) E MI LI DU PE PI　阿彌利都婆毗

5) E MI LI DWO　阿彌利哆

6) SYI DAN PE PI　悉耽婆毗

7) E MI LI DWO　阿彌唎哆

8) PI JYA LAN DI　毗迦蘭帝

9) E MI LI DWO　阿彌唎哆

10) PI JYA LAN DWO　毗迦蘭多

11) CHYE MI LI　伽彌膩

12) CHYE CHYE NWO　伽伽那

13) JR DWO JYA LI　枳多迦利

14) SWO PE HE　娑婆訶

GOOD GODDESS MANTRA 大吉祥天女咒

1) NA MWO FWO TWO　南無佛陀

2) NA MWO DA MWO　南無達摩

3) NA MWO SENG CHYE　南無僧伽

4) NA MWO SHR LI　南無室利

5) MWO HE TI BI YE　摩訶提鼻耶

6) DA NI YE TWO 怛你也他

7) BWO LI FU LOU NWO 波利富樓那

8) JE LI SAN MAN TWO 遮利三曼陀

9) DA SHE NI 達舍尼

10) MWO HE PI HE LWO CHYE DI 摩訶毗訶羅伽帝

11) SAN MAN TWO 三曼陀

12) PI NI CHYE DI 毗尼伽帝

13) MWO HE JA LI YE 摩訶迦利野

14) BWO MI 波禰

15) BWO LA 波囉

16) BWO MI 波禰

17) SA LI WA LI TWO 薩利嚩栗他

18) SAN MAN TWO 三曼陀

19) SYOU BWO LI DI 修鉢犂帝

20) FU LI NWO 富隸那

21) E LI NWO 阿利那

22) DA MWO DI 達摩帝

23) MWO HE PI GU BI DI 摩訶毗鼓畢帝

24) MWO HE MI LEI DI 摩訶彌勒帝

    LOU BWO SENG CHI DI 婁簸僧祇帝

25) SYI DI SYI 醯帝簁

26) SENG CHI SYI DI 僧祇醯帝

27) SAN MAN TWO 三曼陀

28) E TWO E OU 阿他阿兜

29) PE LWO NI 婆羅尼

43

THE HEART OF PRAJNA PARAMITA SUTRA ◎

般若波羅蜜多心經 ◎

Bwo re bwo lwo mi dwo syin jing

WHEN BODHISATTVA AVALOKITESHVARA WAS PRACTICING THE PROFOUND PRAJNA PARAMITA,

觀自在菩薩，行深般若波羅蜜多時，

Gwan dz dzai pu sa sying shen bwo re bwo lwo mi dwo shr.

HE ILLUMINATED THE FIVE SKANDHAS AND SAW THAT THEY ARE ALL EMPTY, AND HE CROSSED BEYOND ALL SUFFERING AND DIFFICULTY.

照見五蘊皆空，度一切苦厄．

Jyau jyan wu yun jye kung. du yi chye ku e.

SHARIPUTRA, FORM DOES NOT DIFFER FROM EMPTINESS; EMPTINESS DOES NOT DIFFER FROM FORM. FORM ITSELF IS EMPTINESS; EMPTINESS ITSELF IS FORM. SO TOO ARE FEELING, COGNITION, FORMATION. AND CONSCIOUSNESS.

舍利子，色不異空，空不異色．色即是空，
空即是色，受想行識亦復如是．

She li dz, shai bu yi kung. kung bu yi shai. shai ji shr kung. kung ji shr shai. shou syang sying shr yi fu ru shr.

SHARIPUTRA, ALL DHARMAS ARE EMPTY OF CHARACTERISTICS. THEY ARE NOT PRODUCED, NOT DESTROYED,

舍利子，是諸法空相，不生不滅，

She li dz. shr ju fa kung syang, bu sheng bu mye,

NOT DEFILED, NOT PURE, AND THEY NEITHER INCREASE NOR DIMINISH.

不垢不淨，不增不減．

Bu gou bu jing. bu dzeng bu jyan.

THEREFORE, IN EMPTINESS THERE IS NO FORM, FEELING, COGNITION, FORMATION, OR CONSCIOUSNESS;

是故空中無色，無受想行識，

Shr gu kung jung wu shai. wu shou syang sying shr.

44

NO EYES, EARS, NOSE, TONGUE, BODY, OR MIND; NO SIGHTS,
SOUNDS, SMELLS, TASTES, OBJECTS OF TOUCH, OR DHARMAS;

無眼耳鼻舌身意，無色聲香味觸法。

Wu yan er bi she shen yi, wu shai sheng syang wei chu fa.

NO FIELD OF THE EYES UP TO AND INCLUDING NO FIELD OF
MIND CONSCIOUSNESS;

無眼界，乃至無意識界。

Wu yan jye, nai jr wu yi shr jye.

AND NO IGNORANCE OR ENDING OF IGNORANCE,

無無明，亦無無明盡。

Wu wu ming, yi wu wu ming jin.

UP TO AND INCLUDING NO OLD AGE AND DEATH OR ENDING OF OLD
AGE AND DEATH.

乃至無老死，亦無老死盡。

Nai jr wu lau sz, yi wu lau sz jin.

THERE IS NO SUFFERING, NO ACCUMULATING, NO EXTINCTION, AND
NO WAY, AND NO UNDERSTANDING AND NO ATTAINING.

無苦集滅道，無智亦無得。

Wu ku ji mye dau, wu jr yi wu de.

BECAUSE NOTHING IS ATTAINED, THE BODHISATTVA

以無所得故，菩提薩埵，

Yi wu swo de gu, pu ti sa two.

THROUGH RELIANCE ON PRAJNA PARAMITA IS UNIMPEDED IN HIS
MIND.

依般若波羅蜜多故，心無罣礙。

Yi bwo re bwo lwo mi dwo gu, syin wu gwa ai,

BECAUSE THERE IS NO IMPEDIMENT, HE IS NOT AFRAID

無罣礙故，無有恐怖，

Wu gwa ai gu, wu you kung bu.

AND HE LEAVES DISTORTED DREAM-THINKING FAR BEHIND.

遠離顛倒夢想，

Ywan li dyan dau meng syang.

ULTIMATELY NIRVANA!

究竟涅槃。

Jyou jing nye pan.

ALL BUDDHAS OF THE THREE PERIODS OF TIME ATTAIN ANUTTARA-
◎

45

SAMYAK-SAMBODHI THROUGH RELIANCE ON PRAJNA PARAMITA.

三世諸佛依般若波羅蜜多故，得阿
耨多羅三藐三菩提。

San shr ju fwo yi bwo re bwo lwo mi dwo gu. de e nwo dwo lwo
san myau san pu ti

THEREFORE KNOW THAT PRAJNA PARAMITA IS A GREAT SPIRITUAL
MANTRA,

故知般若波羅蜜多，是大神咒，

Gu jr bwo re bwo lwo mi dwo.shr da shen jou

A GREAT BRIGHT MANTRA, A SUPREME MANTRA, AN UNEQUALLED
MANTRA.

是大明咒，是無上咒，是無等等咒。

Shr da ming jou. shr wu shang jou. shr wu deng deng jou.

IT CAN REMOVE ALL SUFFERING:IT IS GENUINE AND NOT FALSE.

能除一切苦，真實不虛。

Neng chu yi chye ku. jen shr bu syu.

THAT IS WHY THE MANTRA OF PRAJNA PARAMITA WAS SPOKEN.
RECITE IT LIKE THIS.

故說般若波羅蜜多咒，即說咒曰：

Gu shwo bwo re bwo lwo mi dwo jou. ji shwo jou ywe:

　　GATE GATE PARAGATE PARASAMGATE BODHI SVAHA!

揭諦揭諦，波羅揭諦，波羅僧揭諦，
菩提薩婆訶。

Jye di jye di. bwo lwo jye di. bwo lwo seng jye di. pu
ti sa pe he.

(END OF THE HEART OF PRAJNA PARAMITA SUTRA)

MAHA PRAJNA PARAMITA

摩訶般若波羅蜜多

MWO HE BWO RE BWO LWO MI DWO

(3 times)

(三稱)

46

PRAISE TO MEDICINE MASTER BUDDHA
藥 師 讚

MEDICINE MASTER THUS COME ONE LAPIS LAZULI LIGHT,

藥師如來琉璃光◎

Yau shr ru lai lyou li gwang

WITH HIS SPLENDID BLAZING NET--HOW MATCHLESSLY ADORNED!

燄網莊嚴無等倫

Yan wang jwang yan wu deng lwun

LIMITLESS PRACTICE, BOUNDLESS VOWS--BENIFIT ALL LIVING BEINGS.

無邊行願利有情

Wu byan heng ywan li you ching

HE ACCORDS WITH EACH ONE'S WISH AND NEVER WILL RETREAT.

各遂所求皆不退

Ge swei swo chyou jye bu twei

NA MO MEDICINE MASTER LAPIS LAZULI LIGHT THUS COME ONE OF
THE EASTERN PURE LAPIS LAZULI LAND

南無東方淨琉璃世界◎藥師琉璃光如來。

Na mwo dung fang jing lyou li shr jye, yau shr lyou li gwang
ru lai

NA MO QUELLING DISASTERS LENGTHNING LIFE MEDICINE MASTER
BUDDHA   *(recite while circumambulating)*

南無消災延壽藥師佛   (繞念)

Na mwo syau dzai yan shou yau shr fwo

(Return to place, put palms together,   (歸位後,合掌跪念)
kneel and recite.)
NA MO UNIVERSAL SHINING SUNLIGHT BODHISATTVA   *(3 times)*

南無日光徧照菩薩◎   (三稱)

Na mwo r gwang byan jau pu sa

NA MO UNIVERSAL SHINING MOONLIGHT BODHISATTVA   *(3 times)*

南無月光徧照菩薩◎   (三稱)

Na mwo ywe gwang byan jau pu sa.

47

NA MO MEDICINE MASTER'S GREAT ASSEMBLY OF BUDDHAS AND
BODHISATTVAS VAST AS THE SEA! *(3 times)*

南無藥師海會佛菩薩 (三稱)

Na mwo yau shr hai hwei fwo pu sa

FIRST IS TO WORSHIP AND RESPECT ALL BUDDHAS.

一者禮敬諸佛

Yi je li jing ju fwo

SECOND IS TO MAKE PRAISES TO THE THUS COME ONES.

二者稱讚如來

Er je cheng dzan ru lai

THIRD IS TO PRACTICE PROFOUNDLY THE GIVING OF OFFERINGS.

三者廣修供養

San je gwang syou gung yang

FOURTH TO REPENT AND REFORM ALL KARMIC HINDRANCE.

四者懺悔業障

Sz je chan hwei ye jang

FIFTH TO REJOICE AND FOLLOW IN MERIT AND VIRTUE.

五者隨喜功德

Wu je swei syi gung de

SIXTH IS TO REQUEST THAT THE DHARMA WHEEL BE TURNED.

六者請轉法輪

Lyou je ching jwan fa lwun

SEVENTH REQUEST THAT THE BUDDHAS REMAIN IN THE
WORLD.

七者請佛住世

Chi je ching fwo ju shr

EIGHTH IS TO FOLLOW THE BUDDHAS' TEACHING ALWAYS.

八者常隨佛學

Ba je chang swei fwo swye

48

NINTH IS TO CONSTANTLY ACCORD WITH ALL LIVING BEINGS.

九者恒順衆生

Jyou je heng shwun jung sheng

TENTH TO TRANSFER ALL MERIT AND VIRTUE UNIVERSALLY.

十者普皆回向

Shr je pu jye hwei syang

HOMAGE! ALL BUDDHAS OF THE TEN QUARTERS AND THREE TIMES;

十方三世一切佛

Shr fang san shr yi chye fwo

ALL BODHISATTVAS, MAHASATTVAS, MAHA PRAJNA PARAMITA!

一切菩薩摩訶薩　摩訶般若波羅蜜

Yi chye pu sa mwo he sa　　Mwo he bwo re bwo lwo mi.

ALL BEINGS OF THE FOUR BIRTHS IN THE NINE WORLDLY REALMS,
MAY THEY TOGETHER GAIN THE SECRET DOOR OF THE FLOWER STORE.

四生九有，同登華藏玄門，

Sz sheng jyou you, tung deng hwa dzang sywan men

THOSE SUFFERING FROM THE EIGHT WOES AND THE THREE PATHS
BELOW, MAY THEY ENTER ONE AND ALL, VAIROCHANA'S NATURE SEA.

八難三途，共入昆盧性海

Ba nan san tu, gung ru pi lu sying hai.

UNIVERSAL WORTHY'S TEN GREAT VOWS

49

Hom - age! All Bud - dhas of the ten quar-ters and three times;

All Bo - dhi-sat-tvas Ma - ha - sat - tvas;

rizard
Ma - ha - praj-na-pa - ra - mi - ta!

1. All be - ings of the four births in the nine world-ly realms,
2. Those suff'r-ing from the eight woes and the three paths be - low,

ritard
May they to-geth-er gain the se - cret door of the Flow - er Store.
May they en - ter one and all, Vai-ro - cha-na's Nat - ure Sea.

THE THREE REFUGES 三皈依

TO THE BUDDHA I RETURN AND RELY, VOWING THAT ALL LIVING BEINGS

自皈依佛，當願眾生，

Dz gwei yi fwo, dang ywan jung sheng

UNDERSTAND THE GREAT WAY PROFOUNDLY,

體解大道，

Ti jye da dau

AND BRING FORTH THE BODHI MIND. (bow)

發無上心。　　　(拜)

Fa wu shang syin.

TO THE DHARMA I RETURN AND RELY, VOWING THAT ALL LIVING BEINGS

自皈依法，當願眾生，

Dz gwei yi fa, dang ywan jung sheng

DEEPLY ENTER THE SUTRA TREASURY, AND HAVE WISDOM LIKE THE SEA.

深入經藏，　　智慧如海。

Shen ru jing dzang　　Jr hwei ru hai.

50

TO THE SANGHA I RETURN AND RELY, VOWING THAT ALL LIVING BEINGS

自皈依僧◎，當願眾生，

Dz gwei yi seng, dang ywan jung sheng

FORM TOGETHER A GREAT ASSEMBLY, ONE AND ALL IN HARMONY.

統理大眾◎，　　一切無礙；

Tung li da jung　　　　Yi chye wu ai.

(bow; rise and half-bow)

和南聖眾◎　　　　　（問訊）

He nan sheng jung.

Wei nwo:　　Assembly:

To ——————　To the Bud-dha I re-turn and re-ly,
To ——————　To the Dhar-ma I re-turn and re-ly,
To ——————　To the San-gha I re-turn and re-ly,

Vow - ing that all liv-ing be-ings Un - der - stand the Great
Vow - ing that all liv-ing be-ings Deep-ly en - ter the
Vow - ing that all liv-ing be-ings Form to-ge-ther a

Way pro-found-ly　And bring forth the Bo-dhi Mind.
Su - tra Treas-'ry　And have wis - dom like the sea.
Great As - sem -bly　One and all in har - mo - ny.

NA MO DHARMA GUARDIAN WEI TOU VENERATED DEVA
BODHISATTVA　　　　　*(3 times)*

南無◎護法韋馱尊天菩薩（三稱）

Na mwo hu fa wei two dzwun tyan pu sa

51

THE GOOD GODDESS MANTRA
大吉祥天女咒

1) NA MWO FWO TWO   南無佛陀⊙³

2) NA MWO DA MWO   南無達摩

3) NA MWO SENG CHYE   南無僧伽

4) NA MWO SHR LI   南無室利

5) MWO HE TI BI YE   摩訶提鼻耶

6) DA NI YE TWO   怛你也他

7) BWO LI FU LOU NWO   波利富樓那

8) JE LI SAN MAN TWO   遮利三曼陀

9) DA SHE NI   達舍尼

10) MWO HE PI HE LWO CHYE DI   摩訶毗訶羅伽帝

11) SAN MAN TWO   三曼陀

12) PI NI CHYE DI   毗尼伽帝

13) MWO HE JA LI YE   摩訶迦利野

14) BWO MI   波禰

15) BWO LA   波囉

16) BWO MI   波禰

17) SA LI WA LI TWO   薩利嚩栗他

18) SAN MAN TWO   三曼陀帝

19) SYOU BWO LI DI   修鉢犂那

20) FU LI NWO   富隸那

21) E LI NWO   阿利帝

22) DA MWO DI   達摩

23) MWO HE PI GU BI DJ 　摩訶毗鼓畢帝

24) MWO HE MI LEI DI 　摩訶彌勒帝

  LOU BWO SENG CHI DI 　婁簸僧祇帝

25) SYI DI SYI 　醯帝徙

26) SENG CHI SYI DI 　僧祇醯帝

27) SAN MAN TWO 　三曼陀

28) E TWO E OU 　阿他阿㝹

29) PE LWO NI   *(3 times)* 　婆羅尼　　　　(三徧)

PRAISE TO VAJRAPANI BODHISATTVA

韋馱讚

WEI TOU MASTER WARRIOR OF THE DEVAS;

韋馱天將

Wei two tyan jyang

TRANSFORMATION BODY BODHISATTVA;

菩薩化身

Pu sa hwa shen

VAST AND DEEP YOUR MIGHTY VOWS TO CHERISH AND GUARD THE BUDDHA'S TEACHING.

擁護佛法誓弘深

Yung hu fwo fa shr hung shen

YOUR VAJRA SWORD CAN QUELL THE DEMON ARMIES!

寶杵鎮魔軍

Bau chu jen mwo jyun

MERIT, VIRTUE--ALL BEYOND COMPARE.

功德難倫

Gung de nan lwun

NOW WE PRAY YOU WILL BE GUARDIAN OF OUR MINDS.

◎祈 禱副羣心，

Chi dau fu chyun syin.

NA MO UNIVERSAL EYE BODHISATTVA MAHASATTVA.

南無普◎眼菩薩摩訶薩，

Na mwo Pu Yan Pu Sa Mwo He Sa.

MAHA PRAJNA PARAMITA!

◎摩訶般若波羅蜜◎.

Mwo he bwo re bwo lwo mi!

BOWING TO THE PATRIARCHS
禮 祖

(With each bow, recite the following repentance verse in
silence:)

> *The worshipped and the worshipper are in*
> *nature empty and still.*
> *The interchange in the path between the influence*
> *and response is difficult to conceive of.*
> *This Way-place of mine is like a wish-fulfilling pearl.*
> *The (name of Patriarch) manifests within it.*
> *My form manifests before (name of Patriarch).*
> *Seeking to eradicate obstacles,*
> *I bow in worship.*

(諸位皆五體投地，勤重致禮，想云:)

能禮所禮性空寂，
感應道交難思議，
我此道場如帝珠，
　(祖師名)　影現中，
我身影現(祖師名)前，
為求滅障接足皈命禮.

54

The leader says: 維那師呼：

I BOW IN WORSHIP TO THE VENERABLE ONE, THE NOBLE HSÜ, PRE-
CEPTOR YÜN, LORD HIGH MASTER OF TRUE SUCHNESS MONASTERY.
(3 times)
頂禮真如堂上，上虛下雲戒源和尚◎(三拜)
Ding li jen ru tang shang, shang Syu, sya Yun, jye ywan
he shang.

I BOW IN WORSHIP TO THE VENERABLE ONE, THE REVEREND CHANG,
THE NOBLE JR, LORD HIGH MASTER OF THREE CONDITIONS MONASTERY.
(3 times)
頂禮三緣堂上，上常下智老和尚◎ (三拜)
Ding li san ywan tang shang, shang Chang, sya Jr, lau he
shang.

I BOW IN WORSHIP TO THE VENERABLE ONE, THE REVEREND CHANG,
THE NOBLE REN, LORD HIGH MASTER OF THREE CONDITIONS MONASTERY.
(3 times)
頂禮三緣堂上，上常下仁老和尚◎ (三拜)
Ding li san ywan tang shang, shang Chang, sya Ren, lau he
shang.

I BOW IN WORSHIP TO THE HOLY ONES, ALL PATRIARCHS OF THE
EAST AND WEST, ALL SAGES OF THE DHARMA REALM.   *(3 times)*
頂禮西天東土歷代祖師◎   (三拜)
Ding li syi tyan dung du li dai dzu shr.

(Conclude with a half-bow. Bow to the Triple Jewel and Abbot.)
(問訊後，禮拜三寶，及住持和尚。)

INCENSE PRAISE
香讚

In- cense in the cen- ser now is

burn- ing; All the Dhar- ma

Realm re- ceives the fra- grance

From a- far the sea- vast

host of Bud- dhas all in-

hale its sweet- ness. In

ev- ery place aus- pi- cious clouds ap-

pear- ing,

Our sin- cere in- ten- tion thus ful-

fill- ing, As all

Bud- dhas now show their Per- fect

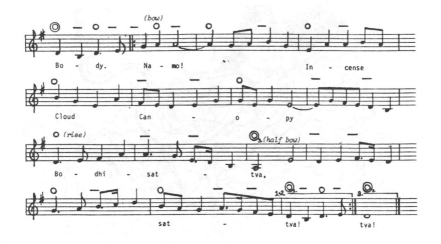

INCENSE IN THE CENSER NOW IS BURNING; ALL THE DHARMA REALM

鑪香乍爇◎　　法界蒙熏

Lyu syang ja re, Fa Jye meng syun.

RECEIVES THE FRAGRANCE, FROM AFAR THE SEA VAST HOST OF
BUDDHAS ALL INHALE ITS SWEETNESS.

諸佛海會悉遙聞◎

Ju Fwo hai hwei syi yau wen.

IN EVERY PLACE AUSPICIOUS CLOUDS APPEARING,

隨處結祥雲　　◎

Swei chu jye syang yun,

OUR SINCERE INTENTION THUS FULFILLING, AS ALL BUDDHAS NOW
SHOW THEIR PERFECT BODY.

誠意方殷　　諸佛現全身◎

Cheng yi fang yin, ju Fwo syan chywan shen.

NA MO! INCENSE CLOUD CANOPY BODHISATTVA, MAHASATTVA!

南無香雲蓋菩薩摩訶薩 (三稱)

Na mwo Syang Yun Gai Pu Sa Mwo He Sa. *(Repeat last line
3 times, bowing each time and ending with a half-bow.)*

57

THE MEAL OFFERING BEFORE THE BUDDHAS
佛前大供

NA MO MAGIC MOUNTAIN ASSEMBLY OF BUDDHAS AND BODHISATTVAS.

南無靈山會上佛菩薩 　（三稱三拜）
Na mwo ling shan hwei shang fwo pu sa

NA MO ETERNALLY ABIDING BUDDHAS OF THE TEN DIRECTIONS.

南無常住十方佛
Na mwo chang ju shr fang fwo

NA MO ETERNALLY ABIDING DHARMA OF THE TEN DIREC TIONS.

南無常住十方法
Na mwo chang ju shr fang fa

NA MO ETERNALLY ABIDING SANGHA OF THE TEN DIREC TIONS.

南無常住十方僧
Na mwo chang ju shr fang seng

58

NA MO FUNDAMENTAL TEACHER SHAKYAMUNI BUD DHA.

南無本師釋迦牟尼佛

Na mwo Ben Shr Shr Jya Mu Ni Fwo

NA MO QUELLING DISASTERS LENGTH'NING LIFE MEDICINE MASTER
BUD DHA.

南無消災延壽藥師佛

Na mwo Syau Dzai Yan Shou Yau Shr Fwo

NA MO IN THE LAND OF ULTIMATE BLISS AMITABHA BUD DHA.

南無極樂世界阿彌陀佛

Na mwo Ji Le Shr Jye E Mi Two Fwo

NA MO MAITREYA HONORED FUTURE BUD DHA.

南無當來下生彌勒尊佛

Na mwo Dang Lai Sya Sheng Mi Lei Dzwun Fwo

NA MO ALL BUDDHAS OF THE TEN QUARTERS AND THREE TIMES.

南無十方三世一切諸佛

Na mwo shr fang san shr yi chye ju Fwo

NA MO MAN JUSRI GREAT WISDOM BODHISAT TVA.

南無大智文殊師利菩薩

Na mwo da jr Wen Shu Shr Li Pu Sa

NA MO UNIVERSAL WORTHY GREAT CONDUCT BODHISAT TVA.

南無大行普賢菩薩

Na mwo da heng Pu Syan Pu Sa

NA MO EARTH TREASURY KING GREAT VOW BODHISAT TVA.

南無大願地藏王菩薩

Na mwo da ywan Di Dzang Wang Pu Sa

NA MO GWAN SHR YIN GREAT COMPASSION BODHISAT TVA.

南無大悲觀世音菩薩

Na mwo da bei Gwan Shr Yin Pu Sa

NA MO GREAT STRENGTH BODHISATTVA.

南無大勢至菩薩
Na mwo Da Shr Jr Pu Sa

NA MO GREAT PURE SEA-LIKE ASSEMBLY OF BODHISATTVAS.

南無清淨大海眾菩薩
Na mwo ching jing da hai jung Pu Sa

NA MO DHARMA GUARDIAN WEI TOU VENERATED DEVA BODHISATTVA.

南無護法韋馱尊天菩薩
Na mwo hu fa Wei Tou dzwun tyan Pu Sa

NA MO ALL DHARMA GUARDING DEVA BODHISATTVAS.

南無護法諸天菩薩
Na mwo hu fa ju tyan Pu Sa

NA MO SANGHARAMA GUARDING HOST OF BODHISATTVAS.

南無伽藍聖眾菩薩
Na mwo Chye Lan sheng jung Pu Sa

NA MO DESCENDING LINE OF PATRIARCHS BODHISATTVAS.

南無歷代祖師菩薩
Na mwo li dai Dzu Shr Pu Sa

NA MO GREAT HOLY KINNARA KING BODHISATTVA.

南無大聖緊那羅王菩薩◎。
Na mwo da sheng Jin Nwo Lwo Wang Pu Sa

(此上各聖號，皆週而復始，三遍) *(recite above text 3 times)*

60

TRANSFORMING THE FOOD TRUE WORDS
變食真言

NA MWO SA WA DAN TWO YE DWO   曩謨薩嚩怛他誐多

WA LU JR DI   嚩嚧枳帝

NAN   唵

SAN BWO LA SAN BWO LA   三跋囉三跋囉

HUNG ◎₃   吽◎₃   *(3 times)*
                                          （三遍）

SWEET DEW TRUE WORDS
甘露水真言

NA MWO SU LU PE YE ◎₃   曩謨蘇嚕婆耶◎₃

DAN TWO YE DWO YE   怛他誐多耶

DA JR TWO   怛姪他

NAN   唵

SU LU SU LU   蘇嚕蘇嚕

BWO LA SU LU BWO LA SU LU   鉢囉蘇嚕鉢囉蘇嚕

SWO PE HE   娑婆訶   *(3 times)*
                                          （三遍）

THE COLOR, SCENT AND FLAVOR OF THIS FOOD, ABOVE IS
OFFERED TO THE BUDDHAS EVERYWHERE,

此食色香味，上供十方佛，

Tsz shr shāi syang wei, shang gung shr fang fwo

BETWEEN TO EVERY SAGE AND WORTHY ONE, BELOW TO LIVING
BEINGS ON THE TURNING WHEEL;

中奉諸聖賢，下及六道品，

Jung feng ju sheng syan, sya ji lyou dau pin

BESTOWED WITHOUT DISTINCTION EQUALLY SO EVERY WISH IS
SATISFIED ACCORDINGLY,

等施無差別，隨願皆飽滿，

Deng shr wu chr bye, swei ywan jye bau man

AND THOSE WHO MADE THIS OFFERING NOW ARE CAUSED, IMMEASURABLE
PARAMITAS TO ATTAIN.

令今施者得，無量波羅蜜，

Ling jin shr je de, wu lyang bwo lwo mi

THE THREE VIRTUES AND SIX FLAVORS ARE OFFERED TO THE BUDDHA
AND SANGHA,

三德六味，供佛及僧，

San de lyou wei, gung fwo ji seng

TO ALL BEINGS OF THE DHARMA REALM
WE RENDER THIS UNIVERSAL OFFERING.

法界有情，普同供養。

Fa jye you ching, pu tung gung yang

UNIVERSAL OFFERING TRUE WORDS 普供養真言

▷ NAN	唵
YE YE NANG ◎₃	誐誐囊 ◎₃
SAN PWO WA ◎₃	三婆嚩 ◎₃
FA DZ LA	伐日囉
HUNG ◎₁	斛 ◎₁

(三遍) (3 times)

62

PRAISE AND MANTRA
讚與咒

WONDROUS OFFERINGS FROM THE HEAVENS' KITCHENS. BLISS OF
DHYANA'S RARE, DELIGHTFUL FLAVOR--

天廚妙供◎，禪悅酥酡

Tyan chu myau gung, chan ywe su two

户唵蘇嚕薩哩嚩◎

HU NAN SU LU SA LI WA

怛他阿誐多　　◎

DAN TWO E YE DWO

怛你也他

DAN NI YE TWO

◎蘇嚕娑嚩訶

SU LU SWO WA HE

NAMO BLISS OF DHYANA TREAS'RY BODHISATTVA, MAHASATTVA,

南無禪悅藏菩薩摩訶薩

Na mwo chan ywe dzang pu sa mwo he sa

MAHA PRAJNA PARAMITA!

◎摩訶般若波羅蜜◎

Mwo he bwo re bwo lwo mi

*(Assembly bows 3½ times, then recites the following praise
with palms together while walking to the dining hall.)*

（大眾三頂禮一問訊後，合掌同念釋迦佛號，舉步往齋堂。）

NAMO FUNDAMENTAL TEACHER SHAKYAMUNI BUDDHA!

南無本師釋迦牟尼佛

Na mwo ben shr shr jya mu ni fwo

*(Seated at table, the assembly with palms together, intone.
the meal offering chant.)*

（桌前坐好，大眾合掌同念臨齋儀。）

MEAL OFFERING CHANT

Now we ren-der these off'-rings to the Pure Dhar-ma-bo-dy Vai-ro-chan-na

Bud-dha; To the Per-fect Re-ward-bo-dy Ni-shyan-da Bud-dha; To the my-

riad Trans-for-ma-tion-bo-dy Shak-ya mu-ni Bud-dha; In the Land of ul-

ti-mate Bliss to A-mi-ta-bha Bud-dha; To Mai-trey-a Hon-ored fu-ture

Bud-dha; And in all times and pla-ces to each and eve-ry Bud-dha; To

Man-jus ri Great Wis-dom Bo-dhi-sat-tva; To U-ni-ver-sal Wor-thy Great

Con-duct Bo-dhi-sat-tva; To Gwan Shr Yin Great Com-pas-sion Bo-dhi-sat-tva;

To Earth Treas'ry King Great Vow Bo-dhi-sat-tva; And to all Hon-ored Bo-

dhi-sat-tvas, Ma-ha-sat-tvas; Ma-ha-pra-jna-pa-ra-mi-ta! The three vir-

tues and the six fla-vors, are of-fered to the Bud-dha and the San-gha;

To all be-ings of the Dhar-ma Realm, We ren-der this u-ni-ver-sal of-fer-

ing. Now as we have this meal be-fore us, we make a vow for all liv-ing

be-ings: May they take Dhy-a-na bliss for food, and be full with the

Joy of the Dhar - ma!

64

臨齋儀
Lin jai yi

NOW WE REN-DER THESE OFF'-RINGS TO THE PURE DHAR-MA BO-DY
VAI-RO-CHAN-NA BUD-DHA.

供養清淨法身毗盧遮那佛
Gung yang ching jing fa shen pi lyu je nwo fwo

TO THE PERFECT REWARD BODY NISHYANDA BUDDHA

圓滿報身盧舍那佛
Ywan man bau shen lyu she nwo fwo

TO THE MY-RIAD TRANS-FOR-MA-TION-BO-DY SHAK-YA-MU-NI BUD-DHA.

千百億化身釋迦牟尼佛
Chyan bai yi hwa shen shr jya mu ni fwo

IN THE LAND OF UL-TI-MATE BLISS TO A-MI-TA-BHA BUD-DHA.

極樂世界阿彌陀佛
Ji le shr jye e mi two fwo

TO MAI-TREY-A HON-ORED FU-TURE BUD-DHA.

當來下生彌勒尊佛
Dang lai sya sheng mi lei dzwun fwo

AND IN ALL TIMES AND PLA-CES TO EACH AND EVE-RY BUD-DHA.

十方三世一切諸佛
Shr fang san shr yi chye ju fwo

TO MAN-JU-SHRI GREAT WIS-DOM BO-DHI-SAT-TVA.

大智文殊師利菩薩
Da jr wen shu shr li pu sa

TO U-NI-VER-SAL WOR-THY GREAT CON-DUCT BO-DHI-SAT-TVA.

大行普賢菩薩
Da heng pu syan pu sa

TO GWAN SHR YIN GREAT COM-PAS-SION BO-DHI-SAT-TVA.

大悲觀世音菩薩
Da bei gwan shr yin pu sa

TO EARTH TREAS'RY KING GREAT VOW BO-DHI-SAT-TVA.

大願地藏王菩薩

Da ywan di dzang wang pu sa

AND TO ALL HON-ORED BO-DHI-SAT-TVAS, MA-HA-SAT-TVAS.
MA-HA-PRA-JNA-PA-RA-MI-TA!

諸尊菩薩摩訶薩，摩訶般若波羅蜜，

Ju dzwun pu sa mwo he sa, mwo he bwo re bwo lwo mi

THE THREE VIR-TUES AND THE SIX FLA-VORS, ARE OF-FERED TO
THE BUD-DHA AND THE SAN-GHA, TO ALL BE-INGS OF THE DHAR-MA
REALM, WE REN-DER THIS U-NI-VER-SAL OF-FER-ING.

三德六味　，　供佛及僧　，
法界有情　，　普同供養　，

San de lyou wei gung fwo ji seng, fa jye you ching pu
tung gung yang

NOW AS WE HAVE THIS MEAL BE-FORE US, WE MAKE A VOW FOR ALL
LIV-ING BE-INGS: MAY THEY TAKE DHY-A-NA BLISS FOR FOOD,
AND BE FULL WITH THE JOY OF THE DHAR-MA!

若飯食時　，　當願眾生　，
禪悅為食　，　法喜充滿　。

Rau fan shr shr, dang ywan jung sheng, chan ywe wei shr,
fa syi chung man

The leader says: 唯那師呼：

THE BUDDHA TOLD THE BHIKSHUS: "WHILE EATING, OBSERVE THE
FIVE CONTEMPLATIONS. A SCATTERED MIND AND CONFUSED TALK
MAKE THE OFFERINGS OF THE FAITHFUL HARD TO DIGEST. GREAT
ASSEMBLY, AT THE SOUND OF THE BELL, EACH BE PROPERLY
MINDFUL.

佛制比丘，食存五觀，散心雜話，
信施難消。大眾聞磬聲，各正念。

All recite together:　（大眾齊念）

AMITABHA!

阿彌陀佛！

E mi two fwo.

66

THREE RECOLLECTIONS AND FIVE CONTEMPLATIONS
三念五觀

When eating, one should perform the following three recollections and five contemplations: (受食時,應作三念五觀:)

THE THREE RECOLLECTIONS: 三念：

1. FIRST SPOON: I VOW TO CUT OFF ALL EVIL.

   初匙： 願斷一切惡．

   Chu chr: Ywan dwan yi chye e.

2. SECOND SPOON: I VOW TO CULTIVATE ALL GOOD.

   二匙： 願修一切善．

   Er chr: Ywan syou yi chye shan.

3. THIRD SPOON: I VOW TO SAVE ALL LIVING BEINGS.

   三匙： 誓度一切眾生．

   San chr: Shr du yi chye jung sheng.

THE FIVE CONTEMPLATIONS: 五觀：

1. CONSIDER THE AMOUNT OF WORK INVOLVED TO BRING THE FOOD
   TO WHERE IT IS EATEN.

   一.記功多少 ，量彼來處 ．

   Ji gung dwo shau, lyang bi lai chu.

2. CONSIDER WHETHER OR NOT ONE'S VIRTUOUS CONDUCT IS SUF-
   FICIENT TO ENABLE ONE TO ACCEPT THE OFFERING.

   二.忖己德行 ，全缺應供 ．

   Tsun ji de heng, chywan chywe ying gung.

3. GUARD THE MIND FROM TRANSGRESSION, OF WHICH GREED IS THE
   PRINCIPLE CAUSE.

   三.防心離過 ，貪等為宗 ．

   Fang syin li gwo, tan deng wei dzung.

4. PROPERLY TAKEN, THE FOOD IS LIKE MEDICINE, TO KEEP THE
   BODY FROM WASTING AWAY.

   四.正事良藥 ，為療形枯 ．

   Jeng shr lyang yau, wei lyau sying ku.

5. THIS FOOD IS ACCEPTED ONLY IN ORDER TO ACCOMPLISH THE WAY.

   五.為成道業 ，應受此食 ．

   Wei cheng dau ye, ying shou tsz shr.

MANTRA AND VERSE TO END THE MEAL: 結齋:

SA DWO NAN　　　　　　　薩多南

SAN MYAU SAN PU TWO　　三藐三菩陀

JYU JR NAN　　　　　　　俱胝南

DA JR TWO　　　　　　　怛姪他

NAN　　　　　　　　　　　唵

JE LI　　　　　　　　　　折隸

JU LI　　　　　　　　　　主隸

JWUN TI　　　　　　　　準提

SWO PE HE　　　　　　　娑婆訶

THEY WHO PRAC-TICE MAK-ING OFF'-RINGS, WILL CER-TAIN-LY
OB-TAIN THEIR RE-WARD:

所謂布施者，必獲其利益，

Swo wei bu shr je,bi hwai chi li yi,

THEY WHO TAKE DE-LIGHT IN GIV-ING, WILL LAT-ER SURE-LY
FIND PEACE AND HAP-PI-NESS.

若為樂故施，後必得安樂，

Rau wei le gu shr, hou bi de an le,

NOW THAT THE MEAL HAS BEEN CON-CLUD-ED, WE MAKE A VOW FOR
ALL LIVING BE-INGS:

飲食已訖，當願眾生，

Fan shr yi chi , dang ywan jung sheng,

MAY THEY HAVE SUC-CESS IN ALL THEY DO, AND BE PER-FECT IN
ALL BUD-DHA-DHARMAS!

所作皆辦，具諸佛法。

Swo dzwo jye ban,jyu ju fwo fa.

68

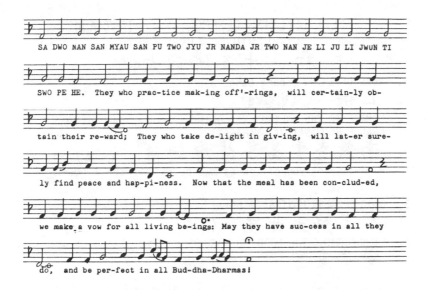

SA DWO NAN SAN MYAU SAN PU TWO JYU JR NANDA JR TWO NAN JE LI JU LI JWUN TI

SWO PE HE. They who prac-tice mak-ing off'-rings, will cer-tain-ly ob-

tain their re-ward; They who take de-light in giv-ing, will lat-er sure-

ly find peace and hap-pi-ness. Now that the meal has been con-clud-ed,

we make a vow for all living be-ings: May they have suc-cess in all they

do, and be per-fect in all Bud-dha-Dharmas!

(Return to Buddha hall while reciting:) (大眾齊念佛號送回佛殿)
NAMO FUNDAMENTAL TEACHER SHAKYAMUNI BUDDHA.

南無本師釋迦牟尼佛.

Na mwo ben shr shr jya mu ni fwo.

MEAL OFFERING CEREMONY FOR FIRST AND FIFTEENTH OF LUNAR MONTH
初一、十五佛前大供

1. MEAL OFFERING (Shang Gung; *see page 56*)
上 供　　（見第56頁）

2. HOMAGE TO THE ENLIGHTENED BEING, CLOUD CANOPY OF FRAGRANCE BODHISATTVA, MAHASATTVA.
南無香雲蓋菩薩摩訶薩　（三稱）
Na mwo syang yun gai pu sa mwo he sa　*(recite 3 times)*

3. GOOD GODDESS MANTRA *(3 times)*
大吉祥天女咒　　（三編）

4. TRANSFORMING THE FOOD TRUE WORDS *(3 times)*
變食真言　　　　（三編）

NA MWO SA WA DAN TWO YE DWO　　曩謨薩嚩怛他誐多

WA LU JR DI　　　　嚩嚧枳帝

NAN　　　　唵

SAN BWO LA SAN BWO LA　　三跋囉三跋囉

HUNG ◎₃　　吽◎₃　　　　*(3 times)*
　　　　　　　　　　　（三遍）

SWEET DEW TRUE WORDS *(3 times*
甘露水真言　　　（三編）

NA MWO SU LU PE YE◎₃　　曩謨蘇嚕婆耶◎₃

DAN TWO YE DWO YE　　怛他誐多耶

DA JR TWO　　怛姪他

70

NAN 唵

SU LU SU LU 蘇嚕蘇嚕

BWO LA SU LU BWO LA SU LU 鉢囉蘇嚕鉢囉蘇嚕

SWO PE HE 娑婆訶 *(3 times)* (三遍)

UNIVERSAL OFFERING TRUE WORDS*(3 times)*
普供養真言 (三徧)

▷ NAN 唵

YE YE NANG ◎₃ 誐誐曩◎₃

SAN BWO WA ◎₃ 三婆嚩◎₃

FA DZ LA 伐日囉

HUNG ◎₁ 斛◎₁

(三遍) *(3 times)*

NAMO DHARMA GUARDIAN WEI TOU VENERATED DEVA BODHISATTVA.
南無護法韋馱尊天菩薩 (三稱)
Na mwo hu fa wei two dzwun tyan pu sa *(3 times)*

5. PRAISE TO WEI TOU BODHISATTVA *(see page 53; bow 1/2 time after praise)*
韋馱讚 (見第53頁；讚畢問訊)

6. HOMAGE TO THE ENLIGHTENED BEING, CLOUD CANOPY OF FRA-GRANCE BODHISATTVA, MAHASATTVA.
南無香雲蓋菩薩摩訶薩 (三稱)
Na mwo syang yun gai pu sa mwo he sa *(recite 3 times)*

7. GREAT COMPASSION MANTRA *(see page 32)*
大悲咒 (一徧；見第32頁)
HOMAGE TO THE HOLY ASSEMBLY OF TEMPLE-GUARDING BODHISATTVAS.

8. *(same as #4)* (同#4)

71

南無伽藍聖眾菩薩◎　　　（三稱）
Na mwo chye lan sheng jung pu sa. *(3 times)*

9. PRAISE TO CHYE LAN BODHISATTVA　伽藍讚

LORD CHYE LAN,

伽藍主者◎
Chye lan ju je

WITH AWESOME POWERS BRINGS HARMONY TO THE TEMPLE.

合寺威靈
He sz wei ling.

RESPECTFULLY HE RECEIVES THE BUDDHA'S COMMANDS.

欽承佛教共輸誠◎
Chin cheng fwo chr gung shu cheng.

AND WITH SINCERITY PROTECTS AND UPHOLDS THE CITY
OF THE DHARMA KING.

擁護法王城　　◎
Yung hu fa wang cheng.

HE ACTS AS A BARRICADE AND SENTRY,

為翰為屏
Wei han wei ping.

SO THAT THE PURE WAY PLACE IS FOREVER PEACEFUL.

◎梵刹永安寧
Fan cha yung an ning.

HOMAGE TO THE BODHISATTVA MAHASATTVA, WHO PROTECTS THE
DHARMA TREASURY, MAHAPRAJNA PARAMITA. ◎

南無護◎法藏菩薩摩訶薩，摩訶般若波羅蜜。
Na mwo hu fa dzang pu sa mwo ne sa, mwo he bwo re
bwo lwo mi. *(bow 3 times)* （三拜）

10. NAMO TO THE SUCCESSIVE GENERATIONS OF PATRIARCHS,
BODHISATTVAS!

(recite while walking to the Patriarch's altar)

南無歷代祖師菩薩 （齊唸名稱，至祖師堂）
Na mo li dai dzu shr pu sa

CEREMONY FOR THE PATRIARCHS
祖師偈讚

HOMAGE TO THE ENLIGHTENED BEING, CLOUD CANOPY OF FRAGRANCE
BODHISATTVA, MAHASATTVA.   *(3 times)*

南無香◎雲蓋菩薩摩訶薩◎ (三稱)

Na mwo syang yun gai pu sa mwo he sa *(3 times)*

HOMAGE TO THE PRAJNA ASSEMBLY OF BUDDHAS AND BODHISATTVAS
AS VAST AS THE SEA.   *(3 times)*

南無般◎若會上佛菩薩◎   (三稱)

Na mwo bwo re hwei shang fwo pu sa.

THE HEART OF PRAJNA PARAMITA SUTRA *(recite 1 time)*

般若波羅蜜多心經◎(一卷,見44頁)

TRANSFORMING THE FOOD TRUE WORDS
變食真言

NA MWO SA WA DAN TWO YE DWO	曩謨薩嚩怛他誐多
WA LU JR DI	嚩嚧枳帝
NAN	唵
SAN BWO LA SAN BWO LA	三跋囉三跋囉
HUNG ◎₃	吽◎₃ *(3 times)*
	(三 遍)

SWEET DEW TRUE WORDS
甘露水真言

NA MWO SU LU PE YE◎₃	曩謨蘇嚕婆耶◎₃
DAN TWO YE DWO YE	怛他誐多耶

73

DA JR TWO　　　　怛姪他

NAN　　　　　　　唵

SU LU SU LU　　　蘇嚕蘇嚕

BWO LA SU LU BWO LA SU LU　鉢囉蘇嚕鉢囉蘇嚕

SWO PE HE　　　娑婆訶　　*(3 times)*
　　　　　　　　　　　　　(三遍)

UNIVERSAL OFFERING TRUE WORDS
普供養真言

NAN　　　　　　　唵

YE YE NANG ◎₃　　　誐誐曩◎₃

SAN BWO WA ◎₃　　三婆嚩◎₃

FA DZ LA　　　　伐日囉

HUNG ◎₁　　　　斛◎₁

　　　　　　　　(三遍)　*(3 times)*

NAMO TO THE SUCCESSIVE GENERATIONS OF PATRIARCHS, BODHI-
SATTVAS!
南無歷◎代祖師菩薩◎ (三稱)
Na mo li dai dzu shr pu sa. (3x)

AS THE FLOWER WAS HELD ALOFT, ENLIGHTENMENT WAS TRANSMITTED,
AND THE PATH OF THE PATRIARCHS FIRST BEGAN.
拈花悟旨◎，祖道初興．
Nyan hwa wu jr, dzu dau chu sying.

CONTINUING THE "4 X 7", THE TRUE VEHICLE IS PROCLAIMED.
縣延四七演真乘◎．
Myan yen sz chi yen jen cheng.

74

SIX GENERATIONS, THE FAR-REACHING TRANSMISSION OF THE LAMP,

六代遠傳燈，

Lyou dai ywan jwan deng

FOR MANY GENERATIONS IT IS SUCCESSIVELY RECEIVED.

奕葉相承，

Yi ye syang cheng,

SO THAT THE PROPER DHARMA MAY FLOURISH GLORIOUSLY FOREVER!

正法永昌明。

Jeng fa yung chang ming.

NAMO TO THE MASTERS WHO CROSS PEOPLE OVER, BODHISATTVAS, MAHASATTVAS.

南無度人師菩薩摩訶薩，

Na mwo du ren shr pu sa mwo he sa.

MAHA-PRAJNA-PARAMITA!

摩訶般若波羅蜜。

Mwo he bwo re bwo lwo mi.

(1/2 bow and recite Fundamental Teacher Shakyamuni Buddha)

****

CEREMONY FOR JYAN TSAI BODHISATTVA
監齋菩薩偈讚

HOMAGE TO THE ENLIGHTENED BEING, CLOUD CANOPY OF FRAGRANCE BODHISATTVA, MAHASATTVA.

南無香雲蓋菩薩摩訶薩 (三稱)

Na mwo syang yun gai pu sa mwo he sa *(3 times)*

JWUN TI SPIRIT MANTRA *(3 times)*

準提神咒 (三徧)

1) NA MWO SA DWO NAN　南無颯哆喃
2) SAN MYAU SAN PU TWO　三藐三菩陀
3) JYU JR NAN　俱胝喃
4) DA JR TWO　怛姪他
5) NAN　唵
6) JE LI JU LI　折戾主戾
7) JWUN TI　準提
8) SWO PE HE　娑婆訶

TRANSFORMING THE FOOD TRUE WORDS *(3 times)*
變食真言　(三徧)

NA MWO SA WA DAN TWO YE DWO　曩謨薩嚩怛他誐多

WA LU JR DI　嚩嚧枳帝

NAN　唵

SAN BWO LA SAN BWO LA　三跋囉三跋囉

HUNG ◎₃　吽◎₃　　　　　*(3 times)*
　　　　　　　　　　　　　(三 徧)

SWEET DEW TRUE WORDS *(3 times)*
甘露水真言(三徧)

NA MWO SU LU PE YE◎₃　曩謨蘇嚕婆耶◎₃

DAN TWO YE DWO YE　怛他誐多耶

DA JR TWO　怛姪他

76

NAN 唵

SU LU SU LU 蘇嚕蘇嚕

BWO LA SU LU BWO LA SU LU 鉢囉蘇嚕鉢囉蘇嚕

SWO PE HE 娑婆訶 *(3 times)*
(三遍)

UNIVERSAL OFFERING TRUE WORDS *(3 times)*
普供養真言 (三遍)

NAN 唵
YE YE NANG ◎₃ 誐誐曩◎₃
SAN BWO WA ◎₃ 三婆嚩◎₃
FA DZ LA 伐日囉
HUNG ◎₁ 斛◎₁

(三遍) *(3 times)*

NAMO TO THE GREAT HOLY KINNARA KING, BODHISATTVA. **(3x)**
南無大◎聖緊那羅王菩薩◎(三稱)
Na mwo da sheng jin nwo lwo wang pu sa.

THE MESSENGER, SUPERINTENDANT OF FOOD, THE AWESOME SPIRIT
OF THE FIRE DIVISION;
監齋使者◎火部威神.
Jyan tsai shr je, hwo bu wei shen

BLENDING THE HUNDRED FLAVORS TO MAKE A FRAGRANT OFFERING.
調和百味薦惟馨◎
Tyau he bai wei jyan wei sying.

STOPPING FOREVER ALL DISASTERS,

77

災耗永無侵,
Dzai hau yung wu chin,

PROTECTING OUR LIVES AND NURTURING OUR BODIES;
護命資身;
Hu ming dz shen

THE PURE ASSEMBLY WILL ALWAYS RECEIVE HIS KINDNESS.
清眾永蒙恩.
Ching jung yung meng en.

NAMO THE FLAMING WISDOM GROUND BODHISATTVA, MAHASATTVA.
南無燄慧地菩薩摩訶薩,
Na mwo yen hwei di pu sa mwo he sa.

MAHA-PRAJNA-PARAMITA!
摩訶般若波羅蜜.
Mwo he bwo re bwo lwo mi.

DEDICATION BEFORE THE REBIRTH PLAQUES
往生位前回向

1. HOMAGE TO THE BODHISATTVA, MAHASATTVA OF THE CLEAR COOL
    GROUND.   *(3 times)*
    南無清涼地菩薩摩訶薩   (三稱)
    Na mwo ching lyang di pu sa mwo he sa

2a. HOMAGE TO THE LOTUS POOL ASSEMBLY OF BUDDHAS AND BODHI-
    SATTVAS AS VAST AS THE SEA.   *(3 times)*
    南無蓮池海會佛菩薩   (三稱)
    Na mwo lyan chr hai hwei fwo pu sa.

3a. THE BUDDHA SPEAKS OF AMITABHA SUTRA *(recite 1 time; see*
    佛說阿彌陀經 (一卷;見第87頁)   *page 87)*

Or, 2b. HOMAGE TO THE PRAJNA ASSEMBLY OF BUDDHAS AND BODHISATTVAS
或   AS VAST AS THE SEA.   *(3 times)*
    南無般若會上佛菩薩   (三稱)
    Na mwo bwo re hwei shang fwo pu sa.

3b. THE HEART OF PRAJNA PARAMITA SUTRA *(recite 1 time or 3*
    般若波羅蜜多心經 (一卷或三卷 見44頁) *times; see pg. 44)*

4. SPIRIT MANTRA FOR REBIRTH IN THE PURE LAND
往生咒（三遍）

NA MWO E MI DWO PE YE ◎	南無阿彌多婆夜 ◎
DWO TWO CHYE DWO YE	哆他伽多夜
DWO DI YE TWO	哆地夜他
E MI LI DU PE PI	阿彌利都婆毗
E MI LI DWO	阿彌利哆
SYI DAN PE PI	悉耽婆毗
E MI LI DWO	阿彌唎哆
PI JYA LAN DI	毗迦蘭帝
E MI LI DWO	阿彌唎哆
PI JYA LAN DWO	毗迦蘭多
CHYE MI LI ◎	伽彌膩 ◎
CHYE CHYE NWO	伽伽那
JR DWO JYA LI	枳多迦利
SWO PE HE *(recite 3 times)*	娑婆訶　　（三遍）

5. TRANSFORMING THE FOOD TRUE WORDS *(3 times)*
變食真言（三遍）

NA MWO SA WA DAN TWO YE DWO	曩謨薩嚩怛他誐多
WA LU JR DI	嚩嚧枳帝
NAN	唵
SAN BWO LA SAN BWO LA	三跋囉三跋囉
HUNG ◎,	吽 ◎,

(3 times)
（三遍）

79

6. SWEET DEW TRUE WORDS *(3 times)*
甘露水真言 (三徧)

NA MWO SU LU PE YE◎₃	曩謨蘇嚕婆耶◎₃
DAN TWO YE DWO YE	怛他誐多耶
DA JR TWO	怛姪他
NAN	唵
SU LU SU LU	蘇嚕蘇嚕
BWO LA SU LU BWO LA SU LU	鉢囉蘇嚕鉢囉蘇嚕
SWO PE HE	娑婆訶 *(3 times)* (三遍)

7. UNIVERSAL OFFERING TRUE WORDS *(3 times)*
普供養真言 (三徧)

▷ NAN	唵
YE YE NANG ◎₃	誐誐曩◎₃
SAN BWO WA ◎₃	三婆嚩◎₃
FA DZ LA	伐日囉
HUNG ◎₁	斛◎₁
	(三遍) *(3 times)*

8. PURE LAND PRAISE
(淨土 讚)
IN THE LOTUS POOL ASSEMBLY AS VAST AS THE SEA, MAY AMITA, THE THUS COME ONE,

蓮池海會◎, 彌陀如來,
Lyan chr hai hwei, mi two ru lai.

80

AVALOKITESHVARA, MAHASTHAMAPRAPTA, AND THE ENTIRE
MULTITUDE OF SAGES.

觀音勢至聖眾偕◎,

Gwan yin shr jr sheng jung jye.

LEAD BEINGS TO ASCEND THE LOTUS DIASES, AND BASED ON
GREAT VOWS, EXPANSIVELY TEACH THEM,

接引上蓮臺．大誓弘開，

Jye yin shang lyan tai. da shr hung kai.

SO THAT ALL WILL VOW TO LEAVE DEFILEMENT.

◎普願離塵埃．

Pu ywan li chen ai。

WE VOW THEY WILL BE BORN IN THE WESTERN PURE LAND,

願生西方淨土中◎,

Ywan sheng syi fang jing du jung.

WITH THE NINE GRADES OF LOTUS FLOWERS AS PARENTS,

九品蓮華為父母，

Jyou pin lyan hwa wei fu mu.

WHEN THE FLOWERS OPEN, THEY WILL SEE THE BUDDHA AND
BECOME ENLIGHTENED TO THE UNPRODUCED,

華開見佛悟無生，

Hwa kai jyan fwo wu wu sheng.

AND IRREVERSIBLE BODHISATTVAS WILL BE THEIR COMPANIONS.

不退菩薩為伴侶．

Bu twei pu sa wei ban lyu.

ALL BUDDHAS OF THE TEN DIRECTIONS AND THE THREE PERIODS
OF TIME.

十方三世一切佛◎

Shr fang san shr yi chye fwo.

81

ALL BODHISATTVAS, MAHASATTVAS.

一切菩薩摩訶薩，

Yi chye pu sa mwo he sa.

MAHA PRAJNA PARAMITA!

◎摩訶般若波羅蜜◎。

Mwo he bwo re bwo lwo mi.

佛亦有疾乳光牛
王獻乳供養大時
婆羅門後此信佛

TRANSFERENCE FOR LENGTHENING LIFE
延生堂回向

1. HOMAGE TO THE BODHISATTVA, MAHASATTVA WHO INCREASES BLESSINGS AND LIFE-SPAN *(3 times)*

南無增福壽菩薩摩訶薩◎　　(三稱)

Na mwo tseng fu shou pu sa mwo he sa

2. HOMAGE TO MEDICINE MASTER BUDDHA WHO ELIMINATES CALAMITIES AND LENGTHENS LIFE *(3 times)*

南無消災延壽藥師佛◎　　(三稱)

Na mwo syau dzai yan shou yau shr fwo

3. MEDICINE MASTER'S TRUE WORDS FOR ANOINTING THE CROWN *(7 times; see page 40)*

藥師灌頂真言　　(七徧；見第40頁)

4. TRANSFORMING THE FOOD TRUE WORDS *(3 times)*

變食真言　(三徧)

NA MWO SA WA DAN TWO YE DWO　　曩謨薩嚩怛他誐多

WA LU JR DI　　嚩嚧枳帝

NAN　　唵

SAN BWO LA SAN BWO LA　　三跋囉三跋囉

HUNG ◎₃　　吽◎₃　　*(3 times)* (三遍)

5. SWEET DEW TRUE WORDS *(3 times)*

甘露水真言(三徧)

NA MWO SU LU PE YE◎₃　　曩謨蘇嚕婆耶◎₃

DAN TWO YE DWO YE　　怛他誐多耶

DA JR TWO　　怛姪他

83

NAN 唵

SU LU SU LU 蘇嚕蘇嚕

BWO LA SU LU BWO LA SU LU 鉢囉蘇嚕鉢囉蘇嚕

SWO PE HE 娑婆訶 *(3 times)*
(三遍)

6. UNIVERSAL OFFERING TRUE WORDS *(3 times)*
普供養真言 (三遍)

NAN 唵

YE YE NANG ◎₃ 誐誐曩 ◎₃

SAN BWO WA ◎₃ 三婆嚩 ◎₃

FA DZ LA 伐日囉

HUNG ◎₁ 斛 ◎₁

(三遍) *(3 times)*

7. PRAISE
(讚偈)
THE BUDDHA'S LIGHT SHINES UPON OUR ORIGINAL LIFE-FORCE.
佛光注照◎, 本命元辰,
Fwo gwang ju jyau, ben ming ywan chen,

THE UNLUCKY STAR RETREATS; A LUCKY STAR ARRIVES.
災星退度福星臨◎
Dzai sying twei du, fu sying lin,

THE NINE PLANETS OFFER PROTECTION AND ENSURE LONG LIFE,
九曜保長生, ◎
Jyou yau bau chang sheng,

SO THAT LANDS ARE PEACEFUL.

運限和平,

Yun syan he ping.

WITH BLESSINGS AND LONGEVITY, MAY WE FLOURISH FOREVER IN
HEALTH AND CONCORD.

◎福壽永康寧.

Fu shou yung kang ning.

I VOW TO ERADICATE THE THREE OBSTRUCTIONS AND ALL AFFLICTIONS,

▽願消三障諸煩惱◎,

Ywan syau san jang ju fan nau.

I VOW TO OBTAIN WISDOM AND TO OBTAIN TRUE UNDERSTANDING,

願得智慧真明了,

Ywan de jr hwei jen ming lyau.

I MAKE A UNIVERSAL VOW THAT THE OBSTACLES OF MY OFFENSES
WILL BE TOTALLY ELIMINATED,

普願罪障悉消除,

Pu ywan dzwei jang syi syau chu.

AND THAT IN LIFE AFTER LIFE WE SHALL CONSTANTLY PRACTICE
THE PATH OF THE BODHISATTVAS,

世世常行菩薩道.

Shr shr chang sying pu sa dau.

ALL BUDDHAS OF THE TEN DIRECTIONS AND THE THREE PERIODS
OF TIME,

▽十方三世一切佛◎,

Shr fang san shr yi chye fwo

ALL BODHISATTVAS, MAHASATTVAS,

一切菩薩摩訶薩,

Yi chye pu sa mwo he sa.

MAHA PRAJNA PARAMITA!

◎摩訶般若波羅蜜◎.

Mwo he bwo re bwo lwo mi.

EVENING CEREMONY
暮時課誦

INCENSE PRAISE (see page 56)　　香讚 (見56頁)

86

NAMO SEA VAST LOTUS POOL ASSEMBLY OF BUDDHAS AND
BODHISATTVAS   *(recite 3 times)*

南無蓮池海會佛菩薩◎　　（三稱）
Na mwo lyan chr hai hwei fwo pu sa.

THE BUDDHA SPEAKS OF AMITABHA SUTRA◎

佛說阿彌陀經◎
Fwo shwo e mi two jing
◎

THUS I HAVE HEARD, AT ONE TIME, THE BUDDHA DWELT AT
SHRAVASTI IN THE JETA GROVE

如是我聞，一時，佛在舍衛國
Ru shr wo wen. Yi shr fwo dzai she wei gwo.

IN THE GARDEN OF THE BENEFACTOR OF ORPHANS AND THE
SOLITARY, TOGETHER WITH A GATHERING OF GREAT BHIKSHUS

祇樹給孤獨園。與大比丘僧。
Chi shu ji gu du ywan. Yu da bi chyou seng.

TWELVE HUNDRED FIFTY IN ALL, ALL GREAT ARHATS WHOM THE
ASSEMBLY KNEW AND RECOGNIZED:

千二百五十人俱，皆是大阿羅漢，
眾所知識。
Chyan er bai wu shr ren jyu. Jye shr da e lwo han. Jung
swo jr shr.

ELDERS SHARIPUTRA, MAHAMAUDGALYAYANA, MAHAKASYAPA,
MAHAKATYAYANA, MAHAKAUSHTILA,

長老舍利弗，摩訶目犍連，摩訶
迦葉，摩訶迦旃延，摩訶俱絺羅，
Jang lau she li fu. Mwo he mu jyan lyan. Mwo he jya she.
Mwo he jya jan yan. Mwo he jyu syi lwo.

REVATA, SUDDHIPANTHAKA, NANDA, ANANDA, RAHULA, GAVAMPATI,
PINDOLA-BHARADVAJA.

離婆多，周利槃陀伽，難陀，阿難陀，
羅睺羅，憍梵波提，賓頭盧頗羅墮。
Li pe dwo. Jou li pan two chye. Nan two. E nan two.
Lwo hou lwo. Jyau fan bwo ti. Bin tou lu pe lwo dwo.

87

KALODAYIN, MAHAKAPHINA, VAKKULA, ANIRUDDHA, AND OTHERS
SUCH AS THESE, ALL GREAT DISCIPLES;

迦留陀夷，摩訶劫賓那，薄拘羅，
阿㝹樓馱。如是等諸大弟子。

Jya lyou two yı. Mwo he jye bin nwo. Bwo jyu lwo. E nou
lou two. Ru shr deng ju da di dz.

TOGETHER WITH ALL THE BODHISATTVAS, MAHASATTVAS:DHARMA
PRINCE MANJUSHRI, AJITA BODHISATTVA, GANDHASTIN
BODHISATTVA.

幷諸菩薩摩訶薩，文殊師利法王子，
阿逸多菩薩，乾陀訶提菩薩，

Bing ju pu sa mwo he sa. Wen shu shr li fa wang dz. E yi
dwo pu sa. Chyan two he ti pu sa.

NITYODUKTA BODHISATTVA, AND OTHERS SUCH AS THESE, ALL
GREAT BODHISATTVAS; AND TOGETHER WITH SHAKRA☺ CHIEF AMONG
GODS, AND THE NUMBERLESS GREAT MULTITUDES FROM ALL THE
HEAVENS.☺

常精進菩薩，與如是等諸大菩薩．
及釋提桓因等◎，無量諸天大眾俱◎．

Chang jing jin pu sa. Yu ru shr deng ju da pu sa. Ji shr
ti hwan yin deng, wu lyang ju tyan da jung jyu.

AT THAT TIME THE BUDDHA TOLD THE ELDER SHARIPUTRA,
"PASSING FROM   HERE THROUGH HUNDREDS OF THOUSANDS OF
MILLIONS OF BUDDHALANDS TO THE WEST, THERE`IS A WORLD
CALLED ULTIMATE BLISS.

爾時佛告長老舍利弗，從是西方，
過十萬億佛土，有世界名曰極樂，

Er shr fwo gau jang lau she li fu. Tsung shr syi fang, gwo
shr wan yi fwo du. You shr jye ming ywe, ji le.

IN THIS LAND A BUDDHA CALLED AMITABHA RIGHT NOW TEACHES
THE DHARMA.

其土有佛，號阿彌陀，今現在說法。

Chi du you fwo hau e mi two. Jin syan dzai shwo fa.

SHARIPUTRA, FOR WHAT REASON IS THIS LAND CALLED ULTIMATE BLISS?

舍利弗，彼土何故名為極樂？

She li fu. Bi du he gu ming wei, ji le.

ALL LIVING BEINGS OF THIS COUNTRY ENDURE NONE OF THE SUFFERINGS, BUT ENJOY EVERY BLISS. THEREFORE IT IS CALLED ULTIMATE BLISS.

其國眾生，無有眾苦，但受諸樂，
故名極樂。

Chi gwo jung sheng. Wu you jung ku. Dan shou ju le.
Gu ming ji le.

MOREOVER, SHARIPUTRA, THIS LAND OF ULTIMATE BLISS IS EVERYWHERE SURROUNDED BY SEVEN TIERS OF RAILINGS, SEVEN LAYERS OF NETTING, AND SEVEN ROWS OF TREES,

又舍利弗，極樂國土，七重欄楯，
七重羅網，七重行樹，皆是四寶

You, she li fu. Ji le gwo du. Chi chung lan shun
Chi chung lwo wang. Chi chung hang shu. Jye shr sz bau.

ALL FORMED FROM THE FOUR TREASURES AND FOR THIS REASON NAMED ULTIMATE BLISS.

周帀圍繞，是故彼國名為極樂。

Joudza wei rau. Shr gu bi gwo ming wei ji le.

MOREOVER, SHARIPUTRA, THE LAND OF ULTIMATE BLISS HAS POOLS OF THE SEVEN JEWELS,

又舍利弗，極樂國土，有七寶池，

You she li fu. Ji le gwo du. You chi bau chr.

FILLED WITH THE EIGHT WATERS OF MERIT AND VIRTUE. THE BOTTOM OF EACH POOL IS PURE, SPREAD OVER WITH GOLDEN SAND.

八功德水充滿其中。池底純以金
沙布地。

Ba gung de shwei chung man chi jung. Chr di chun yi jin
sha bu di.

ON THE FOUR SIDES ARE STAIRS OF GOLD, SILVER, LAPIS LAZULI
AND CRYSTAL; ABOVE ARE RAISED PAVILIONS

四邊階道，金、銀、瑠璃、玻瓈，
合成。上有樓閣，

Sz byan jye dau. Jin, yin, lyou li, bwo li, he cheng,
shang you lou ge.

ADORNED WITH GOLD, SILVER, LAPIS LAZULI, CRYSTAL, MOTHER-
OF-PEARL, RED PEARLS AND CARNELIAN.

亦以金、銀、琉璃、玻瓈、硨磲、
赤珠、瑪瑙，而嚴飾之。

Yi yi jin, yin, lyou li, bwo li, che jyu, chr ju, ma nau,
er yan shr jr.

IN THE POOLS ARE LOTUSES AS LARGE AS CARRIAGE WHEELS:
GREEN COLORED OF GREEN LIGHT; YELLOW COLORED OF YELLOW
LIGHT;

池中蓮華，大如車輪，青色青光，
黃色黃光，

Chr jung lyan hwa. Da ru che lwun. Ching shai ching gwang.
Hwang shai hwang gwang.

RED COLORED OF RED LIGHT; WHITE COLORED OF WHITE LIGHT;
SUBTLY, WONDERFULLY FRAGRANT AND PURE.

赤色赤光，白色白光，微妙香潔。

Chr shai chr gwang. Bai shai bai gwang. Wei myau syang jye.

SHARIPUTRA, THE REALIZATION OF THE LAND OF ULTIMATE BLISS
IS THUS MERITORIOUSLY ADORNED.

舍利弗，極樂國土，成就如是功德
莊嚴。

She li fu. Ji le gwo du, cheng jyou ru shr gung de
jwang yan.

MOREOVER, SHARIPUTRA, IN THAT BUDDHALAND THERE IS ALWAYS
HEAVENLY MUSIC,

又舍利弗，彼佛國土，常作天樂，

You she li fu. Bi fwo gwo du. Chang dzwo tyan ywe.

AND THE GROUND IS YELLOW GOLD. IN THE SIX PERIODS OF THE
DAY AND NIGHT A HEAVENLY RAIN OF MANDARAVA FLOWERS FALLS,
AND THROUGHOUT THE CLEAR MORNING EACH LIVING BEING OF
THIS LAND,

黃金為地，晝夜六時，雨天曼陀羅
華。其土眾生，常以清旦，

Hwang jin wei di. Jou ye lyou shr, yu tyan man two lwo hwa.
Chi du jung sheng chang yi ching dan,

WITH SACKS FULL OF THE MYRIADS OF WONDERFUL FLOWERS, MAKES
OFFERINGS TO THE HUNDREDS OF THOUSANDS OF MILLIONS OF
BUDDHAS OF THE OTHER DIRECTIONS. AT MEALTIME THEY RETURN
TO THEIR OWN COUNTRY, AND HAVING EATEN THEY STROLL AROUND.

各以衣裓，盛眾妙華，供養他方十萬
億佛，即以食時，還到本國，飯食經行。

Ge yi yi sye. sheng jung myau hwa. gung yang ta fang. shr
wan yi fwo. ji yi shr shr hwan dau ben gwo. fan shr jin
sying.

   SHARIPUTRA, THE REALIZATION OF THE LAND OF ULTIMATE
BLISS IS THUS MERITORIOUSLY ADORNED.

舍利弗，極樂國土，成就如是功德
莊嚴。

She li fu. Ji le gwo du, cheng jyou ru shr gung de jwang
yan

   MOREOVER, SHARIPUTRA, IN THIS COUNTRY THERE ARE ALWAYS
RARE AND WONDERFUL VARICOLORED BIRDS:

復次舍利弗，彼國常有種種奇妙雜
色之鳥，

Fu tsz, she li fu. Bi gwo chang you jung jung chi myau
dza shai jr nyau.

WHITE CRANES, PEACOCKS, PARROTS AND EGRETS, KALAVINKAS,
AND TWO HEADED BIRDS.

白鶴、孔雀、鸚鵡、舍利、迦陵頻伽、共命之鳥。

Bai he, kung chyau, ying wu, she li, jya ling pin chye,
gung ming jr nyau.

IN THE SIX PERIODS OF THE DAY AND NIGHT, THE FLOCKS OF
BIRDS SING FORTH HARMONIOUS AND ELEGANT SOUNDS.

是諸眾鳥 ， 晝夜六時 ， 出和雅音 。

Shr ju jung nyau, jou ye lyou shr chu he ya yin.

THEIR CLEAR AND JOYFUL SOUNDS PROCLAIM THE FIVE ROOTS, THE
FIVE POWERS, THE SEVEN BODHI SHARES, THE EIGHT SAGELY WAY
SHARES, AND DHARMAS SUCH AS THESE.

其音演暢五根、五力 、 七菩提分、
八聖道分 ，如是等法 。

Chi yin yan chang wu gen, wu li, chi pu ti fen, ba sheng
dau fen, ru shr deng fa.

WHEN LIVING BEINGS OF THIS LAND HEAR THESE SOUNDS, THEY
ARE ALTOGETHER MINDFUL OF THE BUDDHA, MINDFUL OF THE
DHARMA, AND MINDFUL OF THE SANGHA.

其土眾生 ， 聞是音已 ， 皆悉念佛、
念法、 念僧 。

Chi du jung sheng wen shr yin yi. Jye syi nyan fwo, nyan
fa, nyan seng.

SHARIPUTRA, DO NOT SAY THAT THESE BIRDS ARE BORN AS
RETRIBUTION FOR THEIR KARMIC OFFENSES. FOR WHAT REASON?

舍利弗 ，汝勿謂此鳥 ， 實是罪報所
生 。所以者何 ？

She li fu. Ru wu wei tsz nyau shr shr dzwei bau swo sheng.
Swo yi je he.

IN THIS BUDDHALAND THERE ARE NO THREE EVIL WAYS OF REBIRTH.
SHARIPUTRA, IN THIS BUDDHALAND NOT EVEN THE NAMES OF THE
THREE EVIL WAYS EXIST,

彼佛國土 ， 無三惡道 。舍利弗 ，其
佛國土 ， 尚無惡道之名 ，

Bi fwo gwo du wu san e dau. She li fu. Chi fwo gwo du
shang wu e dau jr ming.

HOW MUCH THE LESS THEIR ACTUALITY! DESIRING THAT THE
DHARMA SOUND BE WIDELY PROCLAIMED, AMITABHA BUDDHA BY

TRANSFORMATION MADE THIS MULTITUDE OF BIRDS.

何況有實。是諸眾鳥，皆是阿彌陀
佛，欲令法音宣流，變化所作。

He kwang you shr. Shr ju jung nyau jye shr e mi two fwo
yu ling fa yin sywan lyou byan hwa swo dzwo.

SHARIPUTRA, IN THAT BUDDHALAND, WHEN THE SOFT WIND BLOWS,
THE ROWS OF JEWELLED TREES AND JEWELLED NETS

舍利弗，彼佛國土，微風吹動，諸
寶行樹，及寶羅網，

She li fu. Bi fwo gwo du. Wei feng chwei dung ju bau hang
shu ji bau lwo wang.

GIVE FORTH SUBTLE AND WONDERFUL SOUNDS, LIKE ONE HUNDRED
THOUSAND KINDS OF MUSIC PLAYED AT THE SAME TIME.

出微妙音,譬如百千種樂,同時俱作。

Chu wei myau yin. Pi ru bai chyan jung yau tung shr jyu
dzwo.

ALL THOSE WHO HEAR THIS SOUND NATURALLY BRING FORTH IN
THEIR HEARTS MINDFULNESS OF THE BUDDHA, MINDFULNESS OF THE
DHARMA, AND MINDFULNESS OF THE SANGHA.

聞是音者，自然皆生念佛。念法、
念僧之心。

Wen shr yin je. Dz ran jye sheng nyan fwo, nyan fa, nyan
seng jr syin.

SHARIPUTRA, THE REALIZATION OF THE LAND OF ULTIMATE BLISS
IS THUS MERITORIOUSLY ADORNED.

舍利弗，其佛國土，成就如是功德
莊嚴。

She li fu. Chi fwo gwo du cheng jyou ru shr gung de jwang
yan.

SHARIPUTRA, WHAT DO YOU THINK?

舍利弗，於汝意云何，

She li fu. Yu ru yi yun he.

WHY IS THIS BUDDHA CALLED AMITABHA? SHARIPUTRA, THE
BRILLIANCE OF THAT BUDDHA'S LIGHT IS MEASURELESS,

彼佛何故號阿彌陀？舍利弗，彼佛
光明無量。

Bi fwo he gu hau e mi two. She li fu. Bi fwo gwang ming
wu lyang.

ILLUMINING THE LANDS OF THE TEN DIRECTIONS EVERYWHERE
WITHOUT OBSTRUCTION; FOR THIS REASON HE IS CALLED AMITABHA.

照十方國，無所障礙，是故號為阿
彌陀。

Jau shr fang gwo wu swo jang ai. Shr gu hau wei e mi two.

MOREOVER, SHARIPUTRA, THE LIFE OF THAT BUDDHA AND THAT OF
HIS PEOPLE EXTENDS FOR MEASURELESS LIMITLESS ASANKHYEYA
KALPAS:

又舍利弗，彼佛壽命，及其人民，
無量無邊阿僧祇劫，

You she li fu. Bi fwo shou ming ji chi ren min. Wu lyang
wu byan e seng chi jye.

FOR THIS REASON HE IS CALLED AMITAYUS. AND SHARIPUTRA,
SINCE AMITABHA REALIZED BUDDHAHOOD, TEN KALPAS HAVE PASSED.

故名阿彌陀。舍利弗，阿彌陀佛成
佛以來，於今十劫。

Gu ming e mi two. She li fu. E mi two fwo cheng fwo yi lai.
Yu jin shr jye.

MOREOVER, SHARIPUTRA, THAT BUDDHA HAS MEASURELESS, LIMITLESS
SOUND-HEARER DISCIPLES, ALL ARHATS,

又舍利弗，彼佛有無量無邊聲聞弟
子，皆阿羅漢，

You she li fu. Bi fwo you wu lyang wu byan sheng wen di dz.
Jye e lwo han.

THEIR NUMBER INCALCULABLE; THUS ALSO IS THE ASSEMBLY

OF BODHISATTVAS.

非是算數之所能知。諸菩薩眾，亦復如是。

Fei shr swan shu jr swo neng jr. Ju pu sa jung yi fu ru shr.

SHARIPUTRA, THE REALIZATION OF THE LAND OF ULTIMATE BLISS IS THUS MERITORIOUSLY ADORNED.

舍利弗，彼佛國土，成就如是功德莊嚴。

She li fu. Bi fwo gwo du cheng jyou ru shr gung de jwang yan,

MOREOVER, SHARIPUTRA, THOSE LIVING BEINGS BORN IN THE LAND OF ULTIMATE BLISS ARE ALL AVAIVARTIKA.

又舍利弗，極樂國土，眾生生者，皆是阿鞞跋致。

You she li fu. Ji le gwo du, jung sheng, sheng je jye shr e bi ba jr.

AMONG THEM ARE MANY WHO IN THIS VERY LIFE WILL DWELL IN BUDDHAHOOD. THEIR NUMBER IS EXTREMELY MANY;

其中多有一生補處。其數甚多，

Chi jung dwo you yi sheng bu chu. Chi shu shen dwo.

IT IS INCALCULABLE AND ONLY IN MEASURELESS, LIMITLESS ASANKHYEYA KALPAS COULD IT BE SPOKEN.

非是算數所能知之，但可以無量無邊阿僧祇說。

Fei shr swan shu swo neng jr jr. Dan ke yi wu lyang wu byan e seng chi shwo.

SHARIPUTRA, THOSE LIVING BEINGS WHO HEAR SHOULD VOW, 'I WISH TO BE BORN IN THAT COUNTRY.'

舍利弗，眾生聞者，應當發願，願生彼國。

She li fu. Jung sheng wen je ying dang fa ywan, ywan sheng bi gwo.

AND WHY? ALL THOSE WHO THUS ATTAIN ARE ALL SUPERIOR AND
GOOD PEOPLE, ALL COMING TOGETHER IN ONE PLACE.

所以者何？得與如是諸上善人俱會
一處。

Swo yi je he. De yu ru shr ju shang shan ren jyu hwei yi
chu.

SHARIPUTRA, ONE CANNOT HAVE FEW GOOD ROOTS, BLESSINGS,
VIRTUES, AND CAUSAL CONNECTIONS TO ATTAIN BIRTH IN THAT
LAND.

舍利弗，不可以少善根福德因緣，
得生彼國。

She li fu. Bu ke yi shau shan gen, fu de, yin ywan, de
sheng bi gwo.

SHARIPUTRA, IF THERE IS A GOOD MAN OR WOMAN WHO HEARS
SPOKEN 'AMITABHA' AND HOLDS THE NAME,

舍利弗，若有善男子善女人，聞說
阿彌陀佛．執持名號，

She li fu. Rau you shan nan dz, shan nyu ren wen shwo e
mi two fwo jr chr ming hau.

WHETHER FOR ONE DAY, TWO DAYS, THREE, FOUR, FIVE DAYS, SIX
DAYS, AS LONG AS SEVEN DAYS, WITH ONE HEART UNCONFUSED,

若一日，若二日，若三日，若四日，
若五日，若六日，若七日，一心不亂。

Rau yi r, rau er r, rau san r, rau sz r, rau wu r, rau
lyou r, rau chi r, yi syin bu lwan.

WHEN THIS PERSON APPROACHES THE END OF LIFE, BEFORE HIM
WILL APPEAR AMITABHA AND ALL THE ASSEMBLY OF HOLY ONES.

其人臨命終時，阿彌陀佛，與諸聖
眾，現在其前。

Chi ren lin ming jung shr. E mi two fwo yu ju sheng jung
syan dzai chi chyan.

WHEN THE END COMES, HIS HEART IS WITHOUT INVERSION;

IN AMITABHA'S LAND OF ULTIMATE BLISS HE WILL ATTAIN REBIRTH.

是人終時，心不顛倒，即得往生阿彌陀佛極樂國土。

Shr ren jung shr. Syin bu dyan dau. Ji de wang sheng e mi two fwo ji le gwo du.

SHARIPUTRA, BECAUSE I SEE THIS BENEFIT, I SPEAK THESE WORDS:

舍利弗，我見是利，故說此言。

She li fu. Wo jyan shr li. Gu shwo tsz yan.

IF LIVING BEINGS HEAR THIS SPOKEN THEY SHOULD MAKE THE VOW, 'I WISH TO BE BORN IN THAT LAND.'

若有眾生，聞是說者，應當發願，生彼國土。

Rau you jung sheng wen shr shwo je ying dang fa ywan, sheng bi gwo du.

SHARIPUTRA, AS I NOW PRAISE THE INCONCEIVABLE BENEFIT FROM THE MERIT AND VIRTUE OF AMITABHA,◎

舍利弗，如我今者，讚歎阿彌陀佛不可思議功德之利◎。

She li fu. Ru wo jin je dzan tan e mi two fwo bu ke sz yi gung de jr li.

◎

THUS IN THE EAST ARE ALSO AKSOBHYA BUDDHA, SUMERU APPEARANCE BUDDHA, GREAT SUMERU BUDDHA, SUMERU LIGHT BUDDHA, WONDERFUL SOUND BUDDHA;

東方亦有阿閦鞞佛，須彌相佛，大須彌佛，須彌光佛，妙音佛，

Dung fang yi you e chu bi fwo, syu mi syang fwo, da syu mi fwo, syu mi gwang fwo, myau yin fwo.

ALL BUDDHAS SUCH AS THESE, NUMBERLESS AS GANGES SANDS. IN HIS OWN COUNTRY EACH BRINGS FORTH THE APPEARANCE OF A

VAST AND LONG TONGUE,

如是等恒河沙數諸佛，各於其國，
出廣長舌相，

Ru shr deng heng he sha shu ju fwo. Ge yu chi gwo chu
gwang chang she syang.

EVERYWHERE COVERING THE THREE THOUSAND GREAT THOUSAND
WORLDS, AND SPEAKS THE SINCERE AND ACTUAL WORDS,

徧覆三千大千世界，說誠實言。

Byan fu san chyan da chyan shr jye. Shwo cheng shr yan.

'ALL YOU LIVING BEINGS SHOULD BELIEVE, PRAISE AND HOLD
IN REVERENCE THE INCONCEIVABLE MERIT AND VIRTUE OF THIS
SUTRA OF THE MINDFUL ONE OF WHOM ALL BUDDHAS ARE
PROTECTIVE.'

汝等眾生，當信是稱讚不可思議功
德，一切諸佛所護念經。

Ru deng jung sheng.dang syin shr cheng dzan bu ke. sz yi
gung de, yi chye ju fwo swo hu nyan jing.

SHARIPUTRA, IN THE SOUTHERN WORLD ARE SUN MOON LAMP
BUDDHA,

舍利弗，南方世界，有日月燈佛，

She li fu. Nan fang shr jye you r ywe deng fwo,

WELL KNOWN LIGHT BUDDHA, GREAT BLAZING SHOULDERS BUDDHA,
SUMERU LAMP BUDDHA, MEASURELESS VIGOR BUDDHA;

名聞光佛，大燄肩佛，須彌燈佛，
無量精進佛，

Ming wen gwang fwo, da yan jyan fwo, syu mi deng fwo, wu
lyang jing jin fwo,

ALL BUDDHAS SUCH AS THESE, NUMBERLESS AS GANGES SANDS.

如是等恒河沙數諸佛，

Ru shr deng heng he sha shu ju fwo.

IN HIS OWN COUNTRY, EACH BRINGS FORTH THE APPEARANCE OF
A VAST AND LONG TONGUE, EVERYWHERE COVERING THE THREE

THOUSAND GREAT THOUSAND WORLDS, AND SPEAKS THE SINCERE AND
ACTUAL WORDS,

各於其國，出廣長舌相，徧覆三千
大千世界，說誠實言。

Ge yu chi gwo chu gwang chang she syang. Byan fu san
chyan da chyan shr jye. Shwo cheng shr yan.

'ALL YOU LIVING BEINGS SHOULD BELIEVE, PRAISE AND HOLD IN
REVERENCE THE INCONCEIVABLE MERIT AND VIRTUE OF THIS
SUTRA OF THE MINDFUL ONE OF WHOM ALL BUDDHAS ARE
PROTECTIVE.'

汝等眾生，當信是稱讚不可思議功
德，一切諸佛所護念經。

Ru deng jung sheng dang syin shr cheng dzan bu ke sz yi
gung de. Yi chye ju fwo swo hu nyan jing.

SHARIPUTRA, IN THE WESTERN WORLD ARE MEASURELESS LIFE
BUDDHA, MEASURELESS APPEARANCE BUDDHA,

舍利弗，西方世界，有無量壽佛，
無量相佛，

She li fu. Syi fang shr jye you wu lyang shou fwo, wu
lyang syang fwo,

MEASURELESS CURTAIN BUDDHA, GREAT LIGHT BUDDHA, GREAT
BRIGHTNESS BUDDHA, JEWELLED APPEARANCE BUDDHA, PURE LIGHT
BUDDHA:

無量幢佛，大光佛，大明佛，寶相
佛，淨光佛，

Wu lyang chwang fwo, da gwang fwo, da ming fwo, bau syang
fwo, jing gwang fwo,

ALL BUDDHAS SUCH AS THESE, NUMBERLESS AS GANGES SANDS.

如是等恆河沙數諸佛，

Ru shr deng heng he sha shu ju fwo.

IN HIS OWN COUNTRY EACH BRINGS FORTH THE APPEARANCE OF
A VAST AND LONG TONGUE, EVERYWHERE COVERING THE THREE

THOUSAND GREAT THOUSAND WORLDS, AND SPEAKS THE SINCERE
AND ACTUAL WORDS,

各於其國，出廣長舌相，徧覆三千
大千世界，說誠實言。

Ge yu chi gwo chu gwang chang she syang. Byan fu san
chyan da chyan shr jye. Shwo cheng shr yan.

'ALL YOU LIVING BEINGS SHOULD BELIEVE, PRAISE AND HOLD
IN REVERENCE THE INCONCEIVABLE MERIT AND VIRTUE OF THIS
SUTRA OF THE MINDFUL ONE OF WHOM ALL BUDDHAS ARE
PROTECTIVE.'

汝等眾生，當信是稱讚不可思議功
德，一切諸佛所護念經。

Ru deng jung sheng dang syin shr cheng dzan bu ke sz yi
gung de, yi chye ju fwo swo hu nyan jing.

SHARIPUTRA, IN THE NORTHERN WORLD ARE BLAZING SHOULDERS
BUDDHA, MOST VICTORIOUS SOUND BUDDHA, HARD TO INJURE
BUDDHA, SUN BIRTH BUDDHA, NET BRIGHTNESS BUDDHA;

舍利弗，北方世界，有燄肩佛，最
勝音佛，難沮佛，日生佛，網明佛，

She li fu. Bei fang shr jye you yan jyan fwo, dzwei sheng
yin fwo, nan jyu fwo, r sheng fwo, wang ming fwo,

ALL BUDDHAS SUCH AS THESE, NUMBERLESS AS GANGES SANDS. IN
HIS OWN COUNTRY EACH BRINGS FORTH THE APPEARANCE OF A
VAST AND LONG TONGUE,

如是等恒河沙數諸佛，各於其國，
出廣長舌相，

Ru shr deng heng he sha shu ju fwo. Ge yu chi gwo chu
gwang chang she syang.

EVERYWHERE COVERING THE THREE THOUSAND GREAT THOUSAND
WORLDS, AND SPEAKS THE SINCERE AND ACTUAL WORDS,

徧覆三千大千世界，說誠實言。

Byan fu san chyan da chyan shr jye. Shwo cheng shr yan.

'ALL YOU LIVING BEINGS SHOULD BELIEVE, PRAISE AND HOLD IN
REVERENCE THE INCONCEIVABLE MERIT AND VIRTUE OF THIS
SUTRA OF THE MINDFUL ONE OF WHOM ALL BUDDHAS ARE
PROTECTIVE.

汝等象生，當信是稱讚不可思議功
德，一切諸佛所護念經。

Ru deng jung sheng dang syin shr cheng dzan bu ke sz yi
gung de. Yi chye ju fwo swo hu nyan jing.

SHARIPUTRA, IN THE WORLD BELOW ARE LION BUDDHA, WELL-KNOWN
BUDDHA, FAMOUS LIGHT BUDDHA,

舍利弗，下方世界，有師子佛，名
聞佛，名光佛，

Shè li fu. Sya fang shr jye you shr dz fwo, ming wen fwo,
ming gwang fwo,

DHARMA BUDDHA, DHARMA CURTAIN BUDDHA, DHARMA MAINTAINING
BUDDHA, ALL BUDDHAS SUCH AS THESE, NUMBERLESS AS GANGES
SANDS.

達摩佛，法幢佛，持法佛，如是等
恒河沙數諸佛，

Da mwo fwo, fa chwang fwo, chr fa fwo, ru shr deng heng
he sha shu ju fwo.

IN HIS OWN COUNTRY, EACH BRINGS FORTH THE APPEARANCE OF A
VAST AND LONG TONGUE, EVERYWHERE COVERING THE THREE THOUS-
AND GREAT THOUSAND WORLDS, AND SPEAKS THE SINCERE AND
ACTUAL WORDS,

各於其國，出廣長舌相，徧覆三千
大千世界，說誠實言。

Ge yu chi gwo chu gwang chang she syang. Byan fu san chyan
da chyan shr jye. Shwo cheng shr yan.

'ALL YOU LIVING BEINGS SHOULD BELIEVE, PRAISE AND HOLD IN
REVERENCE THE INCONCEIVABI.E MERIT AND VIRTUE OF THIS SUTRA

汝等象生,當信是稱讚不可思議功德,

Ru deng jung sheng dang syin shr cheng dzan bu ke sz yi
gung de,

OF THE MINDFUL ONE OF WHOM ALL BUDDHAS ARE PROTECTIVE.

一切諸佛所護念經 。

Yi chye ju fwo swo hu nyan jing.

SHARIPUTRA, IN THE WORLD ABOVE ARE PURE SOUND BUDDHA, KING
OF STARS BUDDHA,

舍利弗，上方世界，有梵音佛，宿
王佛，

She li fu. Shang fang shr jye you fan yin fwo, syu wang fwo,

SUPERIOR FRAGRANCE BUDDHA, FRAGRANT LIGHT BUDDHA, GREAT
BLAZING SHOULDERS BUDDHA, VARICOLORED JEWELS AND FLOWER
ADORNMENT BODY BUDDHA,

香上佛，香光佛，大燄肩佛，雜色
寶華嚴身佛，

Syang shang fwo, syang gwang fwo, da yan jyan fwo, dza shai
bau hwa yan shen fwo,

SALA TREE KING BUDDHA, JEWELLED FLOWER VIRTUE BUDDHA,
VISION OF ALL MEANING BUDDHA, SUCH AS MOUNT SUMERU BUDDHA;

娑羅樹王佛，寶華德佛，見一切義
佛，如須彌山佛，

Swo lwo shu wang fwo, bau hwa de fwo, jyan yi chye yi fwo,
ru syu mi shan fwo,

ALL BUDDHAS SUCH AS THESE, NUMBERLESS AS GANGES SANDS. IN
HIS OWN COUNTRY EACH BRINGS FORTH THE APPEARANCE OF A VAST
AND LONG TONGUE,

如是等恒河沙數諸佛，各於其國，
出廣長舌相，

Ru shr deng heng he sha shu ju fwo. Ge yu chi gwo chu
gwang chang she syang.

EVERYWHERE COVERING THE THREE THOUSAND GREAT THOUSAND
WORLDS AND SPEAKS THE SINCERE AND ACTUAL WORDS,

徧覆三千大千世界，說誠實言 。

Byan fu san chyan da chyan shr jye. Shwo cheng shr yan.

'ALL YOU LIVING BEINGS SHOULD BELIEVE, PRAISE AND HOLD
IN REVERENCE THE INCONCEIVABLE MERIT AND VIRTUE OF THIS
SUTRA OF THE MINDFUL ONE OF WHOM ALL BUDDHAS ARE
PROTECTIVE.'◎

汝等眾生 ， 當信是稱讚不可思議功
德 ， 一切諸佛所護念經◎

Ru deng jung sheng dang syin shr cheng dzan bu ke sz yi
gung de. Yi chye ju fwo swo hu nyan jing.
◎

SHARIPUTRA, WHAT DO YOU THINK? WHY IS IT CALLED SUTRA OF
THE MINDFUL ONE OF WHOM ALL BUDDHAS ARE PROTECTIVE?

舍利弗 ， 於汝意云何 ， 何故名為一
切諸佛所護念經 。

She li fu. Yu ru yi yun he. He gu ming wei yi chye ju
fwo swo hu nyan jing.

SHARIPUTRA, IF A GOOD MAN OR GOOD WOMAN HEARS THIS SUTRA
AND HOLDS TO IT,

舍利弗 ， 若有善男子善女人 ， 聞是
經受持者 ，

She li fu. Rau you shan nan dz, shan nyu ren. Wen shr
jing, shou chr je.

AND HEARS THE NAMES OF ALL THESE BUDDHAS, THIS GOOD MAN
OR WOMAN WILL BE THE MINDFUL ONE OF WHOM ALL BUDDHAS ARE
PROTECTIVE,

及聞諸佛名者 ， 是諸善男子善女人,
皆為一切諸佛之所護念 ，

Ji wen ju fwo ming je. Shr ju shan nan dz shan nyu ren.
Jye wei yi chye ju fwo jr swo hu nyan.

AND WILL IRREVERSIBLY ATTAIN TO ANNUTARA-SAMYAK-SAMBODHI.

皆得不退轉於阿耨多羅三藐三菩提。

Jye de bu twei jwan yu enou dwo lwo san myau san pu ti.

THEREFORE, SHARIPUTRA, ALL OF YOU SHOULD BELIEVE AND

ACCEPT MY WORDS, AND THOSE WHICH ALL BUDDHAS SPEAK.

是故舍利弗，汝等皆當信受我語，
及諸佛所說。

Shr gu she li fu. Ru deng jye dang syin shou wo yu. Ji
ju fwo swo shwo.

SHARIPUTRA, IF THERE ARE PEOPLE WHO HAVE ALREADY MADE THE
VOW, WHO NOW MAKE THE VOW, OR WHO ARE ABOUT TO MAKE THE
VOW, 'I DESIRE TO BE BORN IN AMITABHA'S COUNTRY',

舍利弗，若有人，已發願，今發願，
當發願，欲生阿彌陀佛國者。

She li fu. Rau you ren yi fa ywan, jin fa ywan, dang fa
ywan, yu sheng e mi two fwo gwo je.

THESE PEOPLE WHETHER BORN IN THE PAST, NOW BEING BORN, OR
TO BE BORN IN THE FUTURE, ALL WILL IRREVERSIBLY ATTAIN
ANNUTARA-SAMYAK-SAMBODHI.

是諸人等，皆得不退轉於阿耨多羅
三藐三菩提。於彼國土，若已生，
若今生，若當生。

Shr ju ren deng, jye de bu twei jwan yu e nou dwo lwo san
myau san pu ti. Yu bi gwo du, rau yi sheng, rau jin sheng,
rau dang sheng.

THEREFORE, SHARIPUTRA, ALL GOOD MEN AND GOOD WOMEN, IF
THEY ARE AMONG THOSE WHO HAVE FAITH, SHOULD MAKE THE VOW,
'I WILL BE BORN IN THAT COUNTRY.'

是故舍利弗，諸善男子善女人，若
有信者應當發願，生彼國土。

Shr gu she li fu. Ju shan nan dz shan nyu ren rau you syin
je. Ying dang fa ywan sheng bi gwo du.

SHARIPUTRA, JUST AS I AM NOW ONE WHO PRAISES THE MERIT AND
VIRTUE OF ALL BUDDHAS,

舍利弗,如我今者, 稱讚諸佛不可思議功德,

She li fu. Ru wo jin je cheng dzan ju fwo bu ke sz yi
gung de.

ALL THOSE BUDDHAS EQUALLY PRAISE MY INCONCEIVABLE MERIT
AND VIRTUE SAYING THESE WORDS:

彼諸佛等，亦稱讚我不可思議功德。
而作是言：

Bi ju fwo deng yi cheng dzan wo bu ke sz yi gung de er
dzwo shr yan.

'SHAKYAMUNI BUDDHA CAN COMPLETE EXTREMELY RARE AND DIFFI-
CULT DEEDS, IN THE SAHA LAND, IN THE EVIL TIME OF THE
FIVE TURBIDITIES,

釋迦牟尼佛能為甚難希有之事．能
於婆婆國土，五濁惡世，

Shr jya mu ni fwo neng wei shen nan syi you jr shr. Neng
yu swo pe gwo du, wu jwo e shr.

IN THE MIDST OF THE KALPA TURBIDITY, THE VIEW TURBIDITY,
THE AFFLICTION TURBIDITY, THE LIVING BEINGS TURBIDITY,
AND THE LIFE TURBIDITY,

劫濁、見濁、煩惱濁、眾生濁、命濁中，

Jye jwo, jyan jwo, fan nau jwo, jung sheng jwo, ming jwo
jung.

HE CAN ATTAIN ANNUTARA-SAMYAK-SAMBODHI AND FOR THE SAKE
OF LIVING BEINGS, SPEAK THIS DHARMA WHICH IN THE WHOLE
WORLD IS HARD TO BELIEVE.'

得阿耨多羅三藐三菩提。為諸眾生，
說是一切世間難信之法．

De e nou dwo lwo san myau san pu ti. Wei ju jung sheng
shwo shr yi chye shr jyan nan syin jr fa.

SHARIPUTRA, YOU SHOULD KNOW THAT I, IN THE EVIL TIME OF
THE FIVE TURBIDITIES, PRACTICE THESE DIFFICULT DEEDS,

舍利弗，當知我於五濁惡世，行此
難事，

She li fu. Dang jr wo yu wu jwo e shr, sying tsz nan shr.

ATTAIN ANNUTTARA-SAMYAK-SAMBODHI, AND FOR ALL THE WORLD
SPEAK THIS DHARMA, DIFFICULT TO BELIEVE, EXTREMELY

DIFFICULT!"

得阿耨多羅三藐三菩提，為一切世
間說此難信之法，是為甚難。

De e nou dwo lwo san myau san pu ti. Wei yi chye shr jyan
shwo tsz nan syin jr fa. Shr wei shen nan.

AFTER THE BUDDHA SPOKE THIS SUTRA, SHARIPUTRA AND ALL THE
BHIKSHUS,

佛說此經已，舍利弗及諸比丘，

Fwo shwo tsz jing yi, she li fu, ji ju bi chyou,

ALL THE GODS, HUMANS AND ASURAS, AND OTHERS FROM ALL THE
WORLDS, HEARING WHAT THE BUDDHA HAD SAID, JOYOUSLY WELCOMED.
FAITHFULLY ACCEPTED, BOWED AND WITHDREW.

一切世間天人阿修羅等，聞佛所說，
歡喜信受，作禮而去。

Yi chye shr jyan tyan, ren, e syou lwo deng, wen fwo swo
shwo. Hwan syi syin shou. Dzwo li er chyu.

END OF THE BUDDHA SPEAKS OF AMITABHA SUTRA

佛說阿彌陀經

Fwo shwo e mi two jing

(DHARANI FOR PULLING OUT KARMIC OBSTRUCTIONS BY THE ROOTS
AND OBTAINING BIRTH IN THE PURE LAND)

拔一切業障根本得生淨土陀羅尼 (即往生咒三編)

Ba yi chye ye jang gen ben de sheng jing du two lwo ni

NA MWO E MI DWO PWO YE ◎ 南無阿彌多婆夜 ◎

DWO TWO CHYE DWO YE 哆他伽多夜

DWO DI YE TWO 哆地夜他

E MI LI DU PE PI 阿彌利都婆毗

E MI LI DWO 阿彌利哆

SYI DAN PE PI 悉耽婆毗

E MI LI DWO 阿彌唎哆

PI JYA LAN DI ◎ 毗迦蘭帝 ◎

E MI LI DWO 阿彌唎哆

PI JYA LAN DWO 毗迦蘭多

CHYE MI LI ◎ 伽彌膩 ◎

CHYE CHYE NWO 伽伽那

JR DWO JYA LI 枳多迦利

SWO PE HE *(recite 3 times)* 娑婆訶　　　(三徧)

(Proceed to Meng Shan offering, see page 129)
(接蒙山施食儀，見第129頁)

EVENING CEREMONY

暮時課誦

EIGHTY-EIGHT BUDDHAS REPENTANCE CEREMONY

禮佛大懺悔文

TO THE GREATLY KIND, COMPASSIONATE ONES WHO RESCUE LIVING
BEINGS,

大慈大悲愍眾生,◎

Da tsz da bei min jung sheng

THE ONES OF GREAT JOYOUS GIVING WHO RESCUE CONSCIOUS BEINGS,

大喜大捨濟含識,

Da syi da she ji han shr

THE ONES ADORNED WITH THE LIGHT OF HALLMARKS AND FINE
CHARACTERISTICS,

相好光明以自嚴,

Syang hau gwang ming yi dz yan

THE ASSEMBLIES RETURN THEIR LIVES IN WORSHIP WITH UTMOST
SINCERITY.

◎眾等至心歸命禮.

Jung deng jr syin gwei ming li.

NA MO. I TAKE REFUGE WITH ALL THE BUDDHAS OF THE TEN

南無. 皈依十方 盡虛空界

Na mo gwei yi shr fang jin syu kung jye

DIRECTIONS TO THE ENDS OF EMPTY SPACE.

一切諸佛.◎

yi chye ju fwo

NA MO. I TAKE REFUGE WITH ALL THE VENERABLE DHARMA OF THE

南無 皈依十方 盡虛空界

Na mo gwei yi shr fang jin syu kung jye

TEN DIRECTIONS TO THE ENDS OF EMPTY SPACE.

一切尊法.

yi chye dzwun fa.

NA MO. I TAKE REFUGE WITH THE SANGHA OF ALL SAGES AND

南無 皈依十方 盡虛空界

Na mo gwei yi shr fang jin syu kung jye

WORTHIES OF THE TEN DIRECTIONS TO THE ENDS OF EMPTY SPACE.

一切賢聖僧.

yi chye syan sheng seng.

NA MO THE THUS COME ONES, WORTHY OF OFFERINGS, OF PROPER
AND UNIVERSAL KNOWLEDGE,

南無 如来◎應供，正徧知，

Na mwo ru lai, ying gung, jeng byan jr,

PERFECT IN UNDERSTANDING AND CONDUCT, SKILLFUL IN LEAVING
THE WORLD THROUGH LIBERATION, UNSURPASSED KNIGHTS.

明行足，善逝世間解，無上士，

ming heng dzu, shan shr shr jyan jye, wu shang shr,

TAMING HEROES, TEACHERS OF GODS AND PEOPLE, BUDDHAS,
WORLD HONORED ONES.

調御丈夫，天人師，佛◎，世尊.

tyau yu jang fu, tyan ren shr, fwo, shr dzwun.

NA MO UNIVERSAL LIGHT BUDDHA

南無普光佛◎

Na mwo pu gwang fwo

NA MO UNIVERSAL UNDERSTANDING BUDDHA

南無普明佛

Na mwo pu ming fwo

NA MO UNIVERSAL PURITY BUDDHA

南無普淨佛

Na mwo pu jing fwo

NA MO TAMALAPATTRA AND CHANDANA FRAGRANCE BUDDHA.

南無多摩羅跋栴檀香佛

Na mwo dwo mwo lwo ba jan tan syang fwo.

NA MO CHANDANA LIGHT BUDDHA

南無栴檀光佛

Na mwo jan tan gwang fwo

NA MO MANI BANNER BUDDHA

南無摩尼幢佛

Na mwo mwo ni chwang fwo

NA MO TREASURY OF HAPPINESS AND ACCUMULATION OF MANI
JEWELS BUDDHA.

南無歡喜藏摩尼寶積佛
Na mwo hwan syi dzang mwo ni bau ji fwo

NA MO SUPREME GREAT VIGOR THAT ALL WORLDS DELIGHT TO SEE
BUDDHA

南無一切世間樂見上大精進佛
Na mwo yi chye shr jyan le jyan shang da jing jin fwo

NA MO MANI BANNER AND LAMPS' LIGHT BUDDHA

南無摩尼幢燈光佛
Na mwo mwo ni chwang deng gwang fwo

NA MO WISDOM TORCHES' SHINING BUDDHA

南無慧炬照佛
Na mwo hwei jyu jau fwo

NA MO SEA-VAST VIRTUE'S RADIANCE BUDDHA

南無海德光明佛
Na mwo hai de gwang ming fwo

NA MO VAJRA-FIRM AND SHEDDING GOLDEN LIGHT EVERYWHERE BUDDHA

南無金剛牢強普散金光佛
Na mwo jin gang lau chyang pu san jin gwang fwo

NA MO GREAT FIRM VIGOR AND COURAGE BUDDHA

南無大強精進勇猛佛
Na mwo da chyang jing jin yung meng fwo

NA MO GREATLY COMPASSIONATE LIGHT BUDDHA

南無大悲光佛
Na mwo da bei gwang fwo

NA MO KING OF KINDNESS AND STRENGTH BUDDHA

南無慈力王佛
Na mwo tsz li wang fwo

NA MO TREASURY OF KINDNESS BUDDHA

南無慈藏佛
Na mwo tsz dzang fwo

NA MO ADORNMENTS AND VICTORY IN CHANDANA CAVE BUDDHA

南無栴檀窟莊嚴勝佛

Na mwo jan tan ku jwang yan sheng fwo

NA MO WORTHY AND WHOLESOME LEADER BUDDHA

南無賢善首佛

Na mwo syan shan shou fwo

NA MO WHOLESOME MIND BUDDHA

南無善意佛

Na mwo shan yi fwo

NA MO KING VAST ADORNMENTS BUDDHA

南無廣莊嚴王佛

Na mwo gwang jwang yan wang fwo

NA MO GOLDEN FLOWERS' LIGHT BUDDHA

南無金華光佛

Na mwo jin hwa gwang fwo

NA MO KING SELF-MASTERY POWER LIKE A JEWELLED CANOPY
SHINING IN SPACE BUDDHA

南無寶蓋照空自在力王佛

Na mwo bau gai jau kung dz dzai li wang fwo

NA MO LIGHT OF PRECIOUS FLOWERS IN SPACE BUDDHA

南無虛空寶華光佛

Na mwo syu kung bau hwa gwang fwo

NA MO KING ADORNED WITH LAPUS LAZULI BUDDHA

南無琉璃莊嚴王佛

Na mwo lyou li jwang yan wang fwo

NA MO FORM-BODY'S LIGHT APPEARING EVERYWHERE BUDDHA

南無普現色身光佛

Na mwo pu syan shai shen gwang fwo

NA MO LIGHT OF UNMOVING WISDOM BUDDHA

南無不動智光佛

Na mwo bu dung jr gwang fwo

NA MO KING DEMON-HORDE-SUBDUER BUDDHA

南無降伏眾魔王佛

Na mwo syang fu jung mwo wang fwo

111

NA MO GIFTED AND BRILLIANT BUDDHA

南無才光明佛

Na mwo tsai gwang ming fwo

NA MO WISDOM VICTORY BUDDHA

南無智慧勝佛

Na mwo jr hwei sheng fwo

NA MO MAITREYA, IMMORTAL LIGHT BUDDHA

南無彌勒仙光佛

Na mwo mi lei syan gwang fwo

NA MO KING WELL-STILLED MOON-SOUND AND WONDERFUL VENERABLE
WISDOM BUDDHA

南無善寂月音妙尊智王佛

Na mwo shan ji ywe yin myau dzwun jr wang fwo

NA MO PURE LIGHT FOR THE WORLD BUDDHA

南無世淨光佛

Na mwo shr jing gwang fwo

NA MO SUPREME AND VENERABLE DRAGON-KING BUDDHA

南無龍種上尊王佛

Na mwo lung jung shang dzwun wang fwo

NA MO LIGHT OF SUN AND MOON BUDDHA

南無日月光佛

Na mwo r ywe gwang fwo

NA MO PEARL-LIGHT OF SUN AND MOON BUDDHA

南無日月珠光佛

Na mwo r ywe ju gwang fwo

NA MO VICTORIOUS KING WISDOM-BANNER BUDDHA

南無慧幢勝王佛

Na mwo hwei chwang sheng wang fwo

NA MO KING LION'S ROAR AND POWER OF SELF-MASTERY BUDDHA

南無師子吼自在力王佛

Na mwo shr dz hou dz dzai li wang fwo

NA MO WONDERFUL VOICE AND VICTORY BUDDHA

南無妙音勝佛

Na mwo myau yin sheng fwo

NA MO BANNER OF ETERNAL LIGHT BUDDHA

南無常光幢佛

Na mwo chang gwang chwang fwo

NA MO LAMP THAT CONTEMPLATES THE WORLD BUDDHA

南無觀世燈佛

Na mwo gwan shr deng fwo

NA MO KING AWESOME LAMP OF WISDOM BUDDHA

南無慧威燈王佛

Na mwo hwei wei deng wang fwo

NA MO KING DHARMA-VICTORY BUDDHA

南無法勝王佛

Na mwo fa sheng wang fwo

NA MO SUMERU LIGHT BUDDHA

南無須彌光佛

Na mwo syu mi gwang fwo

NA MO SUMANA FLOWER LIGHT BUDDHA

南無須曼那華光佛

Na mwo syu man nwo hwa gwang fwo

NA MO KING RARE AS THE UDUMBARA FLOWER BUDDHA

南無優曇鉢羅華殊勝王佛

Na mwo you tan bwo lwo hwa shu sheng wang fwo

NA MO KING GREAT WISDOM-POWER BUDDHA

南無大慧力王佛

Na mwo da hwei li wang fwo

NA MO AKSHOBYA, LIGHT OF JOY BUDDHA

南無阿閦毗歡喜光佛

Na mwo e chu bi hwan syi gwang fwo

NA MO KING INFINITE VOICES BUDDHA

南無無量音聲王佛

Na mwo wu lyang yin sheng wang fwo

NA MO GIFTED AND BRIGHT BUDDHA

南無才光佛

Na mwo tsai gwang fwo

NA MO GOLDEN SEA OF LIGHT BUDDHA

南無金海光佛

Na mwo jin hai gwang fwo

NA MO KING WISDOM LIKE MOUNTAINS AND SEAS AND SELF-MASTERY'S
PENETRATIONS BUDDHA

南無山海慧自在通王佛

Na mwo shan hai hwei dz dzai tung wang fwo

NA MO LIGHT OF GREAT PENETRATIONS BUDDHA

南無大通光佛

Na mwo da tung gwang fwo

NA MO KING FOREVER REPLETE IN ALL DHARMAS BUDDHA,

南無一切法常滿王佛

Na mwo yi chye fa chang man wang fwo

NA MO SHAKYAMUNI BUDDHA

南無釋迦牟尼佛◎

Na mwo shr jya mu ni fwo

NA MO VAJRA-INDESTRUCTIBLE BUDDHA

南無金剛不壞佛

Na mwo jin gang bu hwai fwo

NA MO PRECIOUS LIGHT BUDDHA

南無寶光佛

Na mwo bau gwang fwo

NA MO VENERABLE DRAGON-KING BUDDHA

南無龍尊王佛

Na mwo lung dzwun wang fwo

NA MO VIGOR'S ARMY BUDDHA

南無精進軍佛

Na mwo jing jin jyun fwo

NA MO VIGOR AND JOY BUDDHA

南無精進喜佛

Na mwo jing jin syi fwo

NA MO PRECIOUS FIRE BUDDHA

南無寶火佛

Na mwo bau hwo fwo

NA MO PRECIOUS MOONLIGHT BUDDHA

南無寶月光佛

Na mwo bau ywe gwang fwo

NA MO MANIFESTING WITHOUT DELUSION BUDDHA

南無現無愚佛

Na mwo syan wu yu fwo

NA MO PRECIOUS MOON BUDDHA

南無寶月佛

Na mwo bau ywe fwo

NA MO UNDEFILED BUDDHA

南無無垢佛

Na mwo wu gou fwo

NA MO APART FROM DEFILEMENT BUDDHA

南無離垢佛

Na mwo li gou fwo

NA MO COURAGEOUS GIVING BUDDHA

南無勇施佛

Na mwo yung shr fwo

NA MO PURITY BUDDHA

南無清淨佛

Na mwo ching jing fwo

NA MO PURE GIVING BUDDHA

南無清淨施佛

Na mwo ching jing shr fwo

NA MO SWO LYU NA BUDDHA

南無娑留那佛

Na mwo swo lyu na fwo

NA MO WATER-DEVA BUDDHA

南無水天佛

Na mwo shwei tyan fwo

NA MO FIRM VIRTUE BUDDHA

南無堅德佛

Na mwo jyan de fwo

NA MO CHANDANA MERIT AND VIRTUE BUDDHA

南無栴檀功德佛

Na mwo jan tan gung de fwo

NA MO INFINITE HANDFULS OF LIGHT BUDDHA

南無無量掬光佛

Na mwo wu lyang ju gwang fwo

NA MO BRIGHT VIRTUE BUDDHA

南無光德佛

Na mwo gwang de fwo

NA MO VIRTUE FREE OF WORRY BUDDHA

南無無憂德佛

Na mwo wu you de fwo

NA MO NARAYANA BUDDHA

南無那羅延佛

Na mwo nwo lwo yan fwo

NA MO FLOWER OF MERIT AND VIRTUE BUDDHA

南無功德華佛

Na mwo gung de hwa fwo

NA MO LOTUS-FLOWER LIGHT, ROAMING IN SPIRITUAL POWER BUDDHA

南無蓮華光遊戲神通佛

Na mwo lyan hwa gwang you syi shen tung fwo

116

NA MO WEALTHY IN MERIT AND VIRTUE BUDDHA

南無財功德佛

Na mwo tsai gung de fwo

NA MO VIRTUE AND MINDFULNESS BUDDHA

南無德念佛

Na mwo de nyan fwo

NA MO MERIT AND VIRTUE AND GOOD RENOWN BUDDHA

南無善名稱功德佛

Na mwo shan ming cheng gung de fwo

NA MO KING BLAZING RED IMPERIAL BANNER BUDDHA

南無紅燄帝幢王佛

Na mwo hung yan di chwang wang fwo

NA MO SKILLFUL TRAVEL AND MERIT AND VIRTUE BUDDHA

南無善遊步功德佛

Na mwo shan you bu gung de fwo

NA MO VICTORIOUS IN BATTLE BUDDHA

南無鬭戰勝佛

Na mwo dou jan sheng fwo

NA MO SKILLFULLY TRAVELING BUDDHA

南無善遊步佛

Na mwo shan you bu fwo

NA MO ENCOMPASSING ADORNMENTS AND MERIT AND VIRTUE BUDDHA

南無周帀莊嚴功德佛

Na mwo jou dza jwang yan gung de fwo

NA MO PRECIOUS FLOWER TRAVELING BUDDHA

南無寶華遊步佛

Na mwo bau hwa you bu fwo

NA MO KING PRECIOUS LOTUS SKILLFULLY DWELLING BENEATH THE
SALA TREE BUDDHA

南無寶蓮華善住娑羅樹王佛

Na mwo bau lyan hwa shan ju swo lwo shu wang fwo

117

NA MO AMITA BUDDHA, WHOSE BODY IS THE TREASURY OF THE DHARMA
REALM

南無法界藏身阿彌陀佛

Na mwo fa jye dzang shen e mi two fwo

AND ALL OTHER BUDDHAS LIKE THEM, WORLD HONORED ONES OF ALL
WORLDS,

如是等◎，一切世界，諸佛世尊，

Ru shr deng, yi chye shr jye, ju fwo shr dzwun,

WHO DWELL IN THE WORLD FOREVER. MAY ALL THE WORLD HONORED
ONES

常住在世，是諸世尊，

Chang ju dzai shr. shr ju shr dzwun,

KINDLY BE MINDFUL OF ME AS I REPENT OF THE OFFENSES I HAVE
COMMITTED IN THIS LIFE AND IN FORMER LIVES

當慈念我，若我此生，若我前生，

Dang tsz nyan wo, rau wo tsz sheng, rau wo chyan sheng,

THROUGHOUT BIRTHS AND DEATHS WITHOUT BEGINNING,

從無始生死以來，所作眾罪，

Tsung wu shr sheng sz yi lai, swo dzwo jung dzwei,

WHETHER I HAVE DONE THEM MYSELF, TOLD OTHERS TO DO THEM,
OR CONDONED THEIR BEING DONE:

若自作，若教他作，見作隨喜．

Rau dz dzwo, rau jyau ta dzwo, jyan dzwo swei syi;

SUCH AS TAKING THINGS FROM STUPAS, FROM A SANGHAN, OR FROM
THE SANGHA OF THE FOUR DIRECTIONS,

若塔若僧，若四方僧物，

Rau ta rau seng, rau sz fang seng wu,

EITHER TAKING THEM MYSELF, TELLING OTHERS TO TAKE THEM, OR
CONDONING THEIR BEING TAKEN;

若自取，若教他取，見取隨喜．

rau dz chyu, rau jyau ta chyu, jyan chyu swei syi.

OR COMMITTING THE FIVE AVICI OFFENSES, EITHER COMMITTING
THEM MYSELF, TELLING OTHERS TO COMMIT THEM, OR CONDONING
THEIR BEING COMMITTED;

五無間罪，若自作，若教他作，見作隨喜，

Wu wu jyan dzwei, rau dz dzwo, rau jyau ta dzwo, jyan dzwo
swei syi;

OR COMMITTING THE TEN EVILS, EITHER COMMITTING THEM MYSELF,
TELLING OTHERS TO COMMIT THEM, OR CONDONING THEIR BEING
COMMITTED;

十不善道，若自作，若教他作，見作隨喜，

Shr bu shan dau, rau dz dzwo, rau jyau ta dzwo, jyan dzwo
swei syi;

ALL SUCH OBSTRUCTING OFFENSES, WHETHER HIDDEN OR NOT,

所作罪障，或有覆藏，或不覆藏，

Swo dzwo dzwei jang, hwei you fu dzang, hwei bu fu dzang,

WHICH MERIT MY FALLING INTO THE HELLS OR AMONG THE HUNGRY
GHOSTS OR ANIMALS OR ANY OTHER EVIL DESTINY,

應墮地獄，餓鬼畜生，諸餘惡趣，

Ying dwo di yu, e gwei chu sheng, ju yu e chyu;

OR INTO A LOWLY LIFE, A LIFE IN THE BORDER REGIONS, OR A
LIFE AS A MLECCHA;

邊地下賤，及篾戾車，

Byan di sya yan, ji mye li che;

I NOW REPENT OF AND REFORM ALL THE OBSTRUCTING OFFENSES
I'VE COMMITTED.

如是等處，所作罪障，今皆懺悔，

Ru shr deng chu, swo dzwo dzwei jang, jin jye chan hwei.

NOW MAY ALL THE BUDDHAS, WORLD HONORED ONES, CERTIFY ME;
MAY THEY BE MINDFUL OF ME.

今諸佛世尊，當證知我，當憶念我。

Jin ju fwo shr dzwun, dang jeng jr wo, dang yi nyan wo.

BEFORE ALL THE BUDDHAS, WORLD HONORED ONES, I FURTHER SPEAK
THESE WORDS:

我復於諸佛世尊前，作如是言，

Wo fu yu ju fwo shr dzwun chyan, dzwo ru shr yan:

ANY GOOD ROOTS THAT I HAVE GAINED IN THIS LIFE, OR IN PAST LIVES,

若我此生，若我餘生，

Rau wo tsz sheng, rau wo yu sheng,

THROUGH GIVING, THROUGH GUARDING PURE PRECEPTS,

曾行布施，或守淨戒，

Tseng sying bu shr, hwei shou jing jye,

SIMPLY THROUGH GIVING A MORSEL OF FOOD TO AN ANIMAL, OR THROUGH CULTIVATING PURE CONDUCT;

乃至施與畜生，一摶之食，或修淨行，

Nai jr shr yu chu sheng, yi twan jr shr, hwei shou jing heng,

ANY GOOD ROOTS FROM BRINGING LIVING BEINGS TO ACCOMPLISHMENT;

所有善根，成就眾生，

Swo you shan gen, cheng jyou jung sheng,

ANY GOOD ROOTS FROM CULTIVATING BODHI;

所有善根，修行菩提，

Swo you shan gen, syou sying pu ti,

AND ANY GOOD ROOTS FROM ATTAINING SUPREME WISDOM:

所有善根，及無上智，

Swo you shan gen, ji wu shang jr,

ALL OF THEM, ACCUMULATED AND RECKONED UP THROUGHOUT MY LIFESPANS,

所有善根，一切合集，校計籌量，

Swo you shan gen, yi chye he ji, jyau ji chou lyang,

I TRANSFER TO ANUTTARASAMYAKSAMBODHI.

皆悉迴向，阿耨多羅，三藐三菩提．

Jye syi hwei shang, e nou dwo lwo, san myau san pu ti.

MY TRANSFERENCE IS LIKE THE TRANSFERENCES MADE BY ALL THE BUDDHAS OF THE PAST, PRESENT, AND FUTURE.

如過去未來，現在諸佛，所作迴向，我亦如是迴向．

Ru gwo chu wei lai, syan dzai ju fwo, swo dzwo hwei syang,
wo yi ru shr hwei syang.

I REPENT OF AND REFORM EVERY OFFENSE, COMPLIANTLY REJOICE
IN ALL BLESSINGS,

眾罪皆懺悔◎ 諸福盡隨喜，

Jung dzwei jye chan hwei, ju fu jin swei syi,

SEEK THE BUDDHA'S MERIT AND VIRTUE, AND VOW TO ACCOMPLISH
THE UNSURPASSED WISDOM.

及請佛功德，願成無上智，

Ji ching fwo gung de, ywan cheng wu shang jr.

TO ALL BUDDHAS OF PAST AND PRESENT, SUPREME AMONG LIVING
BEINGS,

去來現在佛，於眾生最勝，

Chyu lai syan dzai fwo, yu jung sheng dzwei sheng,

WITH SEAS OF INFINITE MERIT AND VIRTUE, I NOW RETURN MY
LIFE IN WORSHIP.

無量功德海，我今歸命禮，

Wu lyang gung de hai, wo jin gwei ming li.

THROUGHOUT THE WORLDS IN THE TEN DIRECTIONS,

所有十方世界中◎，

Swo you shr fang shr jye jung

BEFORE ALL LIONS AMONG MEN IN THE PAST, IN THE PRESENT, AND
ALSO IN THE FUTURE,

三世一切人師子，

San shr yi chye ren shr dz

WITH BODY, MOUTH, AND MIND ENTIRELY PURE,

我以清淨身語意，

Wo yi ching jing shen yu yi,

I BOW BEFORE THEM ALL, OMITTING NONE.

一切徧禮盡無餘，

Yi chye byan li jin wu yu.

WITH THE AWESOME SPIRITUAL POWER OF SAMANTABHADRA'S VOWS,

普賢行願威神力,

Pu syan heng ywan wei shen li,

I APPEAR AT THE SAME TIME BEFORE EVERY THUS COME ONE,

普現一切如來前,

Pu syan yi chye ru lai chyan,

AND IN TRANSFORMED BODIES AS MANY AS MOTES OF DUST IN LANDS,

一身復現剎塵身,

Yi shen fu syan cha chen shen,

BOW TO BUDDHAS AS MANY AS MOTES OF DUST IN LANDS.

一一徧禮剎塵佛,

Yi yi byan li cha chen fwo.

IN EVERY MOTE OF DUST ARE BUDDHAS AS MANY AS MOTES OF DUST,

於一塵中塵數佛,

Yu yi chen jung chen shu fwo,

EACH DWELLING AMID A HOST OF BODHISATTVAS.

各處菩薩眾會中,

Ge chu pu sa jung hwei jung,

THROUGHOUT MOTES OF DUST IN ENDLESS DHARMA REALMS IT IS THE
SAME:

無盡法界塵亦然,

Wu jin fa jye chen yi ran

I DEEPLY BELIEVE THEY ALL ARE FILLED WITH BUDDHAS.

深信諸佛皆充滿,

Shen syin ju fwo jye chung man.

WITH SEAS OF EACH AND EVERY SOUND, I EVERYWHERE LET FALL

各以一切音聲海,

Ge yi yi chye yin sheng hai,

WORDS AND PHRASES, WONDERFUL AND ENDLESS.

普出無盡妙言辭，

Pu chu wu jin myau yan tsz.

WHICH EXHAUST ALL KALPAS OF THE FUTURE, AND

盡於未來一切劫，

Jin yu wei lai yi chye jye,

PRAISE THE WIDE, DEEP SEA OF THE BUDDHAS' MERIT AND VIRTUE.

讚佛甚深功德海，

Dzan fwo shen shen gung de hai.

FLOWER GARLANDS SUPREME AND WONDERFUL,

以諸最勝妙華鬘，

Yi ju dzwei sheng myau hwa man,

MUSIC, PERFUMES, PARASOLS, AND CANOPIES,

伎樂塗香及傘蓋，

Ji le tu syang ji san gai,

AND OTHER DECORATIONS RICH AND RARE,

如是最勝莊嚴具，

Ru shr dzwei sheng jwang yan jyu,

I OFFER UP TO EVERY THUS COME ONE.

我以供養諸如來，

Wo yi gung yang ju ru lai.

FINE CLOTHING, SUPERIOR INCENSE,

最勝衣服最勝香，

Dzwei sheng yi fu dzwei sheng syang,

POWDERED AND BURNING INCENSE, LAMPS AND CANDLES

末香燒香與燈燭，

Mo syang shau syang yu deng ju,

EACH ONE HEAPED AS HIGH AS WONDERFULLY HIGH MOUNTAIN,

一一皆如妙高聚，

Yi yi jye ru myau gau jyu,

I OFFER COMPLETELY TO ALL TATHAGATAS.

我 悉 供 養 諸 如 來 ,

Wo syi gung yang ju ru lai.

WITH A VAST, GREAT, SUPREMELY LIBERATED MIND,

我 以 廣 大 勝 解 心 ,

Wo yi gwang da sheng jye syin,

I BELIEVE IN ALL THE BUDDHAS OF THE THREE PERIODS OF TIME:

深 信 一 切 三 世 佛 ,

Shen syin yi chye san shr fwo,

WITH THE STRENGTH OF SAMANTABHADRA'S CONDUCT AND VOWS,

悉 以 普 賢 行 願 力 ,

Syi yi pu syan heng ywan li,

I MAKE OFFERINGS TO ALL THUS COME ONES EVERYWHERE.

普 徧 供 養 諸 如 來 ,

Pu byan gung yang ju ru lai.

FOR ALL THE EVIL DEEDS I HAVE DONE IN THE PAST

我 昔 所 造 諸 惡 業 ◎

Wo syi swo dzau ju e ye

BASED ON BEGINNINGLESS GREED, ANGER, AND DELUSION,

皆 由 無 始 貪 瞋 癡 ,

Jye you wu shr tan chen chr

AND CREATED BY BODY, SPEECH, AND MIND,

從 身 語 意 之 所 生 ,

Tsung shen yu yi jr swo sheng,

I NOW KNOW SHAME AND REPENT OF THEM ALL.

一 切 我 今 皆 懺 悔 ,

Yi chye wo jin jye chan hwei.

OF ALL BEINGS IN THE TEN DIRECTIONS,

十方一切諸眾生，

Shr fang yi chye ju jung sheng,

THE LEARNERS AND THOSE PAST STUDY IN THE TWO VEHICLES,

二乘有學及無學，

Er cheng you sywe ji wu sywe,

AND ALL THUS COME ONES AND BODHISATTVAS,

一切如來與菩薩，

Yi chye ru lai yu pu sa,

I REJOICE IN ALL THEIR MERIT AND VIRTUES.

所有功德皆隨喜，

Swo you gung de jye swei syi

BEFORE THE LAMPS OF THE WORLDS OF THE TEN DIRECTIONS,

十方所有世間燈，

Shr fang swo you shr jyan deng,

THOSE WHO FIRST ACCOMPLISHED BODHI,

最初成就菩提者，

Dzwei chu cheng jyou pu ti je,

I NOW REQUEST AND BESEECH THEM ALL

我今一切皆勸請，

Wo jin yi chye jye chywan ching,

TO TURN THE FOREMOST, WONDROUS DHARMA WHEEL.

轉於無上妙法輪，

Jwan yu wu shang myau fa lwun.

IF THERE ARE BUDDHAS WHO WISH FOR NIRVANA,

諸佛若欲示涅槃，

Ju fwo rau yu shr nye pan,

125

I REQUEST WITH DEEP SINCERITY,

我悉至誠而勸請，

Wo syi jr cheng er chywan ching,

THAT THEY DWELL IN THE WORLD FOR AS MANY KALPAS AS THERE ARE
DUST MOTES IN KSHETRAS,

唯願久住刹塵劫，

Wei ywan jyou ju cha chen jye,

TO BRING BENEFIT AND BLISS TO EVERY BEING.

利樂一切諸衆生，

Li le yi chye ju jung sheng.

ALL GOOD ROOTS FROM WORSHIPPING, PRAISING, AND MAKING
OFFERINGS TO BUDDHAS,

所有禮讚供養佛，

Swo you li dzan gung yang fwo

FROM REQUESTING THAT BUDDHAS DWELL IN THE WORLD TO TURN THE
DHARMA WHEEL,

請佛住世轉法輪，

Ching fwo ju shr jwan fa lwun,

FROM COMPLIANTLY REJOICING, FROM REPENTING AND REFORMING,

隨喜懺悔諸善根，

Swei syi chan hwei ju shan gen,

I TRANSFER TO LIVING BEINGS' ATTAINING THE BUDDHA'S WAY.

迴向衆生及佛道◎

Hwei syang jung sheng ji fwo dau.

MAY THIS SUPREME MERIT AND VIRTUE,

願將以此勝功德，

Ywan jyang yi tsz sheng gung de,

BE TRANSFERRED THROUGHOUT THE UNSURPASSED TRUE DHARMA REALM.

迴向無上真法界，

Hwei syang wu shang jen fa jye,

TO THE NATURE AND APPEARANCE OF THE BUDDHA, DHARMA, AND
SANGHA,

性相佛法及僧伽，

Sying syang fwo.fa ji seng chye,

THESE TWO TRUTHS ARE FUSED AND UNDERSTOOD BY THE IMPRESS OF
SAMADHI'S SEA.

二諦融通三昧印，

Er di yung tung san mei yin.

OF ALL SUCH INFINITE SEAS OF MERIT AND VIRTUE,

如是無量功德海，

Ru shr wu lyang gung de hai,

I NOW MAKE COMPLETE TRANSFERENCE.

我今皆悉盡迴向，

Wo jin jye syi jin hwei syang.

MAY ALL THE KARMIC OBSTRUCTION OF LIVING BEINGS'

所有眾生身口意，

Swo you jung sheng shen kou yi,

BODY, MOUTH, AND MIND--VIEW DELUSIONS,

見惑彈謗我法等，

Jyan hwei tan bang wo fa deng,

FALSE ACCUSATIONS, SELF, DHARMAS, AND SO FORTH--

如是一切諸業障，

Ru shr yi chye ju ye jang,

BE ENTIRELY EXTINGUISHED WITHOUT REMAINDER.

悉皆消滅盡無餘，

Syi jye syau mye jin wu yu.

IN EVERY THOUGHT MAY MY WISDOM ENCOMPASS THE DHARMA REALM,

念念智周於法界，

Nyan nyan jr jou yu fa jye,

AND WIDELY CROSS OVER LIVING BEINGS TO IRREVERSIBILITY,

廣度眾生皆不退，

Gwang du jung sheng jye bu twei.

TILL THE EXHAUSTION OF THE REALM OF EMPTY SPACE,

乃至虛空世界盡，

Nai jr syu kung shr jye jin,

AND THE EXHAUSTION OF LIVING BEINGS, OF KARMA AND OF AFFLICTIONS.

眾生及業煩惱盡，

Jung sheng ji ye fan nau jin,

JUST AS THESE FOUR DHARMAS ARE VAST AND BOUNDLESS,

如是四法廣無邊，

Ru shr sz fa gwang wu byan

I NOW VOW THAT MY TRANSFERENCE WILL BE SO, TOO.

願今迴向亦如是。

Ywan jin hwei syang yi ru shr.

NA MO UNIVERSAL WORTHY, BODHISATTVA OF GREAT CONDUCT.

南無大行普賢菩薩◎

Na mwo da heng pu syan pu sa

NA MO UNIVERSAL WORTHY, BODHISATTVA OF GREAT CONDUCT.

南無大行普賢菩薩

Na mwo da heng pu syan pu sa

NA MO UNIVERSAL WORTHY, BODHISATTVA OF GREAT CONDUCT.

南無大行普賢菩薩◎

Na mwo da heng pu syan pu sa

MENG SHANG OFFERING CEREMONY

蒙山施食儀
Meng shan shr shr yi

(Recite each section marked with a ▲ 3 times) (以下俱各三徧.
每段以▲為記.)

▲ IF PEOPLE WISH TO FULLY UNDERSTAND

若人欲了知
Rau ren yu lyau jr

ALL BUDDHAS OF THE THREE PERIODS OF TIME,

三世一切佛 ◎,
San shr yi chye fwo,

THEY SHOULD CONTEMPLATE THE NATURE OF THE DHARMA-REALM:

應觀法界性
Ying gwan fa jye sying,

EVERYTHING IS MADE FROM MIND ALONE.

一切唯心造 ◎,
yi chye wei syin dzau.

▲ *HELL-SMASHING TRUE WORDS:* (破地獄真言)

NAN, CHYE LA DI YE　　　　　唵　伽囉帝耶

SWO PWO HE　　　*(3 times)*　娑婆訶　　　(三徧)

▲ *UNIVERSAL INVITATION TRUE WORDS:* (普召請真言)

NA MWO BU BU DI LI CHYE LI DWO LI 南無部部帝唎伽哩哆哩

DAN DWO YE DWO YE　*(3 times)*　怛哆誐哆耶　(三徧)

▲ *UNTYING THE KNOT OF HATRED TRUE WORDS:* (解怨結真言)

NAN, SAN TWO LA,　　　　　唵　三陀囉

CHYE TWO SWO PWO HE *(3 times)* 伽陀娑婆訶 ◎, (三徧)

▲ *(Put palms together.)* (合掌)
HOMAGE TO THE GREAT MEANS EXPANSIVE BUDDHA FLOWER ADORNMENT SUTRA.

南無大方廣佛華嚴經
Na mwo Da Fang Gwang Fwo Hwa Yen Jing.

▲ HOMAGE TO THE ETERNALLY DWELLING BUDDHAS OF THE TEN DIREC-
TIONS.

南無常住十方佛

Na mwo chang ju shr fang fwo.

HOMAGE TO THE ETERNALLY DWELLING DHARMA OF THE TEN DIREC-
TIONS.

南無常住十方法

Na mwo chang ju shr fang fa.

HOMAGE TO THE ETERNALLY DWELLING SANGHA OF THE TEN DIREC-
TIONS.

南無常住十方僧

Na mwo chang ju shr fang seng.

HOMAGE TO OUR ORIGINAL TEACHER SHAKYAMUNI BUDDHA.

南無本師釋迦牟尼佛

Na mwo ben shr shr jya mwo ni fwo.

*(the attendant makes 1/2 bow and leaves his position at
third time)* (於第三徧時,行者問訊出位。)
*(The attendant walks slowly to the middle, when reciting to
the word "Je (者)", the attendant turns his face to the
front and listens.)* (徐步至中,到「者」字轉臉向上聽。)

HOMAGE TO GREATLY COMPASSIONATE CONTEMPLATOR OF THE WORLDS'
SOUNDS BODHISATTVA.

南無大悲觀世音菩薩

Na mwo da bei gwan shr yin pu sa.

HOMAGE TO EARTH STORE KING BODHISATTVA, WHO RESCUES THE
LIVING AND THE DEAD FROM SUFFERING.

南無冥陽救苦地藏王菩薩

Na mwo ming yang jyou ku di dzang wang pu sa.

HOMAGE TO THE VENERABLE ANANDA WHO STATED THE TEACHINGS.

南無啓教阿難陀尊者

Na mwo chi jyau e nan two dzwun je. *(release palm)*
(放掌)

*(As the attendant leaves his position and bows to the Buddha,
he should make this contemplation, "By the original vow-power*

of Shakyamuni Buddha, Gwan Yin, Earth Store, and Ananda, of
the Triple Jewel, may they hear me intone their names and
appear in empty space to save and pull these hungry ghosts
from suffering。")

(行者出位禮佛,必須觀想三寶釋迦.觀音.地藏.阿難,以本願力
閒我稱名,顯現虛空濟拔餓鬼離苦.)

(bow)
▲ I TAKE REFUGE WITH THE BUDDHA, I TAKE REFUGE WITH THE DHARMA,
I TAKE REFUGE WITH THE SANGHA.

皈 依 佛(下拜), 皈 依 法, 皈 依 僧.
Gwei yi fwo, gwei yi fa, gwei yi seng.

I TAKE REFUGE WITH THE BUDDHA, THE DOUBLY PERFECTED
HONORED ONE. *(turn over palms)*

皈 依 佛 兩 足 尊 (反掌)
Gwei yi fwo, lyang dzu dzwun.

I TAKE REFUGE WITH THE DHARMA, WHICH IS HONORABLE AND APART
FROM DESIRE.

皈 依 法 離 欲 尊
Gwei yi fa, li yu dzwun.

I TAKE REFUGE WITH THE SANGHA, THE HONORED AMONG ASSEMBLIES.

皈 依 僧 衆 中 尊
Gwei yi seng, jung jung dzwun.

(stand)
I HAVE COMPLETED TAKING REFUGE WITH THE BUDDHA, I HAVE
COMPLETED TAKING REFUGE WITH THE DHARMA, AND I HAVE COM-
PLETED TAKING REFUGE WITH THE SANGHA.

皈 依 佛 竟 (起立), 皈 依 法 竟, 皈 依 僧 竟 (三拜畢 問訊復位)
Gwei yi fwo jing, gwei yi fa jing, gwei yi seng jing.
(3 times for this entire section)

(After 3 bows, the attendant makes 1/2 bow and returns to
the original place.)

▲ DISCIPLES OF THE BUDDHA
SENTIENT BEINGS   ,   THE EVIL KARMA WHICH YOU
SOLITARY SPIRITS

HAVE CREATED, IS ALL BECAUSE OF BEGINNINGLESS GREED, HATRED,
AND STUPIDITY,

佛子
有情 所 造 諸 惡 業, 皆 由 無 始 貪 瞋 癡.
孤魂

131

Fwo dz
You ching swo dzau ju e ye, jye you wu shr tan chen chr,
Gu hwun

WHICH HAS BEEN PRODUCED IN BODY, MOUTH, AND MIND,

DISCIPLES OF THE BUDDHA
SENTIENT BEINGS   REPENT OF IT ALL.
SOLITARY SPIRITS

從身語意之所生，一切 佛子 皆懺悔．
            有情
            孤魂

Tsung shen yu yi jr swo sheng, yi chye You ching jye tsan
                                     Fwo Dz
                                     Gu hwun

hwei.

▲LIVING BEINGS ARE LIMITLESS, I VOW TO CROSS THEM OVER.

眾生無邊誓願度

Jung sheng wu byan shr ywan du.

AFFLICTIONS ARE INEXHAUSTIBLE, I VOW TO CUT THEM OFF.

煩惱無盡誓願斷

Fan nau wu jin shr ywan dwan.

DHARMA-DOORS ARE IMMEASURABLE, I VOW TO LEARN THEM.

法門無量誓願學

Fa men wu lyang shr ywan sywe.

THE BUDDHA-PATH IS UNSURPASSED, I VOW TO REALIZE IT.

佛道無上誓願成

Fwo dau wu shang shr ywan cheng.*(3 times for this enire
                                     section)*

▲THE LIVING BEINGS OF THE SELF-NATURE, I VOW TO CROSS
  OVER.

自性眾生誓願度

Dz sying jung sheng shr ywan du.

132

THE AFFLICTIONS OF THE SELF-NATURE, I VOW TO CUT OFF.

自 性 煩 惱 誓 願 斷 ▽₃

Dz sying fan nau shr ywan dwan,

THE DHARMA-DOORS OF THE SELF-NATURE, I VOW TO ENTIRELY LEARN.

自 性 法 門 誓 願 學 (行者問訊出位)

Dz sying fa men shr ywan sywe.
  (the attendant makes a 1/2 bow and leaves his position.)

THE BUDDHA-PATH OF THE SELF NATURE, I VOW TO REALIZE.

自 性 佛 道 誓 願 成 ◎₃

Dz sying fwo dau shr ywan cheng. *(3 times for this entire*
                    ◎₃   *section)*

▲ *EXTINGUISHING FIXED KARMA TRUE WORDS:* (滅定業真言)

NAN, BWO LA MWO LIN TWO NING 唵 鉢囉末鄰陀顙

SWO PWO HE *(3 times)* 娑婆訶 (三徧)
(1/2 bow to the center on the third round) (第三徧向中問訊)

▲ *ERADICATING KARMIC OBSTACLES TRUE WORDS:* (滅業障真言)

NAN, E LU LE JI 唵 阿嚕勒繼

SWO PWO HE *(3 times)* 娑婆訶 (三徧)

▲ *OPENING THE THROAT TRUE WORDS:* (開咽喉真言)

NAN, BU BU DI LI CHYE DWO LI, 唵 步步底哩伽哆哩

DAN DWO YE DWO YE *(3 times)* 怛哆誐哆耶 (三徧)
(1/2 bow to the Buddha on the third round) (第三徧佛前問訊)

▲ *SAMAYA PRECEPTS TRUE WORDS:* (三昧耶戒真言)

NAN, SAN MEI YE, 唵 三昧耶

SA TWO WAN. *(3 times)* 薩錘鎫 (三徧)

133

▲ *TRANSFORMATION OF FOOD TRUE WORDS:* （變食真言）

NA MWO SA WA DAN TWO YE DWO 南無薩嚩怛他誐哆
(place pure vase in hand) （取淨盂在手中）

WA LU JR DI, NAN, 嚩嚕枳帝唵
(hold fingers in flower mudra) （扣手指花印）

SAN BWO LA, SAN BWO LA, 三跋囉　三跋囉

HUNG *(3 times)* 吽 （三徧）

(The left hand upholds the food offering and the right hand lightly presses on the food. Make the following contemplation, "I now recite this sublime, wondrous Dharma of limitless awesome virtue and tranquil brightness to aid this food. Just this single portion multiplies into limitless portions. It's neither one nor limitless, yet at the same time it is one and limitless. And each portion increases layer upon layer without exhaustion, filling up empty space and pervading the Dharma realm, so that it universally rescues those hungry beings and causes them to leave suffering and attain bliss.")

（以左手擎食，右手按食上，作觀˚我今誦此無量威德自在
光明勝妙羅尼，加持此食，即此一食出無量食，咸趣一食，
非一非無量，而一而無量，一一出生重重無盡充塞虛空，
周徧法界，普濟飢虛，離苦得樂˚）

▲ *SWEET DEW TRUE WORDS:* （甘露水真言）

NA MWO SU LU PWO YE, 南無蘇嚕婆耶
(Place pure vase on the rim of （取淨瓶壓盂口上）
the cup which contains seven
grains of rice.)

DAN TWO YE DWO YE, 怛他誐哆耶

DA JR TWO, NAN, 怛姪他唵

SU LU, SU LU 蘇嚕蘇嚕
(Swirl the pure vase around （此當香頭上繞二匝）
the incense twice.)

134

BWO LA SU LU, BWO LA SU LU,   鉢囉蘇嚕鉢囉蘇嚕
  swirl the pure vase around   (盃口上繞二臣)
  the cup twice.)

SWO PWO HE.   *(3 times)*   娑婆詞   (三徧)

(Pour 1/3 of water into the cup.)   (滹水)

(The first pour of water, swirl   (其滹水第一遍右繞向外,
outside to the right. The second   二遍左繞向裡,
and the third pour of water,swirl   三首遍同)
inside to the left.)

(Contemplate how this water, aided by the power of mantras, becomes pure and clean and completely pervades the Dharma realm. It enables the throats of all hungry ghosts to open by themselves. Living beings throughout the Dharma realm attain the food and drink of sweet dew all in an instant.)

(觀想此水咒力加持,清淨湛然,周徧法界,令諸餓鬼咽喉
自開,法界眾生,一時皆得,甘露飲食.)

▲*THE ONE CHARACTER WATER WHEEL TRUE WORDS:* (一字水輪真言)

NAN, WAN, WAN, WAN WAN WAN.   唵 鑁 鑁 鑁鑁鑁
      (3 times)   (三徧)

▲*MILK OCEAN TRUE WORDS:*   (乳海真言)

NA MWO SAN MAN DWO,   南無三滿哆

MWO TWO NAN,   沒馱喃

NAN, WAN.   *(3 times)*   唵 鑁 (三徧)

(After the third recitation of the mantra, the attendant presses his finger on the rim of the cup. Upon the first recitation (of the seven Buddhas' names), at the word "li", the attendant turns to the left and walks to the left corner, facing outside. Upon the second recitation, at the word "li", the attendant walks back to his original position, facing right. Upon the third recitation, at the word "li", the attendant turns and walks to the middle of the hall, facing the front. The attendant gets his cues from the sound of the handbell.) (三遍畢,指壓盃口至灑字一轉臉,
一舉轉臉向左,走至左角面上外,二遍"灑"字一舉走下本位,轉臉向
右,三遍"灑"字一舉走至居中,向上舉步,皆聽,引磬.

135

▲ HOMAGE TO THE THUS COME ONE MANY JEWELS,

南 無 多 寶 如 來

Na mwo dwo bau ru lai.

HOMAGE TO THE THUS COME ONE JEWELLED VICTORY.

南 無 寶 勝 如 來

Na mwo bau sheng ru lai.

HOMAGE TO THE THUS COME ONE WONDROUS FORM.

南 無 妙 色 身 如 來

Na mwo myau shai shen ru lai.

HOMAGE TO THE THUS COME ONE VAST AND EXTENSIVE BODY.

南 無 廣 博 身 如 來

Na mwo gwang bwo shen ru lai.

HOMAGE TO THE THUS COME ONE APART FROM FEAR.

南 無 離 怖 畏 如 來

Na mwo li bu wei ru lai.
(1, 2, 3 step forward at the first time)

HOMAGE TO THE THUS COME ONE SWEET DEW KING.

南 無 甘 露 王 如 來

Na mwo gan lu wang ru lai.

HOMAGE TO THE THUS COME ONE AMITABHA.

南 無 阿 彌 陀 如 來 。 (散掌)

Na mwo e mi two ru lai. *(3 times for this entire section)*
(release palms)

▲ THESE SPIRITUAL MANTRAS AID AND UPHOLD THE

PURE DHARMA FOOD,
DHARMA-OFFERING FOOD,
SWEET DEW WATER,

(戒指寫水中吽字) 淨 法 食 ，
神 咒 加 持 法 施 食 ，
甘 露 水 ，

jing fa·shr *(At the first time: With the*
Shen jou jya chr fa shr shr , *index finger write the "hung 吽"*
gan lu shwei *character over the water.)*

UNIVERSALLY GIVEN TO THE MULTITUDES OF THE

DISCIPLES OF THE BUDDHA
SENTIENT BEINGS   LIKE SAND GRAINS IN A RIVER.
SOLITARY SPIRITS

佛子　　(佛字再慮吽)
普施河沙象有情 ，
(一彈水)　　孤魂
　　　　　fwo dz　　(When the word "Buddha(fwo)" is
Pu shr he sha jung you ching.　recited, write "hung 吽" again.)
　　　　　gu hwun
(flick the water)

I VOW THAT THEY WILL ALL BE SATISFIED AND RENOUNCE STINGI-
NESS AND GREED,
願皆飽滿捨慳貪，
Ywan jye bau man she chyan tan,

AND QUICKLY BE FREED FROM DARKNESS AND BE REBORN IN THE
PURE LAND, (flick the water and kneel)(彈水胡跪)
速脫幽冥生淨土 ，
Su two you ming sheng jing du.

AND TAKE REFUGE WITH THE TRIPLE JEWEL AND GIVE RISE TO BODHI,
皈依三寶發菩提，
Gwei yi san bau fa pu ti, ◎₃

AND ULTIMATELY REALIZE THE UNSURPASSED PATH,
究竟得成無上道 ，
Jyou jing de cheng wu shang dau.

WITH THE LIMITLESS MERIT AND VIRTUE WHICH EXHAUSTS THE
FUTURE,
功德無邊盡未來，
Gung de wu byan jin wei lai,◎₃

　　　　DISCIPLES OF THE BUDDHA
MAY ALL SENTIENT BEINGS   SHARE IN THE FOOD OF DHARMA.
　　　SOLITARY SPIRITS   (flick it three times, to the
　　佛子　　　　　　　　　　left, right, and center)
一切有情 同法食.(左右中共三彈)
　　孤魂
　　fwo dz
Yi chye you ching tung fa shr. (3 times for this entire
　　gu hwun   section)

137

(At this time the attendant holds the pure food and goes outdoors to put it on the offering platform. He divides it into three shares: the first share to creatures of the sea, so that they attain the emptiness of people; the second share to the fur group, so that they attain the stillness of dharmas; and the third share to those who possess consciousness and barrel-like appearances, throughout other lands, causing them all to be full and content, and to attain the patience of non-production. If there's no platform, then place the food on clean ground or upon a big stone. Do not place it under either a pomegranate or peach tree, because ghosts and spirits are afraid of these kinds of trees, and will not dare to partake of the food. Also, according to the manual of Dharma Master Yun-ch'i, one does not divide the food into three portions--which is the right method. But now we just go along with the general custom.)

（是時行者持淨食出，置生臺上，分為三分，一施水族，令獲人空。二施毛羣，令獲法寂，三施他方稟識陶形，悉令充足，獲無生忍。如無生臺，置淨地上或大石山亦得，不得濕於石榴．挑樹之下，鬼神慳怕，不得食之．又雲棲本不分三種，甚是今，姑徙俗。）

▲ ALL OF YOU MULTITUDES OF SENTIENT BEINGS

DISCIPLES OF THE BUDDHA
SOLITARY SPIRITS   ,

佛子
汝等有情　眾，
　孤魂

fwo dz
Ru deng you ching jung,
　gu hwun

I NOW MAKE THIS OFFERING TO YOU. THIS FOOD PERVADES THE TEN DIRECTIONS,

我今施汝供，　　此食徧十方，
Wo jin shr ru gung.　　Tsz shr byan shr fang,

DISCIPLES OF THE BUDDHA
TO ALL THE SENTIENT BEINGS　　　　TOGETHER.
SOLITARY SPIRITS

　　佛子
一切有情　共，
　孤魂

138

fwo dz
Yi chye you ching gung.
　　gu　hwun

I VOW THAT THE MERIT AND VIRTUE FROM THIS,

願以此功德，

Ywan yi tsz gung de,

WILL GO EVERYWHERE AND REACH EVERY ONE.

普及於一切，

Pu ji yu yi chye,

　　　　　　　　　　　　　　　　DISCIPLES OF THE BUDDHA
THIS FOOD OFFERING IS GIVEN TO THE SENTIENT BEINGS　　　　，
　　　　　　　　　　　　　　　　SOLITARY SPIRITS

施食與 佛子
　　　 有情 ，
　　　 孤魂

fwo dz
Shr shr yu you ching,
　　gu　hwun

SO THAT THEY WILL ALL REALIZE THE BUDDHA-PATH.

皆共成佛道。 （三編）

Jye gung cheng fwo dau. *(3 times for this entire section)*

▲ *GIVING UNOBSTRUCTED FOOD TRUE WORDS:* (施無遮食真言)

NAN, MU LI LING,　　　　唵　穆力陵
SWO PWO HE. 　(3 times)　婆婆詞 （三編）

▲ *UNIVERSAL OFFERING TRUE WORDS:* 　（普供養真言）

NAN, YE YE NANG,　　　唵 誐誐曩
SAN PWO WA,　　　　　三 婆嚩
FA DZ LA, HUNG.　　　伐日囉斛 （三編）

139

HEART SUTRA *(1 time; see page 44)*

般若波羅蜜多心經 (一編見第44頁)

SPIRIT MANTRA FOR REBIRTH IN THE PURE LAND *(3 times;*

往生咒 (三編;見第107頁) *page 107)*

PRAISE
讚偈

MAY ALL THE FOUR KINDS OF BEINGS REACH THE JEWELLED LAND,

四生登於寶地◎

Sz sheng deng yu bau di.

AND THE BEINGS OF ALL THREE REALMS BE BORN FROM LOTUS
BLOOMS.

三有托化蓮池

San you two hwa lyan chr.

MAY ALL THE MYRIAD GHOSTS ATTAIN THE THREE-FOLD WORTHINESS,

河沙餓鬼證三賢

He sha e gwei jeng san syan.

AND THE COUNTLESS SENTIENT ONES ASCEND THE TEN GROUNDS.

萬類有情登十地

Wan lei you ching deng shr di.

AMITABHA'S BODY IS THE COLOR OF GOLD

阿彌陀佛身金色◎

E mi two fwo shen jin shai.

THE SPLENDOR OF HIS HALLMARKS HAS NO PEER.

相好光明無等倫

Syang hau gwang ming wu deng lwun.

THE LIGHT OF HIS BROW SHINES ROUND A HUNDRED WORLDS,

白毫宛轉五須彌

Bai hau wan jwan wu syu mi.

140

WIDE AS THE SEAS ARE HIS EYES PURE AND CLEAR.

紺目澄清四大海

Gan mu cheng ching sz da hai.

SHINING IN HIS BRILLIANCE BY TRANSFORMATION

光中化佛無數億

Gwang jung hwa fwo wu shu yi.

ARE COUNTLESS BODHISATTVAS AND INFINITE BUDDHAS.

化菩薩衆亦無邊◎

Hwa pu sa jung yi wu byan.

HIS FORTY-EIGHT VOWS WILL BE OUR LIBERATION,

四十八願度衆生

Sz shr ba ywan du jung sheng.

IN NINE LOTUS-STAGES WE REACH THE FARTHEST SHORE.

九品咸令登彼岸

Jyou pin syan ling deng bi an.

HOMAGE TO THE BUDDHA OF THE WESTERN PURE LAND, KIND AND
COMPASSIONATE AMITABHA. *(repeat this line 3 times)*

「南無西方極樂世界◎大慈大悲阿彌陀佛.

Na mwo syi fang ji le shr jye, da tsz da bei, e mi two fwo.

NA MO AMITA BUDDHA   *(recite and circumambulate)*

南無阿彌陀佛 (繞念)

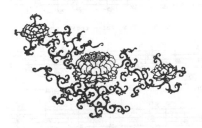
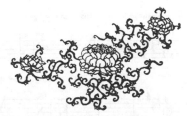

141

Praise to Amitabha

A - mi - ta - bha's bod - y is the co - lor of gold—— The

splen - dor of his hall - marks has no peer———— The

light of his brow shines 'round a hun - dred worlds———

Wide as the seas are his eyes pure and clear———

shin - ing in his bril - liance by trans - for - ma - tion Are

count-less Bo - dhi - satt - vas and in - fin - ite Bud - dhas His

for - ty eight vows will be our li - ber - a - tion In

nine lo - tus sta - ges we reach the far - thest shore

Hom - age to the Bud - dha of the west - ern Pure Land——

Kind and com - pas - sion- ate A - mi - ta - bha.

PRAISE TO AMITA BUDDHA
彌 陀 讚

AMITABHA'S BODY IS THE COLOR OF GOLD

阿彌陀佛身金色◎

E mi two fwo shen jin shai

THE SPLENDOR OF HIS HALLMARKS HAS NO PEER.

相好光明無等倫

Syang hau gwang ming wu deng lwun

THE LIGHT OF HIS BROW SHINES 'ROUND A HUNDRED WORLDS,

白毫宛轉五須彌

Bai hau wan jwan wu syu mi

WIDE AS THE SEAS ARE HIS EYES PURE AND CLEAR.

紺目澄清四大海

Gan mu cheng ching sz da hai

SHINING IN HIS BRILLIANCE BY TRANSFORMATION

光中化佛無數億

Gwang jung hwa fwo wu shu yi

ARE COUNTLESS BODHISATTVAS AND INFINITE BUDDHAS.

化菩薩眾亦無邊◎

Hwa pu sa jung yi wu byan

HIS FORTY-EIGHT VOWS WILL BE OUR LIBERATION,

四十八願度眾生

Sz shr ba ywan du jung sheng

IN NINE LOTUS-STAGES WE REACH THE FARTHEST SHORE.

九品咸令登彼岸

Jyou pin syan ling deng bi an

HOMAGE TO THE BUDDHA OF THE WESTERN PURE LAND, KIND AND
COMPASSIONATE AMITABHA. *(repeat this line 3 times)*

南無西方極樂世界◉大慈大悲阿彌陀佛

Na mwo syi fang ji le shr jye da tsz da bei e mi two fwo.

NA MO AMITA BUDDHA   *(Recite while circumambulating.)*

南無阿彌陀佛   (持名繞念)

Na mwo e mi two fwo

143

VERSE FOR TRANSFERING MERIT
回向偈

I VOW THAT THIS MERIT

願以此功德

Ywan yi tsz gung de

WILL ADORN THE BUDDHA'S PURE LAND,

莊嚴佛淨土

Jwang yan fwo jing du

REPAYING FOUR KINDS OF KINDNESS ABOVE

上報四重恩

Shang bau sz chung en

AIDING THOSE BELOW IN THE THREE PATHS OF SUFFERING.

下濟三途苦

Sya ji san tu ku

MAY THOSE WHO SEE AND HEAR

若有見聞者

Rau you jyan wen je

ALL BRING FORTH THE BODHI HEART

悉發菩提心

Syi fa pu ti syin

AND WHEN THIS RETRIBUTION BODY IS DONE

盡此一報身

Jin tsz yi bau shen

BE BORN TOGETHER IN THE LAND OF ULTIMATE BLISS.

同生極樂國 （開示後唱誦）

Tung sheng ji le gwo.

(sung after lecture)

CEREMONY FOR PURIFYING THE BOUNDARIES
淨壇儀規
PRAISE FOR PURIFYING THE WATER
楊枝淨水讚

USING THE WILLOW BRANCH, THE PURE WATER IS SPRINKLED EVERY-WHERE IN THREE THOUSAND WORLDS.

楊枝淨水、徧灑三千

Yang jr jing shwei, byan sa san chyan.

ITS NATURE IS EMPTY, YET ITS EIGHT VIRTUES BENEFIT HUMANS AND GODS,

性空八德利人天◎

Sying kung ba de li ren tyan,

*SO THEIR BLESSINGS AND LIFE SPAN WILL BE INCREASED GREATLY.

＊福壽廣增延　　　◎

fu shou gwang dzeng yan.

*CAUSING HUNGRY GHOSTS TO AVOID HAVING NEEDLE-SIZED THROATS.

＊餓鬼免針咽

e gwei myan jen yan.

ERADICATING OFFENSES AND GETTING RID OF FAULTS,

滅罪除愆

mye dzwei chu chyan,

IT TURNS THEIR FLAMES INTO RED LOTUSES.

火燄化紅蓮◎

hwo yan hwa hung lyan.

HOMAGE TO THE BODHISATTVAS, MAHASATTVAS OF THE CLEAR COOL GROUND.

南無清涼地菩薩摩訶薩◎ (三稱)

Na mwo ching lyang di pu sa mwo he sa (recite 3 times)

＊此兩句只誦其一

*Recite only one of these two lines.

145

HOMAGE TO THE BODHISATTVA WHO OBSERVES THE SOUNDS OF THE
WORLD

南無大悲觀世音菩薩 (三稱)

na mwo da bei gwan shr yin pu sa *(recite 3 times)*

VERSE SPOKEN BY·THE DHARMA HOST WHILE HOLDING
THE WATER　　　主法持水說文

THE BODHISATTVA WITH HIS WILLOW BRANCH AND SWEET DEW WATER,

菩薩柳頭甘露水

Pu sa lwo tou gan lu shwei,

CAN MAKE A SINGLE DROP PÉRVADE THE TEN DIRECTIONS 'ROUND.

能令一滴徧十方

Neng ling yi di byan shr fang,

ENTIRELY WASHED AWAY ARE ALL DEFILEMENT AND FOUL ODOR;

腥羶垢穢盡蠲除

Sying shan gou hwei jin jywan chu;

COMPLETELY CLEANSED AND PURIFIED, THIS HOLY PRACTICE-GROUND.

令此壇場悉清淨

Ling tsz tan chang syi ching jing.

THE TEACHINGS CONTAIN THESE TRUE WORDS, WHICH WE SHOULD
REVERENTLY HOLD AND RECITE:

敎有真言謹當持誦

Jyau you jen yan jin dang chr sung:

GREAT COMPASSION MANTRA *(recite continuously until instructed
to stop; see page 32)*

大悲咒　(持續誦念,至提示始歇;見第32頁)

TEN SMALL MANTRA'S *(see page 36)*

十小咒　(見第36頁)

THE HEART OF PRAJNA PARAMITA SUTRA *(see page 44)*

般若波羅蜜多心經　(見第44頁)

MAHA PRAJNA PARAMITA

摩訶般若波羅蜜多 (三稱)

Mwo he bwo re bwo lwo mi dwo *(recite 3 times)*

ALL THE NAMES OF THE GREAT ONE, AVALOKITESVARA, PERVADES EVERYWHERE.

觀音大士 慈號圓通

Gwan Yin da shr, syi hau ywan tung.

HIS TWELVE GREAT VOWS ARE GRAND AND PROFOUND.

十二大願誓弘深

Shr er da ywan shr hung shen.

HE FERRIES THE CONFUSED ACROSS THE SEA OF SUFFERING,

苦海度迷津

Ku hai du mi jin,

RESCUING THE SUFFERING BY SEARCHING OUT THEIR SOUNDS.

救苦尋聲

jyou ku syun sheng.

THERE ARE NO LANDS WHERE HE DOES NOT APPEAR.

無刹不現身

Wu cha bu syan shen.

VERSE OF DEDICATION

回 向 偈

MAY THESE ADORNMENTS AND PURE MERIT AND VIRTUE,

以此嚴淨功德

Yi tsz yan jing gung de

BE DEDICATED TO THE DHARMA PROTECTING DRAGONS AND GODS,

回向護法龍天

hwei syang hu fa lung tyan,

TO THE MOUNTAIN AND RIVER SPIRITS OF THE THREE REALMS.

三界嶽瀆靈聰

san jye ywe du ling tsung,

AND TO THE GUARDIANS WHO WATCH OVER OUR SANGHARAMAS.

守護伽藍真宰

shou hu chye lan jen dzai.

WE PRAY THAT BLESSINGS, PEACE AND GOODNESS

祈福保安平善

Chi fu bau an ping shan,

BE AN ADORNMENT TO BODHI WHICH IS UNSURPASSED,

莊嚴無上菩提

jwang yan wu shang pu ti,

VOWING THAT ALL, BOTH OUR ENEMIES AND THOSE WE ARE CLOSE TO
THROUGHOUT THE DHARMA REALM.

普願法界冤親

pu ywan fa jye ywan chin,

WILL ENTER THE SEA OF VAIROCANA'S NATURE TOGETHER.

◎共入毘盧性海◎

gung ru pi lu sying hai.

GREAT TRANSFERENCE OF MERIT
大 回 向
Da hwei syang

(Kneel and recite)
(跪念)

WE DISCIPLES ARE COMMON PEOPLE, SUBJECT TO BIRTH AND DEATH.

弟子眾等◎，現是生死凡夫，

Di dz jung deng, syan shr sheng sz fan fu.

BURDENED BY DEEP AND HEAVY OFFENSES, REVOLVING IN SIX DESTINIES,

罪障深重，輪迴六道，

Dzwei jang shen jung, lwun hwei lyou dau.

WE SUFFER UNSPEAKABLE PAIN. BUT NOW WE HAVE MET A GOOD TEACHER.

苦不可言，今遇知識，

Ku bu ke yan, jin yu jr shr.

WE HAVE HEARD AMITABHA'S NAME AND THE MERIT OF HIS VOWS.

得聞彌陀名號，本願功德。

De wen mi two ming hau, ben ywan gung de.

SINGLEMINDEDLY RECITING HIS NAME, AND SEEKING REBIRTH IN HIS LAND,

一心稱念，求願往生。

Yi syin cheng nyan, chou ywan wang sheng.

WE HOPE THE BUDDHA WILL NOT RENOUNCE US, BUT WILL KINDLY GATHER US IN.

願佛慈悲不捨，哀憐攝受。

Ywan fwo tsz bei bu she, ai lyan she shou.

WE DISCIPLES DO NOT RECOGNIZE HIM, HIS BODY, HIS HALLMARKS, HIS LIGHT.

弟子眾等◎，不識佛身，相好光明。

Di dz jung deng, bu shr fwo shen, syang hau gwang ming.

WE HOPE THE BUDDHA WILL MANIFEST, LET US SEE GWAN YIN, GREAT STRENGTH,

願佛示現，令我得見，及見觀音勢至，

Ywan fwo shr syan, ling wo de jyan, ji jyan gwan yin shr jr.

149

AND ALL OF THE BODHISATTVAS IN THAT LAND OF PURE ADORNMENT,

諸菩薩眾，彼世界中，清淨莊嚴，

Ju pu sa jung, bi shr jye jung, ching jing jwang yan.

THEIR LIGHT, THEIR HALLMARKS AND CHARACTERISTICS; AND
CAUSE US ALL AT LAST

光明妙相等◎，令我了了，

Gwang ming myau syang deng, ling wo lyau lyau.

TO SEE AMITABHA.

得見阿彌陀佛◎

De jyan e mi two fwo.

(Circumambulate the Buddha, reciting:)　　　(繞念)

NA MO AMITABHA

南無阿彌陀佛

Na mwo e mi two fwo

NA MO GWAN SHR YIN BODHISATTVA

南無觀世音菩薩

Na mwo gwan shr yin pu sa

NA MO GREAT STRENGTH BODHISATTVA

南無大勢至菩薩

Na mwo da shr jr pu sa

NA MO GREAT PURE SEA OF BODHISATTVAS

南無清淨大海眾菩薩

Na mwo ching jing da hai jung pu sa

(All kneel) (跪念)

WHEN DEATH COMES MAY WE HAVE NO OBSTRUCTIONS. MAY AMITABHA
COME TO WELCOME US.

願我臨終無障礙◎阿彌陀佛遠相迎，

Ywan wo lin jung wu janq ai. E mi two fwo ywan syang ying.

MAY GWAN YIN SPRINKLE SWEET DEW ON OUR HEADS, AND GREAT
STRENGTH PLACE A GOLDEN DIAS BENEATH OUR FEET.

觀音甘露灑吾頭，勢至金臺安我足，
Gwan yin gan lu sa wu tou. Shr jr jin tai an wo dzu.

SO IN AN INSTANT WE LEAVE THE FIVE TURBIDITIES AND ARRIVE
AT THE LOTUS POOL.

一刹那中離五濁，屈伸臂頃到蓮池，
Yi cha na jung li wu jwo. Chyu shen bei ching dau lyan chr.

WHEN OUR FLOWERS OPEN, MAY WE SEE THE BUDDHA,

蓮華開後見慈尊◎，
Lyan hwa kai hou jyan tsz dzwun.

AND DRAWING NEAR, HEAR THE SOUNDS OF DHARMA WITH CLEAR
UNDERSTANDING.

親聽法音可了了，
Chin ting fa yin ke lyau lyau.

MAY WE AWAKEN TO PATIENCE WITH NON-PRODUCTION.

聞已即悟無生忍，
Wen yi ji wu wu sheng ren.

THEN, NOT LEAVING PEACE, WE WILL ENTER THE SAHA WORLD,

不違安養入娑婆，
Bu wei an yang ru swo pe.

TEACH LIVING BEINGS THROUGH SKILL IN MEANS,

善知方便度眾生，
Shan jr fang byan du jung sheng.

AND WITHIN THE WEARISOME DUST, DO THE BUDDHA'S WORK.

巧把塵勞為佛事◎，
Chyau ba chen lau wei fwo shr.

MAY THE BUDDHA KNOW OF THESE VOWS WE'VE MADE. MAY WE
FINALLY REALIZE BUDDHAHOOD.

我願如斯佛自知◎，畢竟當來得成就◎。
Wo ywan ru sz fwo dz jr. Bi jing dang lai de cheng jyou.

SINGLEMINDED WE BOW TO SHAKYA-THUS-COME-ONE WHO PROPAGATES
　THE VAST, PURE, AND BLISSFUL LAND.

一心頂禮，宏揚淨樂土，釋迦如來，

Yi syin ding li, hung yang jing le du, shr jya ru lai.

HIS HUNDRED-THOUSAND KOTIS OF TRANSFORMATION BODIES PERVADE
ALL BUDDHAS OF THE DHARMA REALM.

千百億化身，徧法界諸佛。

Chyan bai yi hwa shen, byan fa jye ju fwo.

SINGLEMINDED WE BOW TO AMITABHA-THUS-COME-ONE OF THE
ETERNAL, STILL, AND BRIGHT PURE LAND.

一心頂禮，常寂光淨土，阿彌陀如來，

Yi syin ding li, chang ji gwang jing du, e mi two ru lai.

HIS PURE AND WONDERFUL DHARMA-BODY PERVADES ALL BUDDHAS OF
THE DHARMA-REALM.

清淨妙法身，徧法界諸佛。

Ching jing myau fa shen, byan fa jye ju fwo.

SINGLEMINDED WE BOW TO AMITABHA-THUS-COME-ONE OF THE
LAND ADORNED WITH REAL REWARDS,

一心頂禮，實報莊嚴土，阿彌陀如來，

Yi syin ding li, shr bau jwang yan du, e mi two ru lai.

HIS SEA OF BODIES WITH MYRIAD HALLMARKS PERVADES ALL
BUDDHAS OF THE DHARMA-REALM.

微塵相海身，徧法界諸佛。

Wei chen syang hai shen, byan fa jye ju fwo.

SINGLEMINDED WE BOW TO AMITABHA-THUS-COME-ONE OF THE LAND OF
SAGELY DWELLING IN EXPEDIENT MEANS.

一心頂禮，方便聖居土，阿彌陀如來，

Yi syin ding li, fang byan sheng jyu du, e mi two ru lai.

HIS BODIES ADORNED WITH LIBERATION PERVADE ALL BUDDHAS OF
THE DHARMA-REALM.

解脫相嚴身，徧法界諸佛。

Jye two syang yan shen, byan fa jye ju fwo.

SINGLEMINDED WE BOW TO AMITABHA-THUS-COME-ONE OF THE
WESTERN LAND OF PEACE AND BLISS.

一心頂禮，西方安樂土，阿彌陀如來，
Yi syin ding li, syi fang an le du, e mi two ru lai.

HIS BODIES FOUNDED UPON THE GREAT VEHICLE PERVADE ALL
BUDDHAS OF THE DHARMA-REALM.

大乘根界身，徧法界諸佛。
Da cheng gen jye shen, byan fa jye ju fwo.

SINGLEMINDED WE BOW TO AMITABHA-THUS-COME-ONE OF THE
WESTERN LAND OF PEACE AND BLISS.

一心頂禮，西方安樂土，阿彌陀如來，
Yi syin ding li, syi fang an le du, e mi two ru lai.

HIS BODIES TRANSFORMING IN ALL DIRECTIONS PERVADE ALL
BUDDHAS OF THE DHARMA-REALM.

十方化往身，徧法界諸佛。
Shr fang hwa wang shen, byan fa jye ju fwo.

SINGLEMINDED WE BOW TO THE THREE ASPECTS OF THE SUTRAS OF:
THE WESTERN LAND OF PEACE AND BLISS--THEIR TEACHINGS,
PRACTICES, AND PRINCIPLES.

一心頂禮，西方安樂土，教行理三經，
Yi syin ding li, syi fang an le du, jyau heng li san jing.

TO THEIR PROCLAMATION AND PROPAGATION IN THE WORLD. THEY
PERVADE THE HONORED DHARMA OF THE DHARMA-REALM.

及依正宣揚，徧法界尊法。
Ji yi jeng sywan yang, byan fa jye dzwun fa.

SINGLEMINDED WE BOW TO GWAN SHR YIN BODHISATTVA OF THE
WESTERN LAND OF PEACE AND BLISS.

一心頂禮，西方安樂土，觀世音菩薩，
Yi syin ding li, syi fang an le du, gwan shr yin pu sa.

HIS MYRIAD KOTIS OF PURPLE-GOLDEN BODIES PERVADE ALL
BODHISATTVAS, MAHASATTVAS OF THE DHARMA-REALM.

萬億紫金身，徧法界菩薩摩訶薩。
Wan yi dz jin shen, byan fa jye pu sa mwo he sa.

TO GREAT STRENGTH BODHISATTVA OF THE WESTERN LAND OF PEACE
AND BLISS.

一心頂禮，西方安樂土，大勢至菩薩，
Yi syin ding li, syi fang an le du, da shr jr pu sa.

153

HIS BOUNDLESS BODIES OF BLAZING LIGHT PERVADE ALL
BODHISATTVAS, MAHASATTVAS OF THE DHARMA-REALM.

無邊光熾身 ， 徧法界菩薩摩訶薩.

Wu byan gwang jr shen, byan fa jye pu sa mwo he sa.

SINGLEMINDED WE BOW TO THE GREAT PURE SEA-VAST ASSEMBLY
OF THE WESTERN LAND OF PEACE AND BLISS.

一心頂禮◎, 西方安樂土 ， 清淨大海眾,

Yi syin ding li, syi fang an le du, ching jing da hai jung,

THEIR BODIES COMPLETE WITH THE TWO ADORNMENTS PERVADE
THE ASSEMBLY OF SAGES OF THE DHARMA-REALM.

滿分二嚴身 ， 徧法界聖眾◎。

Man fen er yan shen, byan fa jye sheng jung.

NA MO AMITA BUDDHA OF THE WESTERN LAND OF ULTIMATE BLISS,
GUIDE AND MASTER WITH GREAT KINDNESS, GREAT COMPASSION,
GREAT POWER, AND GREAT VOWS. *(recite 3 times. 3 bows)*

南無西方極樂世界 ， 大慈大悲 ，
大願大力接引導師 ， 阿彌陀佛◎.(三稱三拜)

Na mwo syi fang, ji le shr jye, da tsz da bei, da ywan
da li, jye yin dau shr, e mi two fwo.

NA MO GWAN SHR YIN BODHISATTVA OF THE WESTERN LAND OF
ULTIMATE BLISS, MAHASATTVA OF A MYRIAD KOTIS OF PURPLE-GOLDEN
BODIES.   *(recite 3 times, 3 bows)*

南無西方極樂世界 ， 萬億紫金身 ，
觀世音菩薩摩訶薩◎. (三稱三拜)

Na mwo syi fang, ji le shr jye, wan yi dz jin shen,
gwan shr yin pu sa mwo he sa.

NA MO GREAT STRENGTH BODHISATTVA OF THE WESTERN LAND OF
ULTIMATE BLISS, MAHASATTVA OF THE BOUNDLESS BODIES OF
BLAZING LIGHT.   *(recite 3 times, 3 bows)*

南無西方極樂世界 ， 無邊光熾身 ，
大勢至菩薩摩訶薩◎. (三稱三拜)

Na mwo syi fang, ji le snr jye, wu byan gwang jr shen,
da shr jr pu sa mwo he sa.

NA MO GREAT PURE SEA OF BODHISATTVAS OF THE WESTERN LAND
OF ULTIMATE BLISS, MAHASATTVAS WITH BODIES COMPLETE WITH
THE TWO ADORNMENTS. *(recite 3 times, 3 bows)*

南無西方極樂世界，滿分二嚴身，
清淨大海眾菩薩摩訶薩。(三稱三拜)

Na mwo syi fang, ji le shr jye, man fen er yan,shen,
ching jing da hai jung pu sa mwo he sa.

THREE REFUGES
三皈依
San Gwei Yi

TO THE BUDDHA I RETURN AND RELY,

自皈依佛

Dz gwei yi fwo

VOWING THAT ALL LIVING BEINGS

當願眾生

Dang ywan jung sheng

UNDERSTAND THE GREAT WAY PROFOUNDLY

體解大道

Ti jye da dau

AND BRING FORTH THE BODHI MIND.   *(bow)* •

發無上心。   (拜) •

Fa wu shang syin.

TO THE DHARMA I RETURN AND RELY,

自皈依法，

Dz gwei yi fa

VOWING THAT ALL LIVING BEINGS

當願眾生

Dang ywan jung sheng

DEEPLY ENTER THE SUTRA TREASURY

深入經藏

Shen ru jing dzang

155

AND HAVE WISDOM LIKE THE SEA.   *(bow)* •

智慧如海◎

Jr Hwei ru hai.

（拜）•

TO THE SANGHA I RETURN AND RELY,

自皈依僧◎

Dz gwei yi seng

VOWING THAT ALL LIVING BEINGS

當願眾生

Dang ywan jung sheng

FORM TOGETHER A GREAT ASSEMBLY,

統理大眾

Tung li da jung

ONE AND ALL IN HARMONY,   *(bow; rise and half-bow)*

一切無礙◎ （拜）•   和南聖眾◎ （問訊）

Yi chye wu ai.   He nan sheng jung.

(On the first and last nights of the session, bow to the Patriarchs; see page 158)

（首晚及末晚禮祖，見第158頁）

Leader says: 維那師呼：

ON BEHALF OF THEIR FATHERS, MOTHERS, TEACHERS, ELDERS, AND RELATIVES AND ENEMIES FROM KALPAS PAST, ALL BOW THREE TIMES TO THE BUDDHA.

各人代為父母師長，暨歷劫怨親，禮佛三拜。

Ge ren dai wei fu mu shr jang, ji li jye ywan chin, li Fwo san bai.

Leader repeats three times: 維那師再呼三次：

SEEKING BIRTH IN THE PURE LAND.

求生淨土◎

Chyou sheng jing du.

After each repetition, the Assembly bows and calls out:

(維那師每呼一次後，大眾答阿彌陀佛，隨即拜下。)

AMITABHA!

阿彌陀佛！

E mi two fwo!

UNIVERSAL WORTHY BODHISATTVA'S VERSE OF EXHORTATION
普賢菩薩警眾偈

THIS DAY IS ALREADY DONE. OUR LIVES ARE THAT MUCH LESS.

是日已過◎，命亦隨減，

Shr r yi gwo. Ming yi swei jyan.

WE'RE LIKE FISH IN A SHRINKING POND. WHAT JOY IS THERE IN THIS?

如少水魚，斯有何樂？

Ru shau shwei yu. Sz you he le.

Leader says: 維那師呼：

GREAT ASSEMBLY!

大眾◎！

Da jung!

WE SHOULD BE DILIGENT AND VIGOROUS, AS IF OUR OWN HEADS
WERE AT STAKE.

當勤精進，如救頭然，

Dang chin jing jin, ru jyou tou ran.

ONLY BE MINDFUL OF IMPERMANENCE AND BE CAREFUL NOT TO BE LAX.

但念無常，慎勿放逸◎。

Dan nyan wu chang shen wu fang yi.

157

AMITABHA!

阿彌陀佛！

E mi two fwo!

BOWING TO THE PATRIARCHS
禮 祖

Leader says:

維那師呼：

WE BOW TO THE GENERATIONS OF PATRIARCHS OF EAST AND WEST.

頂禮西天東土歷代祖師◎

Ding li syi tyan dung du li dai dzu shr.

TO ALL THE GREAT GOOD KNOWING ONES THROUGHOUT THE WORLD WHO
PROPAGATE THE SCHOOLS AND PROCLAIM THE TEACHINGS.

頂禮天下宏宗演教諸大善知識

Ding li tyan sya hung dzung yan jyau ju da shan jr shr.

WE BOW TO THE FIRST PATRIARCH THE NOBLE YWAN, GREAT MASTER
OF EASTERN GROVE MONASTERY AT LU MOUNTAIN.

頂禮初祖廬山東林遠公大師

Ding li chu dzu lu shan dung lin ywan gung da shr.

WE BOW TO THE SECOND PATRIARCH THE NOBLE DAU, GREAT MASTER
OF RADIANT LIGHT MONASTERY AT CHANG AN.

頂禮二祖長安光明導公大師

Ding li er dzu chang an gwang ming dau gung da shr.

WE BOW TO THE THIRD PATRIARCH THE NOBLE YWAN, GREAT MASTER
OF PRAJNA BOAT MONASTERY AT NAN YWE.

頂禮三祖南嶽般舟遠公大師

Ding li san dzu nan ywe bwo jou ywan gung da shr.

WE BOW TO THE FOURTH PATRIARCH THE NOBLE JAU, GREAT MASTER
OF BAMBOO GROVE MONASTERY AT WU TAI.

頂禮四祖五臺竹林照公大師

Ding li sz dzu wu tai ju lin jyau gung da shr.

WE BOW TO THE FIFTH PATRIARCH THE NOBLE KANG, GREAT MASTER
OF BLACK DRAGON MONASTERY AT SYIN DING.

頂禮五祖新定烏龍康公大師

Ding li wu dzu syin ding wu lung kang gung da shr.

WE BOW TO THE SIXTH PATRIARCH THE NOBLE SHOU, GREAT MASTER
OF ETERNAL BRILLIANCE MONASTERY AT HANG JOU.

頂禮六祖杭州永明壽公大師

Ding li lyou dzu hang jou yung ming shou gung da shr.

WE BOW TO THE SEVENTH PATRIARCH THE NOBLE CHANG, GREAT
MASTER OF BRIGHT JOY MONASTERY AT HANG JOU.

頂禮七祖杭州昭慶常公大師

Ding li chi dzu hang jou jau ching chang gung da shr.

WE BOW TO THE EIGHTH PATRIARCH THE NOBLE HUNG, GREAT MASTER
OF CLOUD PERCH MONASTERY OF HANG JOU.

頂禮八祖杭州雲棲宏公大師

Ding li ba dzu hang jou ywun chi hung gung da shr.

WE BOW TO THE NINTH PATRIARCH THE NOBLE SYU, GREAT MASTER
OF SPIRIT PEAK MONASTERY AT BEI TYAN MU.

頂禮九祖北天目靈峯旭公大師

Ding li jyou dzu bei tyan mu ling feng syu gung da shr.

WE BOW TO THE TENTH PATRIARCH THE NOBLE TSE, GREAT MASTER
OF UNIVERSAL BENEVOLENCE MONASTERY AT YU MOUNTAIN.

頂禮十祖虞山普仁策公大師

Ding li shr dzu yu shan pu ren tse gung da shr.

WE BOW TO THE ELEVENTH PATRIARCH THE NOBLE SYAN, GREAT
MASTER OF BRAHMA HEAVEN MONASTERY AT HANG JOU.

頂禮十一祖杭州梵天賢公大師

Ding li shr yi dzu hang jou fan tyan syan gung da shr.

WE BOW TO THE TWELFTH PATRIARCH THE NOBLE SYING, GREAT
MASTER OF ENDOWED-WITH-BLESSINGS MONASTERY AT HUNG LWO.

頂禮十二祖紅螺資福醒公大師

Ding li shr er dzu hung lwo dz fu sying gung da shr.

WE BOW TO THE THIRTEENTH PATRIARCH THE NOBLE YIN, GREAT
MASTER OF HOLY MEASURE TEMPLE AT SPIRIT CAVE MOUNTAIN
AT SU JOU.

頂禮十三祖蘇州靈巖聖量印公大師

Ding li shr san dzu su jou ling yan sheng lyang yin gung
da shr.

WE BOW TO THE FOURTEENTH PATRIARCH THE NOBLE YUN, GREAT
MASTER OF TRUE SUCHNESS MONASTERY AT JYANG SYI.

頂禮十四祖江西真如雲公大師

Ding li shr sz dzu jyang syi jen ru yun gung da shr.

WE BOW TO THE PAST AND PRESENT MASTERS OF THE LOTUS
SOCIETY.

頂禮古今蓮社宗師

Ding li gu jin Tyan she dzung shr.

WE BOW TO THE HOST DHARMA MASTER OF THIS SEVEN DAY SESSION.

頂禮主七和尚◎

Ding li ju chi he shang.

160

VERSE FOR TRANSFERRING THE MERIT FROM TAKING REFUGE

皈依功德回向

Gwei yi gung de hwei syang

I DEDICATE THE MERIT AND VIRTUE FROM THE PROFOUND ACT OF TAKING REFUGE.

皈依功德殊勝行

gwei yi gung de shu sheng heng

WITH ALL ITS SUPERIOR, LIMITLESS BLESSINGS,

無邊勝福皆回向

Wu byan sheng fu jye hwei syang

WITH THE UNIVERSAL VOW THAT ALL BEINGS SUNK IN DEFILEMENT,

普願沉溺諸眾生

Pu ywan chen ni ju jung sheng

WILL QUICKLY GO TO THE LAND OF THE BUDDHA OF LIMITLESS LIGHT (AMITABHA).

速往無量光佛刹

Su wang wu lyang gwang fwo cha

ALL BUDDHAS OF THE TEN DIRECTIONS AND THE THREE PERIODS OF TIME.

十方三世一切佛

Shr fang san shr yi chye fwo

ALL BODHISATTVAS, MAHASATTVAS,

一切菩薩摩訶薩

Yi chye pu sa mwo he sa

MAHA PRAJNA PARAMITA!

摩訶般若波羅蜜

Mwo he bwo re bwo lo mi.

UNIVERSAL BOWING
拜願

INSTRUCTIONS FOR CONDUCTING THE UNIVERSAL BOWING CEREMONY

Refer to the ceremonies for the Holy Days (pp. 164 -179) to find the names to be recited. The assembly is divided into two equal groups: "side one" (of the hall) and "side two." The very first recitation of the entire ceremony is sung by both sides together. After that very first recitation, "side one" bows and contemplates while "side two" recites. Then "side two" bows and contemplates while "side one" recites, and so on. Throughout the rest of the ceremony, the only note sung by both sides together is on the syllable "fwo" (or "sa"), until the very last recitation of the final name when the entire assembly stands and sings together.

The *wei nwo* leads the two sides in bowing, using the *yin ching* (hand bell) to signal when one side rises (on the next to last syllable of each recitation) and the other side bows down (on the final syllable of each recitation). The *wei nwo* also signals the end of each name's recitation by sounding the *da ching* (large bell) on the word "fwo" or "sa" of "side one's" third (or twelfth, or ninth) recitation. Following the sound of the large bell, "side two" recites the name for the final time.

The drum and bell accompaniment has several variations for the different names being recited. Each variation has two versions: the version marked "(A)" is played while "side one" recites; the version marked "(B)" is played while "side two" recites.

拜願儀規

釋迦聖號十二拜，如時間不許，
六拜、三拜均可，餘皆三拜。
小楗子每兩拍敲一次。
○表鼓，一表鐘。所有普佛拜願
板眼皆同此。

163

佛 fwo.
薩 sa.
尚 shang.

****

9. 南 Na　　無 mwo　　阿 e　普 pu　彌 mi
10. 南 Na　　無 mwo　　普 pu　彌 mi
11. 南 Na　　無 mwo　　彌 mi

9 彌 mi　　陀 two　　佛 fwo.
10 賢 syan　菩 pu　　薩 sa.
11 勒 lei　　菩 pu

****

12. 南 Na　　無 mwo　　觀 gwan　世 shr
13. 南 Na　　無 mwo　　大 da　　勢 shr
14. 南 Na　　無 mwo　　地 di　　藏 dzang

12. 音 yin　　菩 pu　　薩 sa.
13. 至 jr　　菩 pu　　薩 sa.
14. 王 wang　菩 pu　　薩 sa.

164

CEREMONY FOR SHAKYAMUNI BUDDHA'S BIRTHDAY
釋迦文佛聖誕祝儀 四月八日

1. JEWELED CENSER PRAISE *(see page 1)*
   寶鼎讚 (見1頁)

2. NAMO SHURANGAMA ASSEMBLY OF BUDDHAS AND BODHISATTVAS
   南無楞嚴會上佛菩薩◎　　(三稱)
   Na mwo leng yan hwei shang fwo pu sa

3. SHURANGAMA MANTRA
   楞嚴咒 (一遍,見3頁)

4. HEART OF PRAJNA PARAMITA SUTRA
   般若波羅蜜多心經 (一遍;見第44頁)

5. MAHA PRAJNA PARAMITA
   摩訶般若波羅蜜多◎　　(三稱)
   Mwo he bwo re bwo lwo mi dwo

6. PRAISE OF BUDDHA JEWEL
   佛寶讚
   IN THE HEAVENS ABOVE, IN ALL THAT IS BELOW, NOTHING
   COMPARES WITH THE BUDDHA,
   天上天下無如佛◎
   Tyan shang tyan sya wu ru fwo.

   THROUGHOUT THE WORLDS OF THE TEN DIRECTIONS HE IS
   MATCHLESS.
   十方世界亦無比
   Shr fang shr jye yi wu bi.

   OF ALL I HAVE SEEN IN THE WORLD,
   世間所有我盡見
   Shr jyan swo you wo jin jyan.

   THERE IS NOTHING AT ALL THAT IS LIKE THE BUDDHA.
   一切無有如佛者
   Yi chye wu you ru fwo je.

HOMAGE TO THE GUIDING MASTER OF THE THREE REALMS OF THE
SAHA WORLD,

南無娑婆世界◎，三界導師，

na mwo swo pwo shr jye, san jye dau shr

COMPASSIONATE FATHER OF THE FOUR KINDS OF BEINGS, TEACHER
OF PEOPLE AND GODS,

四生慈父，人天教主，

sz sheng tsz fu, ren tyan jyau ju

WHOSE TRANSFORMATION BODIES ARE OF THREE KINDS; OUR ORIGINAL
TEACHER SHAKYAMUNI BUDDHA.

三類化身，本師釋迦牟尼佛◎

san lei hwa shen ben shr shr jya mu ni fwo

NAMO FUNDAMENTAL TEACHER SHAKYAMUNI BUDDHA

南無本師釋迦牟尼佛 (繞念)

na mwo ben shr shr jya mu ni fwo *(recite while circumambulating)*

6. UNIVERSAL BOWING *(Recite the names below; for music,*
   拜願   *see page 163.)* (參考音譜見163頁)

HOMAGE TO OUR ORIGINAL TEACHER SHAKYAMUNI BUDDHA

南無本師釋迦牟尼佛　　(十二拜)

na mwo ben shr shr jya mu ni fwo *(bow 12 times)*

HOMAGE TO MANJUSHRI BODHISATTVA

南無文殊師利菩薩　　　(三拜)

na mwo wen shu shr li pu sa *(bow 3 times)*

HOMAGE TO UNIVERSAL WORTHY BODHISATTVA

南無普賢菩薩　　　　(三拜)

na mwo pu syan pu sa *(bow 3 times)*

HOMAGE TO MAITREYA BODHISATTVA

南無彌勒菩薩　　　　(三拜)

na mwo mi lei pu sa *(bow 3 times)*

HOMAGE TO THE BODHISATTVAS MAHASATTVAS OF THE TEN DIRECTIONS

南無十方菩薩摩訶薩　（三拜）

na mwo shr fang pu sa mwo he sa (bow 3 times)

7. THREE REFUGES (see page 50) 三皈依（見第50頁）

PRAISE FOR BATHING THE BUDDHA
浴 佛 讚 偈

I NOW BATHE ALL THUS COME ONES

我今灌浴諸如來

wo jin gwan yu ju ru lai

WHO ARE ADORNED WITH PURE WISDOM, WHO HAVE AMASSED MERIT AND VIRTUE.

淨智莊嚴功德聚

jing jr jwang yan gung de jyu

MAY LIVING BEINGS OF THE FIVE TURBID REALMS BE LED FROM FILTH,

五濁眾生令離垢

wu jwo jung sheng ling li gou

AND TOGETHER REALIZE THE PURE DHARMA BODY OF THE THUS COME ONE.

同證如來淨法身　　　　（三徧）

tung jeng ru lai jing fa shen 　(3 times)

TRUE WORDS FOR BATHING THE BUDDHA
沐浴真言

唵底沙底沙僧伽娑訶（持續誦念）

nän di sha di sha samgha swo he (repeat continuously)

167

VERSE FOR TRANSFERRING THE MERIT
FROM BATHING THE BUDDHA

浴佛功德回向

Yu fwo gung de hwei syang

I DEDICATE THE MERIT AND VIRTUE OF THE PROFOUND ACT OF
BATHING THE BUDDHA

浴佛功德殊勝行◎

Yu fwo gung de shu sheng heng

WITH ALL ITS SUPERIOR LIMITLESS BLESSINGS,

無邊勝福皆回向

Wu byan sheng fu jye hwei syang

WITH THE UNVERSAL VOW THAT ALL BEINGS SUNK IN DEFILEMENT

普願沉溺諸眾生

Pu yuan chen ni ju jung sheng

WILL QUICKLY GO TO THE LAND OF THE BUDDHA OF LIMITLESS
LIGHT (AMITABHA).

速往無量光佛刹

Su wang wu lyang gwang fwo cha

ALL BUDDHAS OF THE TEN DIRECTIONS AND THE THREE PERIODS
OF TIME.

十方三世一切佛◎

Shr fang san shr yi chye fwo

ALL BODHISATTVAS, MAHASATTVAS.

一切菩薩摩訶薩

Yi chye pu sa mwo he sa

MAHA PRAJNA PARAMITA!

◎摩訶般若波羅蜜

Mwo he bwo re bwo lo mi.

CEREMONY FOR MEDICINE MASTER BUDDHA'S BIRTHDAY
藥師佛聖誕祝儀 (九月三十日)

1. JEWELED CENSER PRAISE *(see page 1)*

   寶鼎讚 (見1頁)

2. RECITE EIGHTY-EIGHT BUDDHAS REPENTANCE *(see page 108)*

   禮佛大懺悔文 （見第108頁）

3. PRAISE *(see page 47)*

   藥師讚 （見第47頁）

   NA MO QUELLING DISASTERS LENGTHNING LIFE MEDICINE MASTER BUDDHA *(recite while circumambulating)*

   南無消災延壽藥師佛 （繞念）

   Na mwo syau dzai yan shou yau shr fwo

5. UNIVERSAL BOWING 拜願 *(Recite the names below; for music see page 163.)* （參考音譜見163頁）

   HOMAGE TO OUR ORIGINAL TEACHER SHAKYAMUNI BUDDHA

   南無本師釋迦牟尼佛 （三拜）

   Na mwo ben shr shr jya mu ni fwo *(bow 3 times)*

   NA MO QUELLING DISASTERS LENGTHNING LIFE MEDICINE MASTER BUDDHA

   南無消災延壽藥師佛 （十二拜）

   Na mwo syau dzai yan shou yau shr fwo *(bow 12 times)*

   NA MO UNIVERSAL SHINING SUNLIGHT BODHISATTVA

   南無日光徧照菩薩 （三拜）

   Na mwo r gwang byan jau pu sa *(bow 3 times)*

   NA MO UNIVERSAL SHINING MOONLIGHT BODHISATTVA

   南無月光徧照菩薩 （三拜）

   Na mwo ywe gwang byan jau pu sa *(bow 3 times)*

   NA MO MEDICINE MASTER'S GREAT ASSEMBLY OF BUDDHAS AND BODHISATTVAS VAST AS THE SEA!

   南無藥師海會佛菩薩 （三拜）

   Na mwo yau shr hai hwei fwo pu sa *(bow 3 times)*

6. THE THREE REFUGES *(see page 49)* 三皈依 (見第50頁)

169

CEREMONY FOR AMITABHA BUDDHA'S BIRTHDAY
阿彌陀佛聖誕祝儀 (十一月十七日)

1. JEWELED CENSER PRAISE *(see page 1)*

   寶鼎讚 (見 1 頁)

2. NA MO HOMAGE TO THE LOTUS POOL ASSEMBLY OF BUDDHAS AND BODHISATTVAS AS VAST AS THE SEA. *(3 times)*

   南無蓮池海會佛菩薩 (三稱)

   THE BUDDHA SPEAKS OF AMITABHA SUTRA *(see page 87)*

   佛說阿彌陀經 (見第87頁)

   SPIRIT MANTRA FOR REBIRTH IN THE PURE LAND *(see page 107)*

   往生咒 (見第107頁)

3. PRAISE *(see page 140)*

   彌陀讚 (見第140頁)

4. CIRCUMAMBULATION (NA MWO E MI TWO FWO)

   南無阿彌陀佛 (繞念)

5. UNIVERSAL BOWING 拜願 *(Recite the names below; for music see page 163.)* (參考音譜見163頁)

   HOMAGE TO OUR ORIGINAL TEACHER SHAKYAMUNI BUDDHA.

   南無本師釋迦牟尼佛 (三拜)

   Na mwo ben shr shr jya mu ni fwo. *(bow 3 times)*

   NAMO AMITABHA BUDDHA

   南無阿彌陀佛 (十二拜)

   Na mwo e mi two fwo. *(bow 12 times)*

   NAMO BODHISATTVA WHO OBSERVES THE WORLD'S SOUNDS.

   南無觀世音菩薩 (三拜)

   Na mwo gwan shr yin pu sa. *(bow 3 times)*

   NAMO GREAT STRENGTH BODHISATTVA.

   南無大勢至菩薩 (三拜)

   Na mwo da shr jr pu sa. *(bow 3 times)*

   NAMO GREAT PURE SEA OF BODHISATTVAS.

   南無清淨大海眾菩薩 (三拜)

   Na mwo ching jing da hai jung pu sa *(bow 3 times)*

6. THE THREE REFUGES *(see page 50)* 三皈依 (見第50頁)

CEREMONY FOR MAITREYA BUDDHA'S BIRTHDAY
彌勒佛聖誕祝儀 (正月初一日)

1. JEWELED CENSER PRAISE *(see page 1)*
   ### 寶鼎讚 (見1頁)
2. RECITATION *(same as Shakyamuni Buddha's birthday; see page 165)*
   ### 念誦：(與釋迦佛誕同,見第165頁)
3. PRAISE
   (彌勒讚)

IN THE PAST HE WAS THE IMMORTAL WISDOM LIGHT.

過去曾做智光仙◎
Gwo chu tseng dzo jr gwang syan,

HIS SAMADHI OF GREAT KINDNESS IS WONDERFUL BEYOND EXPRESSION.

大慈三昧妙難宣
Da tsz san mei myau nan sywan.

BORN IN THE SOUTH, IN A COUNTRY OF ADORNMENT CALLED SEA SHORE,

莊嚴南有海岸國
Jwang yan nan you hai an gwo,

HE ASCENDS TO THE TUSHITA HEAVEN, AND BUDDHA IN HIS NEXT LIFE HE'LL BE.

補處上生兜率天
Bu chu shang sheng dou shwai tyan.

WITH PERFECTED MIND AND CONSCIOUSNESS WHOSE BRIGHTNESS SPANS THE REALMS OF THE TEN DIRECTIONS,

心識圓明十方界
Syin shr ywan ming shr fang jye,

THE MERIT AND VIRTUE CULTIVATED IN HIS NATURE HE SIMULTANEOUSLY FULFILLED.

性修功德一時圓◎
Sying syou gung de yi shr ywan.

MANY ARE THOSE WHO OBTAIN REBIRTH IN THE INNER COURTYARD,

幾多內院往生輩

Ji dwo nei ywan wang sheng bei,

AS THEY ASSEMBLE AT THE DRAGON-FLOWER ASSEMBLY AND FIRST
RECEIVE A PREDICTION.

會啓龍華授記先

Hwei chi lung hwa shou ji syan.

HOMAGE TO MATIREYA HONORED BUDDHA WHO DWELLS IN THE INNER
COURTYARD OF THE TUSHITA HEAVEN, WHO WITH TEN THOUSAND
VIRTUES REPLETE, WAITS TO BECOME BUDDHA IN HIS NEXT LIFE.

「南無兜率內院，萬德周圓，位居補處，
當來下生」彌勒尊佛◎

Na mwo dou shwai nei ywan, wan de jou ywan, wei jyu bu chu
dang lai sya sheng mi lei dzwun fwo.

4. NA MO THE HONORED BUDDHA MAITREYA, SOON TO BE BORN IN THE
WORLD. *(recite while circumambulating)*

南無當來下生彌勒尊佛 （繞念）

Na mwo dang lai sya sheng mi lei dzwun fwo.

5. UNIVERSAL BOWING 拜願 *(Recite the names below; for music
see page 163.)* （參考音譜見163頁）

HOMAGE TO OUR ORIGINAL TEACHER SHAKYAMUNI BUDDHA.

南無本師釋迦牟尼佛 （三拜）

Na mwo ben shr shr jya mu ni fwo. *(bow 3 times)*

NA MO THE HONORED BUDDHA MAITREYA, SOON TO BE BORN IN THE
WORLD.

南無當來下生彌勒尊佛 （十二拜）

Na mwo dang lai sya sheng mi lei dzwun fwo。 *(bow 12 times)*

HOMAGE TO MANJUSHRI BODHISATTVA

南無文殊師利菩薩 （三拜）

Na mwo wen shu shr li pu sa *(bow 3 times)*

HOMAGE TO UNIVERSAL WORTHY BODHISATTVA

南無普賢菩薩　　　　　(三拜)

Na mwo pu syan pu sa *(bow 3 times)*

HOMAGE TO THE BODHISATTVAS MAHASATTVAS OF THE TEN DIREC-
TIONS.

南無十方菩薩摩訶薩　　(三拜)

Na mwo shr fang pu sa mwo he sa *(bow 3 times)*

7. THREE REFUGES *(see page 50)*　　三皈依 (見第50頁)

****

CEREMONY FOR GWAN YIN BODHISATTVA'S BIRTHDAY

觀世音菩薩聖誕祝儀　二月十九日
　　　　　　　　　　　　六月十九日

1. JEWELED CENSER PRAISE *(see page 1)*　九月十九日

寶鼎讚 (見1頁)

2. NA MO GWAN SHR YIN BODHISATTVA OF GREAT COMPASSION.

南無大悲觀世音菩薩◎　(三稱)

Na mwo da bei gwan shr yin pu sa *(3 times)*

GREAT COMPASSION MANTRA *(7 times; see page 32)*

大悲咒　　　　(七徧;見第32頁)

3. PRAISE

觀音讚

BODHISATTVA GWAN SHR YIN IS WONDERFUL PAST GRATITUDE.

觀音菩薩妙難酬◎,

Gwan yin pu sa myau nan chou.

PURE AND CLEAR ARE HER ADORNMENTS, GAINED THROUGH
PRACTICE AGES LONG.

清淨莊嚴累劫修 ,

Ching jing jwang yan lei jye syou.

SEA-VAST A RED LOTUS FLOWER FRAGRANT RESTS BENEATH
HER FOOT.

浩浩紅蓮安足下 ,

Hau hau hung lyan an dzu sya.

173

BAY-CURVE OF AN AUTUMN MOON IS IN THE CRESCENT OF HER BROWS

灣灣秋月鎖眉頭，

Wan wan chyou ywe sou mei tou.

EVERYWHERE AND CONSTANTLY, SWEET DEW SPRINKLES FROM HER VASE.

瓶中甘露常徧洒，

Ping jung gan lu chang byan sa.

IN HER HAND, THE WILLOW BRANCH, THROUGH THE COUNTLESS AUTUMNS.

手内楊枝不計秋◎

Shou nei yang jr bu ji chyou.

PRAYERS DEPART A THOUSAND HEARTS, IN A THOUSAND HEARTS SHE ANSWERS,

千處祈求千處應，

Chyan chu chi chyou chyan chu ying.

SAILING THE SEA OF SUFFERING, CROSSING PEOPLE OVER.

苦海常作度人舟，

Ku hai chang dzwo du ren jou.

NA MO GREATLY KIND AND COMPASSIONATE BODHISATTVA OF THE CRYSTAL LAND, WHO DWELLS ON POTOLA MOUNTAIN AND OBSERVES THE SOUNDS OF THE WORLD.   *(3 times)*

南無普陀山琉璃世界◎，
大慈大悲觀世音菩薩◎。

Gwan Yin Praise

Bo- dhi - satt - va Gwan Shr Yin is won - der - ful past

gra- ţi - tude_____ Pure and clear are her a - dorn - ments

Gained through prac - tice a - ges long. Sea- vast a red´

lo - tus flow - er Fra - grant rests be - neath her foot____

Bay- curve of an au - tumn moon is in the cres - cent

of her brows_____ Ev - 'ry where and con - stant-ly sweet dew

sprin-kles from her vase In her hand the wil - low branch

Thru' the count - less au -tumns Prayers de -part a thou-sand hearts

In a thou-sand hearts she an - swers Sail___ - ing the sea of

suf - fer - ing Cross - ing peo - ple ov - er.

Na - mo great - ly kind and com-pas-sion- ate Bo - dhi - satt- va

of the Cry-stal Land—— Who dwells on Po - to - la Moun - tain

And ob - serves the sounds of the world. sounds of the world.——

4. NA MWO GWAN SHR YIN PU SA. *(recite and circumambulate)*
南無觀世音菩薩　　　　　　(繞念)

5. UNIVERSAL BOWING 拜願 *(Recite the names below; for music, see page 163.)*(參考音譜見163頁)

HOMAGE TO OUR ORIGINAL TEACHER SHAKYAMUNI BUDDHA.
南無本師釋迦牟尼佛　　　(三拜)
Na mwo ben shr shr jya mu ni fwo. *(bow 3 times)*

NAMO AMITABHA BUDDHA.
南無阿彌陀佛　　　　　(三拜)
Na mwo e mi two fwo. *(bow 3 times)*

NAMO BODHISATTVA WHO OBSERVES THE WORLD'S SOUNDS.
南無觀世音菩薩　　　(十二拜)
Na mwo gwan shr yin pu sa. *(bow 12 times)*

NAMO GREAT STRENGTH BODHISATTVA.
南無大勢至菩薩　　　(三拜)
Na mwo da shr jr pu sa. *(bow 3 times)*

NAMO GREAT PURE SEA OF BODHISATTVAS.
南無清淨大海眾菩薩　(三拜)
Na mwo ching jing da hai jung pu sa. *(bow 3 times)*

6. THE THREE REFUGES *(see page 50)* 三皈依(見第50頁)

****

CEREMONY FOR UNIVERSAL WORTHY BODHISATTVA'S BIRTHDAY

普賢菩薩聖誕祝儀 (二月二十一日)

1. JEWELED CENSER PRAISE *(see page 1)*

寶鼎讚 (見1頁)

2. RECITE EIGHTY-EIGHT BUDDHAS REPENTANCE *(see page 108)*

禮佛大懺悔文 (見第108頁)

3. PRAISE

(普賢讚)

THE BODHISATTVA OF GREAT CONDUCT IS CALLED UNIVERSAL WORTHY,

大行菩薩稱普賢◎

Da heng pu sa cheng pu syan,

THE SEA OF HIS VOW POWER IS MULTI-LAYERED WITHOUT BOUNDS.

重重願海浩無邊

Chung chung ywan hai hau wu byan.

WITH DIGNITY HE REPOSES UPON A SIX-TUSKED ELEPHANT;

端嚴示坐六牙象

Dwan yan shr dzo lyou ya syang,

BY WISDOM HE IS BORN, TRANSFORMATIONALLY FROM A LOTUS OF
THE SEVEN GEMS.

智慧化生七寶蓮

Jr hwei hwa sheng chi bau lyan.

IN ALL SAMADHIS HE ATTAINS SOVEREIGNTY,

一切三昧皆自在

Yi chye san mei jye dz dzai,

HIS ORIGINALLY WONDERFUL VIRTUE IS PERVASIVE AND PERFECTED.

本來妙德盡周圓◎

Ben lai myau de jin jou ywan.

PRAISES OF HIS JEWELED AWESOMENESS ARRIVES TO TEACH THE
SAHA WORLD;

寶威來贊娑婆化

Bau wei lai dzan swo pe hwa.

HIS EFFICACIOUS RESPONSE AND SPIRITUAL POWERS SHAKE THE
GREAT-THOUSAND REALM.

靈感神通震大千

Ling gan shen tung jen da chyan.

HOMAGE TO UNIVERSAL WORTHY BODHISATTVA OF GREAT
CONDUCT, WHO DWELLS IN THE SILVER WORLD OF E MEI MOUNTAIN.

南無峨嵋山銀色世界◎大行普賢王菩薩。

Na mwo O mei shan, yin shai shr jye, da heng pu syan
pu sa.

4. NA MWO PU SYAN WANG PU SA   *(recite and circumambulate)*

南無普賢王菩薩   (繞念)

5. UNIVERSAL BOWING 拜願 *(Recite the names below; for music,*
                        see page 163.) (參考音譜見163頁)
HOMAGE TO OUR ORIGINAL TEACHER SHAKYAMUNI BUDDHA.

南無本師釋迦牟尼佛   (三拜)

Na mwo ben shr shr jya mu ni fwo. *(bow 3 times)*

HOMAGE TO MANJUSHRI BODHISATTVA

南無文殊師利菩薩　　　(三拜)

Na mwo wen shu shr li pu sa *(bow 3 times)*

HOMAGE TO UNIVERSAL WORTHY BODHISATTVA

南無普賢菩薩　　　(十二拜)

Na mwo pu syan pu sa *(bow 12 times)*

HOMAGE TO MAITREYA BODHISATTVA

南無彌勒菩薩　　　(三拜)

Na mwo mi lei pu sa *(bow 3 times)*

HOMAGE TO THE BODHISATTVAS MAHASATTVAS OF THE TEN DIREC-
TIONS.

南無十方菩薩摩訶薩　(三拜)

Na mwo shr fang pu sa mwo he sa *(bow 3 times)*

7.　THREE REFUGES *(see page 50)*　三皈依(見第50頁)

＊＊＊＊＊＊＊＊＊＊＊＊＊＊＊＊＊＊＊＊＊＊＊＊

CEREMONY FOR MANJUSHRI BODHISATTVA'S BIRTHDAY
文殊菩薩聖誕祝儀

1.　JEWELED CENSER PRAISE *(see page 1)*
寶鼎讚(見1頁)

2.　RECITE EIGHTY-EIGHT BUDDHAS REPENTANCE *(see page 108)*
禮佛大懺悔文　(見第108頁)

3.　PRAISE
(文殊讚)
"WONDERFUL AUSPICIOUS" IS REPLETE WITH GREAT KINDNESS.

具大慈心妙吉祥◎

Ju da tsz syin myau ji syang.

MOTHER OF ENLIGHTENED ONES THROUGHOUT THE THREE PERIODS
OF TIME, HIS WISDOM IS BEYOND MEASURE.

三世覺母智難量

San shr jyau mu jr nan lyang.

HIS LEFT HAND BRANDISHES A SHARP SWORD THAT SEVERS ALL
AFFLICTIONS;

179

左持利劍煩惱斷
Dso chr li jyan fan nau dwan,

AND HIS RIGHT HAND HOLDS THE BLUE LOTUS WHICH REFLECTS
THE MARK OF HIS VIRTUE.
右執青蓮德相彰
Yu jr ching lyan de syang chang.

A PEACOCK AND LION-SPIRIT ACT AS HIS CARRIAGE,
孔雀神獅供乘馭
Kung chywe shen shr gung cheng yu,

POISONOUS DRAGONS AND FIERCE BEASTS ARE SUBDUED AND
BECOME PURE AND COOL.
毒龍猛獸伏清涼◎
Du lung meng shou fu ching lyang.

THE PURE YOUTH WITH THE FIVE TOPKNOTS--THIS IS A
PROVISIONAL MANIFESTATION.
童形五髻知權現
Tung sying wu ji jr chwyan syan,

ORIGINALLY, HE IS THE HAPPY TREASURY OF THE THUS COME
ONE.
本是如來歡喜藏
Ben shr ru lai hwan syi dzang.

HOMAGE TO MANJUSHRI BODHISATTVA OF GREAT WISDOM, WHO
DWELLS IN THE GOLDEN WORLD OF PURE COOL MOUNTAIN.
南無清涼山金色世界◎大智文殊師利菩薩◎

Na mwo ching lyang shan, jin shai shr jye, da jr wen
shu shr li pu sa.

4. HOMAGE TO WONDERFUL AUSPICIOUS BODHISATTVA
南無妙吉祥菩薩   (繞念)
Na mwo myau ji syang pu sa. *(recite and circumambulate)*

5. UNIVERSAL BOWING 拜願 *(Recite the names below; for music,*
                         see page 163.) (參考音譜見163頁)

180

HOMAGE TO OUR ORIGINAL TEACHER SHAKYAMUNI BUDDHA.

南無本師釋迦牟尼佛　(三拜)

Na mwo ben shr shr jya mu ni fwo *(bow 3 times)*

HOMAGE TO MANJUSHRI BODHISATTVA

南無文殊師利菩薩　(十二拜)

Na mwo wen shu shr li pu sa *(bow 12 times)*

HOMAGE TO UNIVERSAL WORTHY BODHISATTVA

南無普賢菩薩　(三拜)

Na mwo pu syan pu sa *(bow 3 times)*

HOMAGE TO MAITREYA BODHISATTVA

南無彌勒菩薩　(三拜)

Na mwo mi lei pu sa *(bow 3 times)*

HOMAGE TO THE BODHISATTVAS MAHASATTVAS OF THE
TEN DIRECTIONS

南無十方菩薩摩訶薩　(三拜)

Na mwo shr fang pu sa mwo he sa *(bow 3 times)*

6. THE THREE REFUGES *(see page 50)*　三皈依 (見第50頁)

****

CEREMONY FOR GREAT STRENGTH BODHISATTVA'S BIRTHDAY
大勢至菩薩聖誕祝儀 (七月十三日)

1. JEWELED CENSER PRAISE *(see page 1)*
    寶鼎讚 (見1頁)
2. RECITE AMITABHA SUTRA *(see page 87)*; SPIRIT MANTRA FOR
    REBIRTH IN THE PURE LAND. *(see page 107)*
    念誦：彌陀經 (見第87頁)；往生咒 (三遍;見第10頁)
3. PRAISE
    (勢至讚)
    HIS WISDOM LIGHT UNIVERSALLY ILLUMINATES, LUCID AND
    JADE-LIKE.
    慧光普照何玲瓏◎
    Hwei gwang pu jyau he ling lung.

181

THE THREE DESTINIES GET OUT OF SUFFERING AS HE CROSSES
OVER SENTIENT BEINGS.

三塗脫苦度含靈

San tu tou ku du han ling.

THE LIGHT FROM FIVE HUNDRED FLORAL PLATFORMS INTER-
REFLECT,

華臺五百交輝映

Hwa tai wu bai jyau hwei ying,

AS HE MANIFESTS A BODY THROUGHOUT BUDDHA KSHETRAS OF THE
TEN DIRECTIONS.

佛刹十方盡現形

Fwo cha shr fang jin syan sying.

WALKING OR SITTING, HE QUAKES THE GREAT-THOUSAND COSMOS;

行坐震搖大千界

Sying dzo jen yau da chyan jye,

ATOP HIS ADORNED SUMMIT, STANDS THE FLASK OF JEWELED
LIGHT.

莊嚴頂峙寶光瓶◎

Jwang yan ding jr bau gwang ping.

HOW DID HE CERTIFY TO SUCH PERFECT PENETRATION AND SELF-
MASTERY?

圓通自在由何證

Ywan tung dz dzai yu he jeng,

PURE MINDFULNESS, CONSTANTLY AWARE--THE UNSURPASSED
VEHICLE!

淨念常惺最上乘

Jing nyan chang sying dzwei shang cheng.

HOMAGE TO GREAT STRENGTH BODHISATTVA OF BOUNDLESS BODIES
OF BLAZING LIGHT, WHO DWELLS IN THE WESTERN WORLD OF
ULTIMATE BLISS.

南無西方極樂世界,無邊光熾身大勢至菩薩.

Na mwo syi fang ji le shr jye, wu byan gwang jr shen,
da shr jr pu sa.

182

4. HOMAGE TO GREAT STRENGTH BODHISATTVA

南無大勢至菩薩　　　(繞念)

Na mwo da shr jr pu sa *(recite while circumambulating)*

5. UNIVERSAL BOWING 拜願 *(Recite the names below; for music,*
see page 163.)(參考音譜見163頁)

HOMAGE TO OUR ORIGINAL TEACHER SHAKYAMUNI BUDDHA.

南無本師釋迦牟尼佛　　(三拜)

Na mwo ben shr shr jya mu ni fwo. *(bow 3 times)*

NAMO AMITABHA BUDDHA.

南無阿彌陀佛　　　(三拜)

Na mwo e mi two fwo. *(bow 3 times)*

NAMO BODHISATTVA WHO OBSERVES THE WORLD'S SOUNDS.

南無觀世音菩薩　　　(三拜)

Na mwo gwan shr yin pu sa. *(bow 3 times)*

NAMO GREAT STRENGTH BODHISATTVA.

南無大勢至菩薩　　　(三拜)

Na mwo da shr jr pu sa. *(bow 12 times)*

NAMO GREAT PURE SEA OF BODHISATTVAS.

南無清淨大海眾菩薩　　(三拜)

Na mwo ching jing da hai jung pu sa. *(bow 3 times)*

6. THREE REFUGES *(see page 50)* 三皈依(見第50頁)

****

CEREMONY FOR EARTH STORE BODHISATTVA'S BIRTHDAY
地藏王菩薩聖誕祝儀(七月三十日)

1. JEWELED CENSER PRAISE *(see page 1)*
寶鼎讚(見1頁)
2. RECITE EIGHTY-EIGHT BUDDHAS REPENTANCE *(see page 108)*
禮佛大懺悔文 (見第108頁)

EARTH STORE BODHISATTVA PRAISE

slowly

1. Earth Store Bo - dhi - satt - va won - der - ful be - yond com-
2. Won - drous Dhar- ma sounds through-out the three paths and six
3. His pearl shin- ing bright- ly lights the way to heav - en's
4. Leads on those with caus - es gar - nered life and life a -

pare; Gold hue'd in his trans -for - ma - tion bo - dy he ap-
realms; Four births and ten kinds of be - ings gain his kind - ly
halls; Six ringed gold - en staff shakes op - en wide the gates of
gain; To bow at the nine flow'rd ter - race of the Hon - ored

pears.
grace.   Na - mo Earth Store, Great Vows and Com-pas-sion, Bo-dhi-satt-va
hell.
One.

of the dark and dis - mal worlds; On Nine Flow - er Moun - tain, Most Hon - ored

One, with Ten Wheels of pow - er You res-cue all the suf - f'ring ones...

184

3. PRAISE
(地藏讚)
EARTH STORE BODHISATTVA WONDERFUL BEYOND COMPARE；

地藏菩薩妙難倫◎
Di dzang pu sa myau nan lwun

GOLD HUED IN HIS TRANSFORMATION BODY HE APPEARS.

化現金容處處分
Hwa syan jin rung chu chu fen.

WONDROUS DHARMA SOUNDS THROUGHOUT THE THREE PATHS AND
SIX REALMS

三途六道聞妙法
San tu lyou dau wen myau fa.

THOSE OF THE FOUR KINDS OF BIRTH AND TEN KINDS OF BEINGS
GAIN HIS KINDLY GRACE.

四生十類蒙慈恩
Sz sheng shr lei meng tsz en.

HIS PEARL SHINING BRIGHTLY LIGHTS THE WAY TO HEAVEN'S
HALLS；

明珠照徹天堂路
Ming ju jyau che tyan tang lu.

SIX-RINGED GOLDEN STAFF SHAKES OPEN WIDE THE GATES OF
HELL.

金錫振開地獄門◎
Jin syi jen kai di yu men.

LEADS ON THOSE WITH CAUSES GARNERED LIFE AND LIFE AGAIN；

累世親因蒙接引
Lei shr chin yin meng jye yin.

TO BOW AT THE NINE-FLOWERED TERRACE OF THE HONORED ONE.

九蓮臺畔禮慈尊
Jyou lyan tai pan li tsz dzwun.

185

NA MO EARTH STORE, BODHISATTVA OF GREAT VOWS AND COMPASSION,
OF THE DARK AND DISMAL WORLDS; ON NINE FLOWER MOUNTAIN,
MOST HONORED ONE, WITH TEN WHEELS OF POWER YOU RESCUE
ALL THE SUFFERING ONES.

南無九華山幽冥世界,大慈大悲
十輪拔苦,本尊地藏王菩薩。

Na mwo jyou hwa shan, yu ming shr jye, da tsz da bei,
shr lun ba ku, ben dzwun di dzang wang pu sa.

4. HOMAGE TO EARTH STORE BODHISATTVA

南無地藏王菩薩　　　　(繞念)

Na mwo di dzang wang pu sa *(recite while circumambulating)*

5. UNIVERSAL BOWING 拜願 *(Recite the names below; for music,*
see page 163.) (參考音譜見163頁)

HOMAGE TO OUR ORIGINAL TEACHER SHAKYAMUNI BUDDHA.

南無本師釋迦牟尼佛　　　(三拜)

Na mwo ben shr shr jya mu ni fwo. *(bow 3 times)*

HOMAGE TO MANJUSHRI BODHISATTVA.

南無文殊師利菩薩　　　　(三拜)

Na mwo wen shu shr li pu sa. *(bow 3 times)*

HOMAGE TO UNIVERSAL WORTHY BODHISATTVA.

南無普賢菩薩　　　　　(三拜)

Na mwo pu syan pu sa *(bow 3 times)*

HOMAGE TO THE BODHISATTVA WHO OBSERVES THE WORLD'S SOUNDS.

南無觀世音菩薩　　　　(三拜)

Na mwo gwan shr yin pu sa *(bow 3 times)*

HOMAGE TO EARTH STORE BODHISATTVA.

南無地藏王菩薩　　　　(十二拜)

Na mwo di dzang wang pu sa *(bow 12 times)*

HOMAGE TO THE BUDDHAS AND BODHISATTVAS OF THE TUSHITA
ASSEMBLY.

南無忉利會上佛菩薩　　(三拜)

Na mwo dau li hwei shang fwo pu sa *(bow 3 times)*

6. THE THREE REFUGES *(see page 50)* 三皈依(見第50頁)

THE BUDDHA SPEAKS THE ULLAMBANA SUTRA◎

佛説盂蘭盆經◎

Fwo shwo yu lan pen jing

NA MO HOMAGE TO THE ULLAMBANA ASSEMBLY OF BUDDHAS AND BODHI-
SATTVAS. *(recite 3 times)*

南無盂蘭盆會佛菩薩◎ (三稱)

Na mwo yu lan pen hwei fwo pu sa

THUS I HAVE HEARD, AT ONE TIME, THE BUDDHA DWELT AT SHRA-

如是我聞，一時佛在舍衛國

Ru shr wo wen, yi shr fwo dzai she wei gwo.

VASTI IN THE GARDEN OF THE BENEFACTOR OF ORPHANS AND THE SOLI-
TARY.

祇樹給孤獨園。

Chi shu ji gu du ywan.

MAHAMAUDGALYAYANA HAD JUST OBTAINED THE SIX PENETRATIONS AND
WISHED TO CROSS OVER HIS FATHER AND MOTHER TO REPAY THEIR
KINDNESS FOR RAISING HIM.

大目乾連始得六通，欲度父母報乳哺之恩。

Da mu jyan lyan, shr de lyou tung, yu du fu mu bau ru bu
jr en.

THUS, USING HIS WAY EYE, HE REGARDED THE WORLD AND SAW THAT
HIS DECEASED MOTHER HAD BEEN BORN AMONG THE HUNGRY GHOSTS,

即以道眼觀視世間，見其亡母生餓鬼中。

Ji yi dau yan, gwan shr shr jyan, jyan chi wang mu sheng
e gwei jung.

HAVING NEITHER FOOD NOR DRINK, SHE WAS BUT SKIN AND BONES.

不見飲食，皮骨連立。

Bu jyan yin shr, pi gu lyan li.

MAHAMAUDGALAYANA FELT DEEP PITY AND SADNESS, FILLED A BOWL
WITH FOOD AND WENT TO PROVIDE FOR HIS MOTHER. SHE GOT THE
BOWL, SCREENED IT WITH HER LEFT HAND, AND WITH HER RIGHT
HAND MADE A FIST OF FOOD. BUT, BEFORE IT ENTERED HER MOUTH,
IT TURNED INTO BURNING COALS WHICH COULD NOT BE EATEN.

目連悲哀,即鉢盛飯,往餉其母.母得鉢
飯,便以左手障飯,右手搏飯,食未入口,
化成火炭,遂不得食。

Mu lyan bei ai. ji bwo sheng fan. wang syang chi mu. mu de
bwo fan. byan yi dzwo shou jang fan. yo shou twan fan.
shr wei ru kou. hwa cheng hwo tan.swei bu de shr.

MAHAMAUDGALYAYANA CALLED OUT AND WEPT SORROWFULLY, AND
HASTENED TO RETURN TO THE BUDDHA TO SET FORTH ALL OF THIS.

目連大叫,悲號啼泣。馳還白佛,具陳如此。

Mu lyan da jyau. bei hau ti chi. chr hwan bai fwo. jyu chen
ru tsz.

THE BUDDHA SAID, "YOUR MOTHER'S OFFENSES ARE DEEP AND FIRMLY
ROOTED. YOU ALONE DO NOT HAVE ENOUGH POWER. ALTHOUGH YOUR
FILIAL SOUNDS MOVE HEAVEN AND EARTH, THE HEAVEN SPIRITS, THE
EARTH SPIRITS, TWISTED DEMONS, AND THOSE OUTSIDE THE WAY,
BRAHMANS, AND THE FOUR HEAVENLY KING GODS, ARE ALSO WITHOUT
SUFFICIENT STRENGTH.

佛言,汝母罪根深結,非汝一人,力所奈
何。汝雖孝順,聲動天地,天神.地神邪魔.
外道.道士.四天王神,亦不能奈何。

Fwo yan. ru mu dzwei gen shen jye, fei ru yi ren.li swo nai
he. ru swei syau shun sheng dung tyan di, tyan shen di shen.
sye mwo. wai dau. dau shr. sz tyan wang shen. yi bu neng
nai he.

THE AWESOME SPIRITUAL POWER OF THE ASSEMBLED SANGHA OF THE
TEN DIRECTIONS IS NECESSARY FOR LIBERATION TO BE ATTAINED.

當須十方眾僧威神之力,乃得解脫。

Dang syu shr fang jung seng wei shen jr li,nai de jye two.

I SHALL NOW SPEAK A DHARMA OF RESCUE WHICH CAUSES ALL THOSE
IN DIFFICULTY TO LEAVE WORRY AND SUFFERING, AND TO ERADICATE
OBSTACLES FROM OFFENSES.

吾今當為汝說救濟之法,令一切難,皆
離憂苦,罪障消除。

Wu jin dang wei ru shwo jyou ji jr fa. ling yi chye nan.jye
li yu ku, dzwei jang syau chu.

THE BUDDHA TOLD MAUDGALYAYANA: "THE FIFTEENTH DAY OF THE
SEVENTH MONTH IS THE PRAVARANA DAY FOR THE ASSEMBLED SANGHA
OF THE TEN DIRECTIONS.

佛告目連：十方眾僧於七月十五日,僧
自恣時。

Fwo gau mu lyan: shr fang jung seng yu chi ywe shr wu r.
seng dz dz shr.

FOR THE SAKE OF FATHERS AND MOTHERS OF SEVEN GENERATIONS
PAST, AS WELL AS FOR FATHERS AND MOTHERS OF THE PRESENT WHO
ARE IN DISTRESS, YOU SHOULD PREPARE AN OFFERING OF CLEAN
BASINS FULL OF HUNDREDS OF FLAVORS AND THE FIVE FRUITS,

當為七世父母,及現在父母厄難中者,
具飯百味五果,汲灌盆器,

Dang wei chi shr fu mu. ji syan dzai fu mu e nan jung je.
ju fan bai wei wu gwo.ji gwan pen chi.

AND OTHER OFFERINGS OF INCENSE, OIL, LAMPS, CANDLES, BEDS,
AND BEDDING, ALL THE BEST OF THE WORLD, TO THE GREATLY
VIRTUOUS ASSEMBLED SANGHA OF THE TEN DIRECTIONS.

香油錠燭床敷臥具,盡世甘美,以著盆中。
供養十方大德眾僧。

Syang. you. teng. chu. chwang fu. wo ju.jin shr gan mei.yi
jau pen jung. gung yang shr fang da de jung seng.

ON THAT DAY, ALL THE HOLY ASSEMBLY, WHETHER IN THE MOUNTAINS
PRACTICING DHYANA SAMADHI, OR OBTAINING THE FOUR FRUITS OF
THE WAY, OR WALKING BENEATH TREES, OR USING THE INDEPENDENCE
OF THE SIX PENETRATIONS, TO TEACH AND TRANSFORM SOUND HEARERS
AND THOSE ENLIGHTENED TO CONDITIONS,

當此之日,一切聖眾或在山間禪定,或
得四道果,或樹下經行,或六通自在,教
化聲聞緣覺,

Dang tsz jr r. yi chye sheng jung hwei dzai shan jyan chan
ding. hwei de sz dau gwo. hwei shu sya jing sying. hwei lyou
tung dz dzai. jyau hwa sheng wen ywan jyau.

OR PROVISIONALLY MANIFESTING AS BHIKSHUS WHEN IN FACT THEY
ARE GREAT BODHISATTVAS ON THE TENTH GROUND--ALL COMPLETE IN
PURE PRECEPTS AND OCEANLIKE VIRTUE OF THE HOLY WAY--SHOULD
GATHER IN A GREAT ASSEMBLY AND ALL OF LIKE MIND RECEIVE THE
PRAVARANA FOOD.

或十地菩薩大人,權現比丘。在大眾中,
皆同一心受鉢和羅飯。具清淨戒,聖眾
之道,其德汪洋。

Hwei shr di pu sa da ren chwyan syan bi chyou dzai da jung jung
jye tung yi syin. shou bwo he lwo fan. ju ching jing jye.
sheng jung jr dau. chi de wang yang.

IF ONE THUS MAKES OFFERINGS TO THESE PRAVARANA SANGHA, ONE'S
PRESENT FATHER AND MOTHER, PARENTS OF SEVEN GENERATIONS, AS
WELL AS THE SIX KINDS OF CLOSE RELATIVES, WILL ESCAPE FROM
THE THREE PATHS OF SUFFERINGS,

其有供養此等自恣僧者。現在父母,七
世父母,六種親屬,得出三途之苦。

Chi you gung yang tsz deng dz dz seng je. syan dzai fu mu.
chi shr fu mu. lyou jung chin shu. de chu san tu jr ku.

AND AT THAT TIME ATTAIN RELEASE. THEIR CLOTHING AND FOOD
WILL SPONTANEOUSLY APPEAR. IF THE PARENTS ARE STILL ALIVE,
THEY WILL HAVE WEALTH AND BLESSINGS FOR A HUNDRED YEARS.

應時解脫,衣食自然。若復有人父母現
在者,福樂百年。

Ying shr jye two. yi shr dz ran. rau fu you ren fu mu syan
dzai je. fu le bai nyan.

PARENTS OF SEVEN GENERATIONS WILL BE BORN IN THE HEAVENS.
TRANSFORMATIONALLY BORN, THEY WILL INDEPENDENTLY ENTER THE
CELESTIAL FLOWER LIGHT, AND EXPERIENCE LIMITLESS BLISS.

若已亡七世父母生天,自在化生,入天
華光,受無量快樂。

Rau yi wang chi shr fu mu sheng tyan. dz dzai hwa sheng ru
tyan hwa gwang. shou wu lyang kwai le.

AT THAT TIME THE BUDDHA COMMANDED THE ASSEMBLED SANGHA OF THE
TEN DIRECTIONS TO RECITE MANTRAS AND VOWS FOR THE SAKE OF THE
DONOR'S FAMILY, FOR PARENTS OF SEVEN GENERATIONS.

190

時佛勅十方眾僧,皆先為施主家呪願.
七世父母.

Shr fwo chr shr fang jung seng. jye syan wei shr ju jya jou
ywan. chi shr fu mu.

AFTER PRACTICING DHYANA CONCENTRATION, THEY THEN MAY ACCEPT
THE FOOD. WHEN FIRST RECEIVING THE BASIN, PLACE IT BEFORE
THE BUDDHA IN THE STUPA. WHEN THE ASSEMBLED SANGHA HAS FI-
NISHED THE MANTRAS AND VOWS, THEN THEY MAY ACCEPT IT.

行禪定意,然後受食.初受盆時,先安在
佛塔前.眾僧呪願竟,便自受食.

Sying chan ding yi.ran hou shou shr. chu shou pen shr. syan
an dzai fwo ta chyan. jung seng jou ywan jing. byan dz shou
shr.

AT THAT TIME THE BHIKSHU MAUDGALYAYANA AND THE ASSEMBLY OF
GREAT BODHISATTVAS WERE ALL EXTREMELY DELIGHTED AND THE
SORROWFUL SOUND OF MAUDGALYAYANA'S CRYING CEASED.

爾時目連比丘,及此大會大菩薩眾,皆
大歡喜.而目連悲啼泣聲,釋然除滅.

Er shr mu lyan bi chyou.ji tsz da hwei da pu sa jung. jye da
hwan syi. er mu lyan bei ti chi sheng. shr ran chu mye.

AT THAT TIME MAUDGALYAYANA'S MOTHER OBTAINED LIBERATION FROM
ONE KALPA OF SUFFERING AS A HUNGRY GHOST.

是時目連其母,即於是日得脱一劫餓
鬼之苦.

Shr shr mu lyan chi mu. ji yu shr r de tou yi jye e gwei jr ku.

MAUDGALYAYANA ADDRESSED THE BUDDHA AND SAID, "THIS DISCIPLE'S
PARENTS HAVE RECEIVED THE POWER OF THE MERIT AND VIRTUE OF
THE TRIPLE JEWEL, BECAUSE OF THE AWESOME SPIRITUAL POWER OF
THE ASSEMBLED SANGHA.

爾時目連復白佛言:「弟子所生父母,得
蒙三寶功德之力,眾僧威神之力故.

Er shr mu lyan fu bai fwo yan. di dz swo sheng fu mu. de
meng san bau gung de jr li. jung seng wei shen jr li gu.

IF IN THE FUTURE THE BUDDHA'S DISCIPLES PRACTICE FILIALITY BY
OFFERING UP THE ULLAMBANA BASINS, WILL THEY BE ABLE TO CROSS
OVER THEIR PRESENT FATHERS AND MOTHERS AS WELL AS THOSE OF
SEVEN GENERATIONS PAST?"

若未來世一切佛弟子,行孝順者,亦應
奉此盂蘭盆,救度現在父母,乃至七世
父母.為可爾不?

Rau wei lai shr yi chye fwo di dz. sying syau shun je. Yi
ying feng tsz yu lan pen. jyou du syan dzai fu mu. nai jr
chi shr fu mu. wei ke er fau?"

THE BUDDHA REPLIED:"GOOD INDEED, I AM HAPPY YOU ASKED THAT
QUESTION. I JUST WANTED TO SPEAK ABOUT THAT AND NOW YOU
HAVE ALSO ASKED ABOUT IT.

佛言:「大善快問.我正欲說,汝今復問.

Fwo yan. da shan kwai wen. wo jeng yu shwo. ru jin fu wen.

GOOD MAN, IF BHIKSHUS, BHIKSHUNIS, KINGS, CROWN PRINCES,
GREAT MINISTERS, GREAT OFFICIALS, CABINET MEMBERS, THE HUN-
DREDS OF OFFICERS, AND THE TENS OF THOUSANDS OF CITIZENS
WISH TO PRACTICE COMPASSIONATE FILIAL CONDUCT,

善男子,若有比丘.比丘尼.國王.太子.王子.
大臣.宰相.三公.百官.萬民.庶人,行孝慈者.

Shan nan dz. rau you bi chyou bi chyou ni. gwo wang. tai dz.
wang dz. da chen. dzai syang. san gung. bai gwan. wan min.
shu ren.sying syau tsz je.

FOR THE SAKE OF THE PARENTS WHO BORE THEM, AS WELL AS FOR
THE SAKE OF FATHERS AND MOTHERS OF SEVEN LIVES PAST, ON THE
FIFTEENTH DAY OF THE SEVENTH MONTH, THE DAY OF THE BUDDHAS'
DELIGHT, THE DAY OF THE SANGHA'S PRAVARANA,

皆應為所生現在父母,過去七世父母,
於七月十五日,佛歡喜日,僧自恣日.

Jye ying wei swo sheng syan dzai fu mu. gwo chu chi shr fu
mu. yu chi ywe shr wu r. fwo hwan syi r. seng dz dz r.

THEY ALL SHOULD PLACE HUNDREDS OF FLAVORS OF FOODS IN THE
ULLAMBANA BASINS, AND OFFER THEM TO THE PRAVARANA SANGHA OF
THE TEN DIRECTIONS. THEY SHOULD VOW TO CAUSE THE LENGTH OF

LIFE OF THE PRESENT FATHER AND MOTHER TO REACH A HUNDRED
YEARS WITHOUT ILLNESS, WITHOUT SUFFERINGS, AFFLICTIONS, OR
WORRIES,

以百味飲食安盂蘭盆中,施十方自恣
僧.乞願便使現在父母,壽命百年無病,
無一切苦惱之患。

Yi bai wei yin shr an yu lan pen jung. shr shr fang dz dz
seng. chi ywan byan shr syan dzai fu mu. shou ming bai nyan
wu bing. wu yi chye ku nau jr hwan.

AND ALSO VOW TO CAUSE SEVEN GENERATIONS OF FATHERS AND
MOTHERS TO LEAVE THE SUFFERINGS OF THE HUNGRY GHOSTS, TO BE
BORN AMONG MEN AND GODS, AND TO HAVE BLESSINGS AND BLISS
WITHOUT LIMIT."

乃至七世父母離餓鬼苦,得生天人中,
福樂無極。

Nai jr chi shr fu mu. li e gwei ku. de sheng tyan ren jung,
fu le wu ji。

THE BUDDHA TOLD ALL THE GOOD MEN AND GOOD WOMEN, "THOSE DI-
SCIPLES OF THE BUDDHA WHO CULTIVATE FILIAL CONDUCT SHOULD
IN THOUGHT AFTER THOUGHT, CONSTANTLY RECALL THEIR PRESENT
FATHERS AND MOTHERS WHEN MAKING OFFERINGS, AS WELL AS THE
FATHERS AND MOTHERS OF SEVEN LIVES PAST.

佛告諸善男子善女人:「是佛弟子修孝
順者,應念念中常憶父母供養,乃至七
世父母。

Fwo gau ju shan nan dz. shan nyu ren. shr fwo di dz. syou
syau shun je. ying nyan nyan jung. chang yi fu mu. gung yang
nai jr chi shr fu mu.

EVERY YEAR, ON THE FIFTEENTH DAY OF THE SEVENTH MONTH, THEY
SHOULD ALWAYS, OUT OF FILIAL COMPASSION, RECALL THEIR PARENTS
WHO BORE THEM AND THOSE OF SEVEN LIVES PAST.

年年七月十五日,常以孝順慈憶所生
父母,乃至七世父母。

Nyan nyan chi ywe shr wu r. chang yi syau shun tsz yi swo
sheng fu mu. nai jr chi shr fu mu.

AND FOR THEIR SAKES PERFORM THE OFFERING OF THE ULLAMBANA
BASIN TO THE BUDDHA AND THE SANGHA AND THUS `REPAY THE LOVING
KINDNESS OF THE PARENTS WHO RAISED AND NOURISHED THEM.

為作盂蘭盆,施佛及僧,以報父母長養
慈愛之恩.

Wei dzwo yu lan pen. shr fwo ji seng. yi bau fu mu jang yang
tsz ai jr en.

ALL BUDDHAS' DISCIPLES SHOULD RESPECTFULLY RECEIVE THIS
DHARMA."

若一切佛弟子,應當奉持是法.」

Rau yi chye fwo di dz。ying dang feng chr shr fa.

AT THAT TIME THE BHIKSHU MAUDGALYAYANA AND THE FOUR-FOLD
ASSEMBLY OF DISCIPLES,HEARING WHAT THE BUDDHA SAID, PRACTICED
IT WITH DELIGHT.

爾時目連比丘,四輩弟子,聞佛所説,
歡喜奉行.

Er shr mu lyan bi chyou sz bei di dz. wen fwo swo shwo.
hwan syi feng sying.

 END OF THE BUDDHA SPEAKS OF ULLAMBANA SUTRA

佛説盂蘭盆經

Fwo shwo yu lan pen jing

TRUE WORDS FOR REPAYING PARENTS' KINDNESS

報父母恩真言

南無密粟多,哆婆曳,莎訶.

Na mwo mi li dwo dwo pe ye swo he.

(Circumambulate and recite)

(繞念)

194

DHARMA GATHERING TO LIBERATE THE LIVING
放生儀規
feng seng yi kuei

PRAISE FOR PURIFYING THE WATER *(see page 145)*

淨水讚 (見第145頁)

HOMAGE TO THE GREATLY COMPASSIONATE BODHISATTVA WHO OBSERVES THE SOUNDS OF THE WORLD. *(recite three times)*

南無大悲觀世音菩薩 (三稱)

Na mwo da bei gwan shr yin pu sa *(recite three times)*

THE GREAT COMPASSION MANTRA *(see page 32; recite three times or many times)*

大悲咒 (見第32頁；三遍或多遍)

THE HEART OF PRAJNA PARAMITA SUTRA *(see page 44; recite once)*

般若波羅蜜多心經 (見第44頁；一遍)

SPIRIT MANTRA FOR REBIRTH IN THE PURE LAND *(see page 42)*

往生淨土神咒 (見第42頁；三遍)

HOMAGE TO SWEET DEW KING BODHISATTVA *(recite three times)*

南無甘露王菩薩摩訶薩 (三稱)

Na mwo gan lu wang pu sa mwo he sa

INVITATION TO THE TRIPLE JEWEL (啓請三寶)

WITH FRAGRANT FLOWERS, WE WELCOME. WITH FRAGRANT FLOWERS, WE MAKE OUR REQUEST. NAMO, WITH ONE HEART WE OFFER UP A REQUEST TO THE ETERNALLY DWELLING TRIPLE JEWEL OF THE TEN DIRECTIONS WHO PERVADE THE DHARMA REALMS TO THE ENDS OF EMPTY SPACE.

香花迎　香花請　南無一心奉請
盡虛空　徧法界　十方常住佛法僧三寶

Syang hwa ying, syang hwa ching, na mwo yi syin feng ching, jin syu kung, byan fa jye, shr fang chang ju fwo fa seng san bau.

Presiding Dharma Master Recites: (法師白云：)

We beseech the Triple Jewel of the ten directions, our Original Teacher Shakyamuni Buddha, Compassionate Father Amitabha, Jewelled Victory Tathagata, Avalokiteshvara Bodhi-

sattva, Flowing Water Elder's Son, Tyan Tai Master Yung-
ming, and all the other Bodhisattvas. We only wish that
they will be compassionate, certify with their knowledge
and protect these proceedings with their mindfulness. Now
there are all manner of living creatures who move in the
water, on land or in the air, who, because they had been
caught in the nets of others, were about to enter the door
of death. Disciple(s) (names of those who purchased the
animals for liberation) have filled their minds with compassion and, having learned about the conduct of the Bodhisattva, have ransomed these doomed animals and will release
them to roam freely. In accord with the teachings of the
Great Vehicle, we repent and reform on behalf of these
animals and transmit to them the Three Refuges. On their
behalf we proclaim the Ten Names and recite the Twelve Links
of Conditioned Causation. Only because the offenses of these
species are so heavy, are their spirits and consciousnesses
obscured so that they are unable to understand the profound
vaipulya Dharma.

We beseech the Triple Jewel of the ten directions to
use their awesome virtue invisibly to infuse them so they
become enlightened and are soon liberated.

Disciples of the Buddha! Be mindful that your heavy
karma of many lives has made you fall among the animals.
Now, on your behalf, before the Triple Jewel, we confess our
offenses and mistakes. You should sincerely follow us in
repentance and reform:

十方三寶,釋迦本師,彌陀慈父,寶勝
如來,觀音菩薩,流水長者子,天台永明
諸大士等,惟願慈悲,證知護念,今有水
陸飛行,諸眾生,為他網捕,將入死門.難
發慈悲心,學菩薩行,贖其身命,放使道
遙.承順大乘經典,代為懺悔,授與三皈,
稱揚十號,及說十二因緣。但以此類,罪
障深重,神識昏迷,不能了知,方等深法,

仰乞 十方三寶,威德冥加,令其開
悟,早得解脫。佛子!念汝多生業重,墮在
畜生。今為汝等,對三寶前,發露罪愆,汝
當志誠,隨我懺悔。

FOR ALL BAD KARMA CREATED IN THE PAST,

▲ 往昔所造諸惡業

Wang syi swo dzau ju e ye

BASED UPON BEGINNINGLESS GREED, HATRED, AND STUPIDITY,

皆由無始貪瞋癡

Jye yo wu shr tan chen chr

AND BORN OF BODY, MOUTH, AND MIND,

從身語意之所生

Tsung shen yu yi jr swo sheng

I NOW REPENT AND REFORM.

一切我今皆懺悔　　（三徧）

Yi chye wo jin jye tsan hwei　　*(recite three times)*

OFFENSES ARISE FROM THE MIND; REPENTANCE IS BY THE MIND.

▲ 罪從心起將心懺

Dzwei tsung syin chi jyang syin tsan

IF THE MIND IS EXTINGUISHED, OFFENSES ARE FORGOTTEN.

心若滅時罪亦忘

Syin rau mye shr dzwei yi wang

THE MIND FORGOTTEN, OFFENSES WIPED OUT--BOTH ARE EMPTY.

心忘罪滅兩俱空

Syin wang dzwei mye lyang ju kung

THIS IS CALLED TRUE REPENTANCE AND REFORM.

是則名為真懺悔　　（三徧）

Shr dze ming wei jen tsan hwei　　*(recite three times)*

HOMAGE TO COOL REFRESHING GROUND BODHISATTVA

▲ 南無⦿清涼地菩薩摩訶薩⦿ （三稱）

Na mwo ching lyang di pu sa mwo he sa *(recite three times)*

▲ *THE SEVEN BUDDHAS' TRUE WORDS FOR ERADICATING OFFENSES*

七佛滅罪真言

LI PE LI PE DI　　　　　離婆離婆帝

CHYOU HE CHYOU HE DI　求訶求訶帝

TWO LA NI DI　　　　　陀羅尼帝

NI HE LA DI　　　　　　尼阿囉帝

PI LI NI DI　　　　　　毗黎你帝

MWO HE CHYE DI　　　　摩訶伽帝

JEN LIN CHYAN DI　　　真陵乾帝

SWO PE HE　*(recite three times)*　莎婆訶　　（三徧）

▲ *LIBERATING THE LIVING MANTRA*

放生咒

NAN　　　　　　　唵

SA WA BA BWO　　薩斡巴鉢

YWE SZ PU JA　　月斯普吃

DA HE LA　　　　怛賀囉

WA DZ LA YE　　斡資囉耶

SWO HE　*(recite three times)*　莎訶　　（三徧）

Presiding Dharma Master recites: （法師白云:）

ALL OF YOU DISCIPLES OF THE BUDDHA! YOU HAVE NOT HEARD
OF THE TRIPLE JEWEL AND DO NOT UNDERSTAND "TAKING REFUGE."
THEREFORE, AFTER REVOLVING IN THE THREE REALMS OF EXISTENCE,
YOU HAVE PRESENTLY FALLEN AMONG THE ANIMALS. I SHALL NOW
TRANSMIT TO YOU THE DHARMA OF THE THREE REFUGES, SO YOU
SHOULD LISTEN ATTENTIVELY. JU FWO DZ DENG!

諸佛子!汝等不聞三寶,不解皈依,所
以輪迴三有.今墮畜生,我今授汝等,三
皈依法,汝今諦聽。 諸佛子等！

198

WE TAKE REFUGE WITH THE BUDDHA.WE TAKE REFUGE WITH THE DHARMA.
WE TAKE REFUGE WITH THE SANGHA.

▲皈依佛，皈依法，皈依僧。
Gwei yi fwo, gwei yi fa, gwei yi seng.

WE TAKE REFUGE WITH THE BUDDHA, THE VENERABLE ONE WHO IS
DOUBLY PERFECTED.

皈依佛，兩足尊。
Gwei yi fwo, lyang dzu dzwun.

WE TAKE REFUGE WITH THE REVERED DHARMA WHICH ALLOWS ONE TO
LEAVE DESIRE.

皈依法，離欲尊。
Gwei yi fa, li yu dzwun.

WE TAKE REFUGE WITH THE SANGHA, THE VENERABLE ONES AMONG
MULTITUDES.

皈依僧，眾中尊。
Gwei yi seng, jung jung dzwun.

WE TAKE REFUGE WITH THE BUDDHA, SO THAT WE SHALL NOT FALL
INTO THE HELLS.

皈依佛，不墮地獄。
Gwei yi fwo, bu dwo di yu.

WE TAKE REFUGE WITH THE DHARMA, SO THAT WE SHALL NOT FALL
AMONG THE HUNGRY GHOSTS.

皈依法，不墮餓鬼。
Gwei yi fa, bu dwo e gwei.

WE TAKE REFUGE WITH THE SANGHA, SO THAT WE SHALL NOT FALL
AMONG THE ANIMALS.

皈依僧，不墮傍生。
Gwei yi seng, bu dwo pang sheng.

WE HAVE COMPLETED TAKING REFUGE WITH THE BUDDHA, WE HAVE COM-
PLETED TAKING REFUGE WITH THE DHARMA, AND WE HAVE COMPLETED
TAKING REFUGE WITH THE SANGHA.

皈依佛竟，皈依法竟，皈依僧竟。(三徧)
Gwei yi fwo jing, gwei yi fa jing, gwei yi seng jing.

Presiding Dharma Master recites: （法師白云：）

> Disciples of the Buddha!
> You have now taken refuge with the Buddha.
> You have now taken refuge with the Dharma.
> You have now taken refuge with the Sangha.

From today onwards you will take the Buddha as your Teacher
and no longer take refuge with demons and those of external
paths. From today onwards you will take the Dharma as your
teacher and no longer take refuge in the scriptures of external paths. From today onwards you will take the Sangha
as your teacher and no longer take refuge in the improper
assemblies of those of external paths.
All of you disciples of the Buddha! Now that you have taken
refuge, on your behalf I will proclaim the characteristics
of both the production and extinction of the Twelve Links
of Conditioned Causation so that you will totally understand
the Dharma of production and extinction and so that you will
awaken to the Dharma of non-production and non-extinction.
In this very place is the ultimate. In this very place is
purity. In this very place is liberation. When one thought
is ultimate, all is ultimate. When one thought is pure, all
is pure. When one thought is liberated, all is liberated.
Together with all Buddhas, one certifies to the great Nirvana. In other words:
> ignorance is the condition for karmic activity;
> karmic activity is the condition for consciousness;
> consciousness is the condition for name and form;
> name and form is the condition for the six entrances;
> the six entrances are the condition for contact;
> contact is the condition for feeling;
> feeling is the condition for emotional love;
> emotional love is the condition for grasping;
> grasping is the condition for existence;
> existence is the condition for birth;
> birth is the condition for old age, death, worry,
>   sadness, suffering, and despair.

In other words:
> When ignorance is extinguished, karmic activity is
extinguished; when karmic activity is extinguished, consciousness is extinguished; when consciousness is extinguished,
name and form are extinguished; when name and form are extinguished, the six entrances are extinguished; when the six

entrances are extinguished, contact is extinguished; when
contact is extinguished, feeling is extinguished; when feeling is extinguished, emotional love is extinguished; when
emotional love is extinguished, grasping is extinguished;
when grasping is extinguished, existence is extinguished;
when existence is extinguished, birth is extinguished; when
birth is extinguished, old age, death, worry, sadness,
suffering and despair are all extinguished.

Ignorance is without a nature. What is fundamental is
the unmoving substance of all Buddhas. You all become
attached and falsely give rise to ignorance. For instance,
a diseased eye may see flowers in empty space, but after
one knows them for what they are, that ignorance is extinguished.

Disciples of the Buddha!

For your sake we will now recite the Four Great Vows
so that you may hear them. By relying on the Buddha, we
make vows; by relying on our vows, we cultivate. Listen
attentively!

汝等佛子,皈依佛竟,皈依法竟,皈依
僧竟。從今以往,稱佛為師,更不皈依,邪
魔外道。從今以往,稱法為師,更不皈依,
外道典籍。從今以往,稱僧為師,更不皈
依,外道邪眾。

諸佛子等,皈依三寶已,我今更為汝
說,十二因緣生相滅相,令汝等,了知生
滅之法,悟不生滅之法,當處究竟,當處
清淨,當處自在。一究竟,一切究竟。一清
淨,一切清淨。一自在,一切自在.同於諸
佛,證大涅槃。所謂無明緣行,行緣識,識
緣名色,名色緣六入,六入緣觸,觸緣受,
受緣愛,愛緣取,取緣有,有緣生,生緣老

死,憂悲苦惱.所謂無明滅,則行滅,行滅
則識滅,識滅則名色滅,名色滅,則六入
滅,六入滅,則觸滅,觸滅則受滅,受滅則
愛滅,愛滅則取滅,取滅則有滅,有滅則
生滅,生滅則老死,憂悲苦惱滅.無明無
性,本是諸佛,不動之體.汝等執著,妄起
無明.譬如病目,見空中花.既知是已,無
明即滅.

　　佛子,再為汝等,稱四弘誓願,令汝得
聞,依佛發願,依願修行.汝今諦聽!

All recite: (大眾齊念)

I VOW TO TAKE ACROSS THE NUMBERLESS LIVING BEINGS.

▲ 眾生無邊誓願度
Jung sheng wu byan shr ywan du.

I VOW TO CUT OFF THE ENDLESS AFFLICTIONS.

煩惱無盡誓願斷
Fan nau wu jin shr ywan dwan.

I VOW TO STUDY THE COUNTLESS DHARMA DOORS.

法門無量誓願學
Fa men wu lyang shr ywan shyau.

I VOW TO REALIZE THE SUPREME BUDDHA WAY.

佛道無上誓願成　(三編)
Fwo dau wu shang shr yang cheng.　*(recite three times)*

I VOW TO TAKE ACROSS THE LIVING BEINGS OF MY OWN NATURE.

▲ 自性眾生誓願度
Dz sying jung sheng shr ywan du.

I VOW TO CUT OFF THE AFFLICTIONS OF MY OWN NATURE.
自性煩惱誓願斷
Dz sying fan nau shr ywan dwan.

I VOW TO STUDY THE DHARMA DOORS OF MY OWN NATURE.
自性法門誓願學
Dz sying fa men shr ywan shyau.

I VOW TO REALIZE THE BUDDHA WAY OF MY OWN NATURE.
自性佛道誓願成　(三徧)
Dz sying fwo dau shr ywan cheng.

Presiding Dharma Master recites: (法師白云：)

　　　All of you disciples of the Buddha! For your sakes I will now recite and praise the auspicious names of Tathagatas which can cause you to leave the sufferings of the three paths and of the eight difficulties so that you will always be pure disciples of the Buddha, the Tathagata.

　　諸佛子，我更為汝，稱讚如來，吉祥名號，
能令汝等，永離三途，八難之苦，常為如來，
真淨佛子。

All recites: (大眾齊念)

HOMAGE TO MANY JEWELS TATHAGATA.
南無多寶如來
Na mwo Dwo Bau Ru Lai.

HOMAGE TO JEWELED VICTORY TATHAGATA.
南無寶勝如來
Na mwo Bau Sheng Ru Lai.

HOMAGE TO WONDERFULLY COLORED BODY TATHAGATA.

南無妙色身如來

Na mwo Myau Shai Shen Ru Lai.

HOMAGE TO EXTENSIVE BODY TATHAGATA.

南無廣博身如來

Na mwo Gwang Bwo Shen Ru Lai.

HOMAGE TO APART FROM FEAR TATHAGATA.

南無離怖畏如來

Na mwo Li Bu Wei Ru Lai.

HOMAGE TO SWEET DEW KING TATHAGATA.

南無甘露王如來

Na mwo Gan Lu Wang Ru Lai.

HOMAGE TO AMITA TATHAGATA.

南無阿彌陀如來 (三徧或多徧)

Na mwo E Mi Two Ru Lai. (recite three times or many times)

Presiding Dharma Master recites: (法師白云：)

All of you disciples of the Buddha! Those seven Tatha-gatas rescue living beings by means of the power of their vows. By reciting their names three times one can avoid suffering for a thousand lives and certify to the supreme Way. We only wish that after you are released you will never again encounter evil demons, be devoured by predators or snared in nets, and that you will live out your natural span of years. We wish that at the end of your lives you will, because you have received the power of the Triple Jewel, be reborn in accord with conditions, maintain the precepts, cultivate, see the Buddha, hear the Dharma, receive the prediction of a Bodhisattva, and transform living beings.

What is more, we wish that those who are liberating the living, Disciple(s)_____,will increase their understand-ing, their Bodhi conduct and Bodhi vows in thought after thought. In rescuing and protecting living beings, they should always think of living beings as of themselves, so all may obtain the rebirth in the Land of Ultimate Bliss, that they may see Amitabha Buddha, and certify to the patience

of non-production.   With division-bodies as numerous as
dust motes in the many lands, to the ends of the boundaries
of the future, may they take across vast numbers of living
beings.
　　We also wish that those people who capture living beings
will turn their minds toward the good and together obtain
liberation and the certification of true permanence.

諸佛子等,此七如來,以誓願力,拔濟
眾生。三稱其名,千生離苦,證無上道,唯
願汝等,既放以後,永不遭遇惡魔吞噉,
網捕相加。獲盡天年,命終之後,承三寶
力,隨緣往生,持戒修行,見佛聞法,授菩
薩記,轉化眾生。

　　更願放生弟子某等,菩提行願,念念增
明,救護眾生,常如己想,得生安養,見阿
彌陀佛,證無生忍,分身塵剎,盡未來際,
廣度眾生。

　　并願捕生人等,回心向善,同得解脫,
共證真常。

All recite: (唱讚)

MAY THOSE BORN FROM WOMBS, FROM EGGS, FROM MOISTURE, OR BY
TRANSFORMATION, WHO FOR MANY AEONS HAVE BEEN SUNK IN CONFUSION,

『胎卵濕化◎, 多劫沉迷 。
Tai lwan shr hwa. dwo jye chen mi.

TAKE REFUGE WITH THE TRIPLE JEWEL, BRING FORTH BODHI, AND
AVOID CAPTURE IN CAGES OR NETS.

皈依三寶發菩提◎, 籠網捕免離 。 ◎
Gwei yi san bau fa pu ti. lung wang bu myan li.

205

MAY THEY BE FREE ON LAND, IN THE SEAS, AND FLYING IN THE
HEAVENS, AND FOLLOW THE BUDDHA TO BE BORN IN THE HEAVEN OF
THE THIRTY-THREE.

海 闊 天 飛 ， 隨 佛 生 忉 利 。
Hai kwo tyan fei. swei fwo sheng dau li.

HOMAGE TO RISING TO THE HEAVENLY REALMS BODHISATTVA MAHASA-
TTVA. MAHA PRAJNA PARAMITA.

南 無 昇 天 界 菩 薩 摩 訶 薩 , 摩 訶 般 若 波 羅 蜜 。
Na mwo sheng tyan jye pu sa mwo he sa. mwo he bwo re bwo lwo
mi.

All recite: (大眾齊念：)

HOMAGE TO THE GREATLY KIND AND COMPASSIONATE AMITA BUDDHA
IN THE LAND OF ULTIMATE BLISS IN THE WEST.

南 無 西 方 極 樂 世 界 , 大 慈 大 悲 , 阿 彌 陀 佛 。
Na mwo syi fang ji le shr jye, da tsz da bei, E MI TWO FWO.

*(Assembly recites Na Mo Amita Buddha or Great Compassion
Mantra while liberating the creatures. Then returns to their
original bowing places for the transference of merit.)*
(放生時念佛或誦大悲咒後回位念回向偈)

****

放 生 功 德 回 向
VERSE FOR TRANSFERRING THE MERIT
FROM LIBERATING THE LIVING

THE MERIT FROM LIBERATING THE LIVING, THIS SUPREME CONDUCT
AND BOUNDLESS SUPREME BLESSINGS ARE ALL TRANSFERRED.

放 生 功 德 殊 勝 行 ， 無 邊 勝 福 皆 回 向 ，
Fang sheng gung de shu sheng heng, wu byan sheng fu jye hwei
syang.

WE UNIVERSALLY WISH THAT ALL DROWNING LIVING BEINGS WILL
QUICKLY GO TO THE LAND OF THE BUDDHA OF INFINITE LIGHT.

普 願 沉 溺 諸 眾 生 ， 速 往 無 量 光 佛 刹 。
Pu ywan chen ni ju jung sheng, su wang wu lyang gwang fwo cha.

ALL BUDDHAS OF THE TEN DIRECTIONS AND THE THREE PERIODS OF
TIME. ALL THE BODHISATTVAS, MAHASATTVAS.

十方三世一切佛，一切菩薩摩訶薩．

Shr fang san shr yi chye fwo, yi chye pu sa mwo he sa.

MAHA PRAJNA PARAMITA!

摩訶般若波羅蜜．

（三拜三寶，三拜住持和尚．）

Mwo he bwo re bwo lwo mi!

(3½ bows to Triple Jewel;
3½ bows to the Master or
"universally")

207

THE DHARMA OF REPENTANCE OF THE GREAT COMPASSION
WITH A THOUSAND HANDS AND A THOUSAND EYES

千手千眼大悲懺法

(DA BEI CHAN)

The Assembly says: 眾云:
NA MWO GWAN SHR YIN BODHISATTVA OF GREAT COMPASSION *(3 times)*

南無大悲觀世音菩薩 (三稱) ◎

Na mwo Da Bei Gwan Shr Yin Pu Sa

The Leader says: 維那師云:
LET ALL BE RESPECTFUL AND REVERENT.

一切恭敬 ◎

Yi chye gung jing.

The Assembly says: 眾云:
WITH ONE MIND I BOW TO THE EVERLASTING TRIPLE JEWEL OF THE
TEN DIRECTIONS *(Bow once, then stand and ½ bow.)*

一心頂禮十方常住三寶 (一拜起立,問訊) ◎

Yi syin ding li shr fang chang ju san bau.

The Leader says: 維那師云:
ALL IN THIS ASSEMBLY, EACH ONE KNEELING, HOLDING IN ADORN-
MENT INCENSE AND A FLOWER, IN ACCORD WITH DHARMA MAKE OFFER-
INGS.

是諸眾等　各各胡跪
嚴持香花　如法供養

Shr ju jung deng, ge ge hu gwei, yan chr syang hwa, ru fa
gung yang.

*(The Assembly kneels holding up incense and a flower, and
then says:)* (眾跪,手持香花云:)
MAY THIS FRAGRANT FLOWER-CLOUD FULLY PERVADE THE TEN DIREC-
TIONS. MAY ONE BY ONE ALL BUDDHALANDS BE ADORNED. MAY THE
BODHISATTVA PATH BE FULFILLED AND THE THUS-COME-ONE FRAGRANCE
PERFECTED.

願此香花雲,遍滿十方界,一一諸佛土,
無量香莊嚴,具足菩薩道,成就如來香.

Ywan tsz syang hwa yun, byan man shr fang jye. Yi yi ju fwo
du, wu lyang syang jwang yan. Jyu dzu Pu Sa Dau, cheng jyou
ru lai syang.
(Bow and reflect silently:) (拜下默念)

*This incense and flower pervade the ten directions, making
a tower of subtle, wonderful light. All heavenly music,
jeweled heavenly incense, rare heavenly delicacies, and
jeweled heavenly garments, all inconceivably wonderful dharma-
objects, each object emitting all objects, each object emitting all dharmas, revolving unobstructed and adorning each
other, are offered everywhere to the Triple Jewel of the ten
directions. Before the Triple Jewel of the Dharma Realm of
the ten directions, my body everywhere makes offerings. Each
one entirely pervades the Dharma Realm, each one unalloyed
and unimpeded, exhausting the bounds of the future, doing
the Buddhas' work, and spreading fragrance everywhere over
all the living beings in the Dharma Realm. Having received
the fragrance, they bring forth the Bodhi-mind, and together
they enter the Unproduced and are certified to the Buddhas'
wisdom.*

我此香花徧十方， 以為微妙光明臺，
諸天音樂天寶香， 諸天肴膳天寶衣，
不可思議妙法塵， 一一塵出一切塵，
一一塵出一切法， 旋轉無礙互莊嚴，
徧至十方三寶前， 十方法界三寶前，
悉有我身修供養， 一一皆悉徧法界，
彼彼無雜無障礙， 盡未來際作佛事，
普熏法界諸眾生， 蒙熏皆發菩提心，
同入無生證佛智。

The Leader says: 維那師云：
THE OFFERING IS NOW COMPLETE. LET ALL BE REVERENT AND RE-
SPECTFUL. *(Stand and half-bow)*

供養已一切恭敬。 (拜起，問訊)
Gung yang yi yi chye gung jing.

NA MO THE FORMER THUS COME ONE LIGHT OF PROPER DHARMA, THE
PRESENT GWAN SHR YIN BODHISATTVA, PERFECT IN MIRACULOUS
MERIT, COMPLETE IN GREAT COMPASSION,

南無過去正法明如來，現前觀世音菩薩，
成妙功德，具大慈悲，

Na mwo gwo chyu jeng fa ming ru lai. Syan chyan gwan shr yin
pu sa. Cheng myau gung de. Jyu da tsz bei.

WHO IN A SINGLE BODY AND MIND MANIFESTS A THOUSAND HANDS, A
THOUSAND EYES, WHO ILLUMINES AND LOOKS UPON THE DHARMA REALM
AND PROTECTS AND UPHOLDS LIVING BEINGS AND CAUSES THEM TO
BRING FORTH THE GREAT MIND OF THE WAY, WHO TEACHES THEM TO
HOLD THE PERFECT SPIRITUAL MANTRA

於一身心，現千手眼，照見法界，護持眾
生，令發廣大道心，教持圓滿神咒。

Yu yi shen syin. Syan chyan shou yan. Jau jyan fa jye.
Hu chr jung sheng. Ling fa gwang da dau syin. Jyau chr
ywan man shen jou.

TO LEAVE FOREVER THE EVIL PATHS, AND TO BE REBORN AT THE
TIME OF A BUDDHA. GRAVE OFFENSES WHICH DESERVE THE UNINTER-
RUPTED HELLS AND EVIL ILLS WHICH BIND THE BODY, FROM WHICH
NO ONE CAN BE SAVED OR EXTRICATED, ARE CAUSED TO MELT AWAY.

永離惡道，得生佛前，無間重愆，纏身惡
疾，莫能救濟，悉使消除。

Yung li e dau. De sheng fwo chyan. Wu jyan jung chyan.
Chan shen e ji. Mwo neng jyou ji. Syi shr syau chu.

SAMADHI, ELOQUENCE, AND WHATEVER IS SOUGHT IN THIS PRESENT
LIFE, ARE ALL BROUGHT TO ACCOMPLISHMENT.

三昧辯才，現生求願，皆令果遂。

San mei byan tsai. Syan sheng chyou ywan. Jye ling gwo swei.

THERE IS NO DOUBT WHATEVER THAT THE THREE VEHICLES CAN BE
QUICKLY ATTAINED AND THAT THE GROUND OF THE BUDDHAS CAN
SOON BE REACHED.

決定無疑，能使速獲三乘，早登佛地。

Jwye ding wu yi. Neng shr su hwai san cheng. Dzau deng fwo
di.

NO ONE CAN EXHAUST THE PRAISES OF HIS AWESOME SPIRITUAL
MIGHT.   THEREFORE WITH ONE MIND I RETURN MY LIFE IN
WORSHIP. *(Bow.)*

威神之力，歎莫能窮，故我一心，歸命頂禮。

Wei shen jr li. Tan mwo neng chyung. Gu wo yi syin gwei(拜)
ming ding li.

(Stand and half-bow) (拜起，問訊) ◎

WITH ONE MIND I BOW TO MY ORIGINAL TEACHER SHAKYAMUNI BUDDHA,
WORLD-HONORED ONE.

一心頂禮本師釋迦牟尼世尊◎

Yi syin ding li ben shr shr jya mu ni shr dzwun. *(3 times)*

*(Bow to each Buddha or group of Buddhas, reflecting
silently in turn:)*

*The worshipped and the worshipper are empty and still in
nature. The response and the Way are intertwined, inconceivably. This Way-place of mine is like a wish-fulfilling
pearl; the Buddha(s) [reflect on name(s)] appear before me.
I appear before (name of Buddha or Buddhas). Bowing down,
I return my life in worship.*

(諸衆皆須五體投地，勤重致禮．想云:)

能禮所禮性空寂 ， 感應道交難思議，
我此道場如帝珠 ， (如來名號) 影現中，
我身影現 (如來名號)前 ， 頭面接足皈命禮．

WITH ONE MIND I BOW TO AMITA BUDDHA OF THE WESTERN LAND OF
ULTIMATE BLISS, WORLD HONORED ONE.

一心頂禮西方極樂世界阿彌陀世尊

Yi syin ding li syi fang ji le shr jye e mi two shr dzwun.

WITH ONE MIND I BOW TO KING OF A THOUSAND LIGHTS BUDDHA OF
COUNTLESS KOTIS OF KALPAS PAST, WORLD HONORED ONE.

一心頂禮過去無量億劫千光王靜住世尊

Yi syin ding li gwo chyu wu lyang yi jye chyan gwang wang
jing ju shr dzwun.

WITH ONE MIND I BOW TO ALL THE BUDDHAS OF THE PAST, MANY AS
THE SANDS OF NINETY-NINE KOTIS OF GANGES RIVERS, WORLD-HONORED
ONES.

一心頂禮過去九十九億殑伽沙諸佛世尊

Yi syin ding li gwo chyu jyou shr jyou yi ji chye sha ju
fwo shr dzwun.

WITH ONE MIND I BOW TO LIGHT OF PROPER DHARMA OF COUNTLESS
KALPAS PAST, WORLD-HONORED ONE.

一心頂禮過去無量劫正法明世尊

Yi syin ding li gwo chyu wu lyang jye jeng fa ming shr dzwun.

WITH ONE MIND I BOW TO ALL THE BUDDHAS OF THE TEN DIRECTIONS,
WORLD-HONORED ONES.

一心頂禮十方一切諸佛世尊

Yi syin ding li shr fang yi chye ju fwo shr dzwun.

WITH ONE MIND I BOW TO ALL THE THOUSAND BUDDHAS OF THE
THREE PERIODS OF TIME IN THE WORTHY KALPA, WORLD HONORED
ONES.

一心頂禮賢劫千佛三世一切諸佛世尊···

Yi syin ding li syan jye chyan fwo san shr yi chye ju fwo
shr dzwun.
(Stand and half-bow.) (拜起.問訊)

WITH ONE MIND I BOW TO THE SPIRITUAL, WONDERFUL WORDS OF THE
DHARANI OF THE GREATLY COMPASSIONATE MIND, PERFECT, FULL,
UNIMPEDED, VAST, AND GREAT.

一心頂禮廣大圓滿無礙大悲心大陀
羅尼神妙章句 (三稱三拜;想云:)

Yi syin ding li gwang da ywan man wu ai da bei syin da two
lwo ni shen myau jang jyu.

(Bow three times, reflecting:)

The Dharma-Nature, like emptiness, cannot be seen. The
everlasting Dharma-Jewel is difficult to conceive of.
With my three karmas now in accord with Dharma, I pray that
it will manifest and accept this offering.

法性如空不可見,常住法寶難思議,
我今三業如法請,唯願顯現受供養。

WITH ONE MIND I BOW TO ALL THE DHARANIS SPOKEN BY GWAN YIN
AND TO ALL THE HONORED DHARMAS OF THE TEN DIRECTIONS AND THE
THREE PERIODS OF TIME.

一心頂禮觀音所説諸陀羅尼及十方三
世一切尊法 *(Bow, stand, and half-bow.)* (拜起,問訊)
Yi syin ding li gwan yin swo shwo ju two lwo ni ji shr fang
san shr yi chye dzwun fa.

(Bow and reflect:) (頂禮想云:)
True emptiness, the Dharma-nature, is like empty space. The
everlasting Dharma-Jewel is difficult to conceive of.
I now manifest before the Dharma-Jewel. With one mind,
in accord with Dharma, I return my life in worship.

真空法性如虛空，常住法寶難思議，
我身影現法寶前，一心如法皈命禮。

WITH ONE MIND I BOW TO THE GREATLY KIND, GREATLY COMPASSION-
ATE GWAN SHR YIN BODHISATTVA, WHO WITH A THOUSAND HANDS AND
A THOUSAND EYES CONTEMPLATES AT EASE THE SOUNDS OF THE
WORLD, MAHASATTVA.

一心頂禮千手千眼大慈大悲觀世音
自在菩薩摩訶薩 (三稱三拜;想云:)
Yi syin ding li chyan shou chyan yan da tsz da bei gwan
shr yin dz dzai pu sa mwo he sa.

(Bow and reflect three times:)
The worshipped and the worshipper are empty and still in
nature. The response and the Way are intertwined, incon-
ceivably. This Way-place of mine is like a wish-fulfilling
pearl. The Greatly Compassionate Bodhisattva manifests in
it; I now manifest before the Greatly Compassionate One
as I seek eradication of obstacles, prostrate and wor-
shipping.

能禮所禮性空寂，感應道交難思議，
我此道場如帝珠，大悲菩薩影現中，
我身影現大悲前，為求滅障接足禮。

WITH ONE MIND I BOW TO THE BODHISATTVA WHO HAS ATTAINED
GREAT STRENGTH, MAHASATTVA.

一心頂禮大勢至菩薩摩訶薩

Yi syin ding li da shr jr pu sa mwo he sa.

(Bow once to Great Strength Bodhisattva and to each subse-
quent Bodhisattva or Bodhisattvas, reflecting as when bowing
to Gwan Yin Bodhisattva, but substituting the appropriate
name or names.)

（頂禮大勢至菩薩及其他菩薩時，默想法句與
觀世音菩薩同，但念至尊號時分別改換。）

WITH ONE MIND I BOW TO DHARANI-KING BODHISATTVA, MAHASATTVA.

一心頂禮總持王菩薩摩訶薩

Yi syin ding li dzung chr wang pu sa mwo he sa.

WITH ONE MIND I BOW TO SUNLIGHT BODHISATTVA AND MOONLIGHT
BODHISATTVA, MAHASATTVAS.

一心頂禮日光菩薩月光菩薩摩訶薩

Yi syin ding li r gwang pu sa ywe gwang pu sa mwo he sa.

WITH ONE MIND I BOW TO KING OF JEWELS BODHISATTVA, PHYSICIAN-
KING BODHISATTVA, AND SUPREME PHYSICIAN BODHISATTVA,
MAHASATTVAS.

一心頂禮寶王菩薩、藥王菩薩、藥上菩
薩摩訶薩

Yi syin ding li bau wang pu sa, yau wang pu sa, yau shang
pu sa, mwo he sa.

WITH ONE MIND I BOW TO FLOWER-ADORNMENT BODHISATTVA, GREAT
ADORNMENT BODHISATTVA, AND TREASURY OF JEWELS BODHISATTVA,
MAHASATTVAS.

一心頂禮華嚴菩薩、大莊嚴菩薩、寶藏
菩薩摩訶薩

Yi syin ding li hwa yan pu sa, da jwang yan pu sa, bau
dzang pu sa, mwo he sa.

WITH ONE MIND I BOW TO MERIT-TREASURY BODHISATTVA, VAJRA-
TREASURY BODHISATTVA, AND EMPTY-SPACE TREASURY BODHISATTVA,
MAHASATTVAS.

一心頂禮德藏菩薩、金剛藏菩薩、虛空
藏菩薩摩訶薩

Yi syin ding li de dzang pu sa, jin gang dzang pu sa, syu
kung dzang pu sa, mwo he sa.

WITH ONE MIND I BOW TO MAITREYA BODHISATTVA, UNIVERSAL WORTHY
BODHISATTVA, AND MANJUSHRI BODHISATTVA, MAHASATTVAS,

一心頂禮彌勒菩薩、普賢菩薩、文殊師利
菩薩摩訶薩

Yi syin ding li mi lei pu sa, pu syan pu sa, wen shu shr li
pu sa, mwo he sa.

WITH ONE MIND I BOW TO ALL THE BODHISATTVAS OF THE TEN
DIRECTIONS AND THE THREE PREIODS OF TIME, MAHASATTVAS.

一心頂禮十方三世一切菩薩摩訶薩

Yi syin ding li shr fang san shr yi chye pu sa mwo he sa.

WITH ONE MIND I BOW TO MAHAKASHYAPA AND THE IMMEASURABLE,
INNUMERABLE GREAT SOUND-HEARER SANGHA.

一心頂禮摩訶迦葉無量無數大聲聞僧

Yi syin ding li mwo he jya she, wu lyang wu shu da sheng
wen seng.
(Stand and half-bow). (拜起,問訊)

WITH ONE MIND I BOW TO THE VENERABLE ONE OF SZ MING MOUNTAIN,
EXPOUNDER OF THE TYAN TAI TEACHINGS AND CONTEMPLATIONS,
GREAT MASTER FA JR.

一心頂禮闡天台教觀四明尊者法智大師

Yi syin ding li chan tyan tai jyau gwan sz ming dzwun je
fa jr da shr.
(Stand and half-bow.) (拜起,問訊)

WITH ONE MIND, ON BEHALF OF THE GOOD GODS JA FAN MWO AND
CHU PWO CHYE,

一心代為善吒梵摩瞿婆伽天子

Yi syin dai wei shan ja fan mwo chu pwo chye tyan dz.

215

THE FOUR WORLD-PROTECTING KINGS, THE GODS, DRAGONS, AND THE
REST OF THE EIGHT DIVISIONS, THE GODDESS PURE EYES,

護世四主、天龍八部、童目天女、

Hu shr sz wang, tyan lung ba bu, tung mu tyan nyu,

THE SPIRITS OF EMPTY SPACE, THE SPIRITS OF RIVERS AND OCEANS,
THE SPIRITS OF FOUNTAINS AND SPRINGS, THE SPIRITS OF STREAMS
AND POOLS,

虛空神、江海神、泉源神、河沼神、

Syu kung shen, jyang hai shen, chywan ywan shen, he jau shen,

THE SPIRITS OF HERBS, GRASSES, AND WOODS, THE HOUSEHOLD
SPIRITS, THE WATER SPIRITS, THE FIRE SPIRITS,

藥草樹林神、舍宅神、水神、火神、

Yau tsau shu lin shen, she jai shen, shwei shen, hwo shen,

THE WIND SPIRITS, THE EARTH SPIRITS, THE MOUNTAIN SPIRITS,
THE GROUND SPIRITS, THE PALACE SPIRITS, AND OTHERS.

風神、土神、山神、地神、宮殿神等,

Feng shen, tu shen, shan shen, di shen, gung dyan shen deng,

ALL THE GODS, DRAGONS, GHOSTS, AND SPIRITS WHO PROTECT
THOSE WHO HOLD MANTRAS, EACH WITH HIS OR HER RETINUE: ON
THEIR BEHALF I BOW TO THE TRIPLE JEWEL.

及守護持咒一切天龍鬼神,各及眷屬,
頂禮三寶。 (Bow, stand, and half-bow.)   ◎
(一拜起, 立, 問訊)

Ji shou hu chr jou yi chye tyan lung gwei shen, ge ji jywan
shu, ding li san bau.

All kneel. The Leader says: (衆跪; 維那師云:)
THE SUTRA SAYS, "IF THERE ARE BHIKSHUS, BHIKSHUNIS, UPASA-
KAS, UPASIKAS, YOUNG MEN, OR YOUNG WOMEN WHO WISH TO RECITE
AND BEAR IN MIND THIS MANTRA AND TO BRING FORTH A HEART
OF KINDNESS AND COMPASSION FOR ALL LIVING BEINGS, THEY
SHOULD FIRST FOLLOW ME IN MAKING THESE VOWS":

經云:若有比丘、比丘尼、優婆塞、優婆夷
童男、童女, 欲誦持者, 於諸衆生, 起
慈悲心, 先當從我, 發如是願.

Jing yun, rau you bi chyou bi chyou ni, you pe sai you pe yi,
tung nan tung nyu yu sung chr je, yu ju jung sheng chi tsz
bei syin, syan dang tsung wo fa ru shr ywan:

NA MO GREATLY COMPASSIONATE GWAN SHR YIN. I VOW THAT I WILL
QUICKLY KNOW ALL DHARMAS.

南無大悲觀世音，願我速知一切法，

Na mwo da bei gwan shr yin. Ywan wo su jr yi chye fa.

NA MO GREATLY COMPASSIONATE GWAN SHR YIN. I VOW THAT I WILL
SOON OBTAIN THE WISDOM-EYE.

南無大悲觀世音，願我卓得智慧眼，

Na mwo da bei gwan shr yin. Ywan wo dzau de jr hwei yan.

NA MO GREATLY COMPASSIONATE GWAN SHR YIN. I VOW THAT I WILL
WILL QUICKLY CROSS ALL LIVING BEINGS OVER.

南無大悲觀世音，願我速度一切眾

Na mwo da bei gwan shr yin. Ywan wo su du yi chye jung

NA MO GREATLY COMPASSIONATE GWAN SHR YIN. I VOW THAT I WILL
SOON OBTAIN GOOD SKILL IN MEANS.

南無大悲觀世音，願我卓得善方便，

Na mwo da bei gwan shr yin. Ywan wo dzau de shan fang byan.

NA MO GREATLY COMPASSIONATE GWAN SHR YIN. I VOW THAT I WILL
QUICKLY BOARD THE PRAJNA BOAT.

南無大悲觀世音，願我速乘般若船，

Na mwo da bei gwan shr yin. Ywan wo su cheng bwo re chwan.

NA MO GREATLY COMPASSIONATE GWAN SHR YIN. I VOW THAT I WILL
SOON CROSS OVER THE SEA OF SUFFERING.

南無大悲觀世音，願我卓得越苦海，

Na mwo da bei gwan shr yin. Ywan wo dzau de ywe ku hai.

NA MO GREATLY COMPASSIONATE GWAN SHR YIN. I VOW THAT I WILL
QUICKLY ATTAIN PRECEPTS, SAMADHI, AND THE WAY.

南無大悲觀世音，願我速得戒定道，

Na mwo da bei gwan shr yin. Ywan wo su de jye ding dau.

NA MO GREATLY COMPASSIONATE GWAN SHR YIN. I VOW THAT I WILL
SOON CLIMB NIRVANA MOUNTAIN.

南無大悲觀世音，願我卓登涅槃山

Na mwo da bei gwan shr yin. Ywan wo dzau deng nye pan shan.

NA MO GREATLY COMPASSIONATE GWAN SHR YIN. I VOW THAT I WILL QUICKLY DWELL IN THE UNCONDITIONED.

南無大悲觀世音，願我速會無為舍，

Na mwo da bei gwan shr yin. Ywan wo su hwei wu wei she.

NA MO GREATLY COMPASSIONATE GWAN SHR YIN. I VOW THAT I WILL SOON UNITE WITH THE DHARMA-NATURE BODY.

南無大悲觀世音，願我早同法性身，

Na mwo da bei gwan shr yin. Ywan wo dzau tung fa sying shen.

IF I FACE THE MOUNTAIN OF KNIVES, THE MOUNTAIN OF KNIVES OF ITSELF BREAKS UP.

我若向刀山，刀山自摧折，

Wo rau syang dau shan, dau shan dz tswei je.

IF I FACE THE BOILING OIL, THE BOILING OIL OF ITSELF DRIES UP.

我若向火湯，火湯自枯竭，

Wo rau syang hwo tang, hwo tang dz ku jye.

IF I FACE THE HELLS, THE HELLS OF THEMSELVES DISAPPEAR.

我若向地獄，地獄自消滅，

Wo rau syang di yu, di yu dz syau mye.

IF I FACE THE HUNGRY GHOSTS, THE HUNGRY GHOSTS BY THEM-SELVES BECOME FULL.

我若向餓鬼，餓鬼自飽滿，

Wo rau syang e gwei, e gwei dz bau man.

IF I FACE THE ASURAS, THEIR EVIL THOUGHTS BY THEMSELVES ARE TAMED.

我若向修羅，惡心自調伏，

Wo rau syang syou lwo, e syin dz tyau fu.

IF I FACE THE ANIMALS, THEY BY THEMSELVES ATTAIN GREAT WISDOM.

我若向畜生，自得大智慧，

Wo rau syang chu sheng, dz de da jr hwei.

NA MO GWAN SHR YIN BODHISATTVA *(Recite ten times)*.

南無觀世音菩薩。 （十聲）

Na mwo gwan shr yin pu sa.

218

NA MO AMITA BUDDHA. *(Recite ten times, then bow once, stand, and half-bow.)*

南無阿彌陀佛 (唸十聲, 拜下, 起立, 問訊)

Na mwo e mi two fwo.

GWAN SHR YIN BODHISATTVA SAID TO THE BUDDHA: "WORLD HONORED ONE.

觀世音菩薩白佛言, 世尊,

Gwan shr yin pu sa bai fwo yan shr dzwun.

IF ANY LIVING BEING WHO RECITES AND HOLDS THE SPIRITUAL MANTRA OF GREAT COMPASSION SHOULD FALL INTO THE THREE EVIL PATHS, I VOW NOT TO ATTAIN THE RIGHT ENLIGHTENMENT.

若諸眾生, 誦持大悲神咒, 墮三惡道者, 我誓不成正覺.

Rau ju jung sheng, sung chr da bei shen jou, dwo san e dau je, wo shr bu cheng jeng jyau.

IF ANY LIVING BEING WHO RECITES AND HOLDS THIS SPIRITUAL MANTRA OF GREAT COMPASSION SHOULD NOT BE REBORN IN ANY BUDDHALAND, I VOW NOT TO ATTAIN THE RIGHT ENLIGHTENMENT.

誦持大悲神咒, 若不生諸佛國者, 我誓不成正覺.

Sung chr da bei shen jou, rau bu sheng ju fwo gwo je, wo shr bu cheng jeng jyau.

IF ANY LIVING BEING WHO RECITES AND HOLDS THE SPIRITUAL MANTRA OF GREAT COMPASSION SHOULD NOT ATTAIN IMMEASURABLE SAMADHIS AND ELOQUENCE, I VOW NOT TO ATTAIN THE RIGHT ENLIGHTENMENT.

誦持大悲神咒, 若不得無量三昧辯才者, 我誓不成正覺.

Sung chr da bei shen jou, rau bu de wu lyang san mei byan tsai je, wo shr bu cheng jeng jyau.

IF ANY LIVING BEING WHO RECITES AND HOLDS THE SPIRITUAL MANTRA OF GREAT COMPASSION SHOULD NOT OBTAIN WHATEVER HE SEEKS IN THIS PRESENT LIFE,

誦持大悲神咒, 於現在生中, 一切所求, 若不果遂者,

Sung chr da bei shen jou, yu syan dzai sheng jung, yi chye swo chyou, rau bu gwo swei je,

219

THEN IT CANNOT BE THE DHARANI OF THE GREAT COMPASSION MIND."

不得為大悲心陀羅尼也.

Bu de wei da bei syin two lwo ni ye.

HAVING SPOKEN THESE WORDS BEFORE THE ASSEMBLY, HE PUT HIS PALMS TOGETHER.

乃至說是語已,於眾會前,合掌正住.

Nai jr shwo shr yu yi, yu jung hwei chyan, he jang jeng ju.

STOOD UPRIGHT, AND BROUGHT FORTH A THOUGHT OF GREAT COMPASSION FOR ALL BEINGS. HE SMILED BROADLY

於諸眾生,起大悲心,開顏含笑,

Yu ju jung sheng, chi da bei syin, kai yan han syau.

AND IN THIS WAY SPOKE THE WONDERFUL SPIRITUAL PHRASES OF THE DHARANI OF GREAT COMPASSION, PERFECT, FULL, UNIMPEDED, VAST AND GREAT. THE DHARANI RUNS LIKE THIS:

即說如是廣大圓滿無礙大悲心大陀羅尼,神妙章句,陀羅尼曰.

Ji shwo ru shr gwang da ywan man wu ai da bei syin da two lwo ni shen myau jang jyu, two lwo ni ywe:

1) NA MWO HE LA DA NWO DWO　　南無喝囉怛那哆

　　LA YE YE ◎　　囉夜耶◎

2) NA MWO E LI YE　　南無阿唎耶

3) PWO LU JYE DI SHAU BWO LA YE　婆盧羯帝爍鉢囉耶

4) PU TI SA TWO PE YE　　菩提薩埵婆耶

5) MWO HE SA TWO PE YE　　摩訶薩埵婆耶

6) MWO HE JYA LU NI JYA YE　　摩訶迦盧尼迦耶

7) NAN　　唵

8) SA PAN LA FA YE　　薩皤囉罰曳

9) SWO DA NWO DA SYE　　數怛那怛寫

10) NA MWO SYI JI LI TWO YI　南無悉吉㗚埵伊

MENG E LI YE	蒙阿唎耶
11) PE LU JI DI SHR FWO LA	婆盧吉帝室佛囉
LENG TWO PE	楞馱婆
12) NA MWO NWO LA JIN CHR	南無那囉謹墀
13) SYI LI MWO HE PAN DWO	醯唎摩訶皤哆
SA MYE	沙咩
14) SA PE E TWO DOU SHU PENG	薩婆阿他豆輸朋
15) E SHR YUN	阿逝孕
16) SA PE SA DWO NA MWO PE SA DWO	薩婆薩哆那摩婆薩多◎
17) NA MWO PE CHYE	◎那摩婆伽
18) MWO FA TE DOU	摩罰特豆
19) DA JR TWO	怛姪他
20) NAN ◎	唵◎
21) E PE LU SYI	阿婆盧醯
22) LU JYA DI	盧迦帝
23) JYA LA DI	迦羅帝
24) YI SYI LI	夷醯唎
25) MWO HE PU TI SA TWO	摩訶菩提薩埵
26) SA PE SA PE	薩婆薩婆
27) MWO LA MWO LA	摩囉摩囉
28) MWO SYI MWO SYI LI TWO YUN	摩醯摩醯唎馱孕
29) JYU LU JYU LU JYE MENG	俱盧俱盧羯蒙
30) DU LU DU LU FA SHE YE DI	度盧度盧罰闍耶帝
31) MWO HE FA SHE YE DI	摩訶罰闍耶帝

32) TWO LA TWO LA	陀囉陀囉
33) DI LI NI	地唎尼
34) SHR FWO LA YE	室佛囉耶
35) JE LA JE LA	遮囉遮囉
36) MWO MWO FA MWO LA	麼麼罰摩囉
37) MU DI LI	穆帝隸
38) YI SYI YI SYI	伊醯伊醯
39) SHR NWO SHR NWO	室那室那
40) E LA SHEN FWO LA SHE LI	阿囉嘇佛囉舍利
41) FA SHA FA SHEN	罰娑罰嘇
42) FWO LA SHE YE	佛囉舍耶
43) HU LU HU LU MWO LA	呼盧呼盧摩囉
44) HU LU HU LU SYI LI	呼盧呼盧醯利
45) SWO LA SWO LA	娑囉娑囉
46) SYI LI SYI LI	悉唎悉唎
47) SU LU SU LU	蘇嚧蘇嚧
48) PU TI YE PU TI YE	菩提夜菩提夜
49) PU TWO YE PU TWO YE	菩馱夜菩馱夜
50) MI DI LI YE	彌帝利夜
51) NWO LA JIN CHR	那囉謹墀
52) DI LI SHAI NI NWO	地利瑟尼那
53) PE YE MWO NWO	婆夜摩那
54) SWO PE HE ◎	娑婆訶 ◎

55) SYI TWO YE　悉陀夜

56) SWO PE HE　娑婆詞

57) MWO HE SYI TWO YE　摩訶悉陀夜

58) SWO PE HE　娑婆詞

59) SYI TWO YU YI　悉陀喻藝

60) SHR PAN LA YE　室皤囉耶

61) SWO PE HE　娑婆詞

62) NWO LA JIN CHR　那囉謹墀

63) SWO PE HE　娑婆詞

64) MWO LA NWO LA　摩囉那囉

65) SWO PE HE　娑婆詞

66) SYI LU SENG E MU CHYWE YE　悉囉僧阿穆佉耶

67) SWO PE HE　娑婆詞

68) SWO PE MWO HE E SYI TWO YE　娑婆摩訶阿悉陀夜

69) SWO PE HE　娑婆詞

70) JE JI LA E SYI TWO YE　者吉囉阿悉陀夜

71) SWO PE HE　娑婆詞

72) BWO TWO MWO JYE SYI TWO YE　波陀摩羯悉陀夜

73) SWO PE HE　娑婆詞

74) NWO LA JIN CHR PAN CHYE LA YE　那囉謹墀皤伽囉耶

75) SWO PE HE　娑婆詞

76) MWO PE LI SHENG JYE LA YE　摩婆利勝羯囉夜

223

77) SWO PE HE　　　　　　　　娑婆訶

78) NA MWO HE LA DA NWO DWO　南無喝囉怛那哆

　　LA YE YE ◎　　　　　　囉夜耶◎

79) NA MWO E LI YE　　　　南無阿利耶

80) PWO LU JYE DI　　　　婆嚧吉帝

81) SHAU PAN LA YE　　　爍皤囉夜

82) SWO PE HE　　　　　　娑婆訶

83) NAN　　　　　　　　　唵

84) SYI DYAN DU　　　　　悉殿都

85) MAN DWO LA　　　　　漫多囉

86) BA TWO YE　　　　　跋陀耶

87) SWO PE HE　　　　　娑婆訶

WHEN GWAN SHR YIN BODHISATTVA HAD FINISHED SPEAKING THIS MANTRA,

觀世音菩薩説此咒已，

Gwan shr yin pu sa shwo tsz jou yi,

THE GREAT EARTH SHOOK IN SIX WAYS. THE HEAVENS RAINED FORTH JEWELED FLOWERS, WHICH FELL IN COLORFUL PROFUSION.

大地六變震動，天雨寶花，繽紛而下，

Da di lyou byan jen dung, tyan yu bau hwa, bin fen er sya.

ALL THE BUDDHAS OF THE TEN DIRECTIONS WERE DELIGHTED,

十方諸佛，悉皆歡喜，

Shr fang ju fwo, syi jye hwan syi.

WHILE THE HEAVENLY DEMONS AND EXTERNALISTS WERE SO AFRAID THEIR HAIR STOOD ON END.

天魔外道，恐怖毛豎，

Tyan mwo wai dau, kung bu mau shu.

EVERYONE IN THE ENTIRE ASSEMBLY WAS CERTIFIED TO THE FRUITION,

一切眾會，皆獲果證，

Yi chye jung hwei, jye hwai gwo jeng,

SOME ATTAINING THE FRUITION OF A STREAM-ENTERER, SOME THE
FRUITION OF A ONCE-RETURNER,

或得須陀洹果,或得斯陀含果

hwo de syu two hwan gwo, hwo de sz two han gwo,

SOME THE FRUITION OF A NEVER-RETURNER, SOME THE FRUITION OF
AN ARHAT,

或得阿那含果,或得阿羅漢果,

Hwo de e nwo han gwo, hwo de e lwo han gwo.

OTHERS ATTAINING THE FIRST GROUND OF A BODHISATTVA, THE
SECOND GROUND, THE THIRD, FOURTH, OR FIFTH GROUND,

或得一地二地,三四五地,

Hwo de yi di er di, san sz wu di.

EVEN UP TO THE TENTH GROUND. INNUMERABLE LIVING BEINGS
BROUGHT FORTH THE BODHI-MIND.

乃至十地者,無量眾生,發菩提心。

Nai jr shr di je, wu lyang jung sheng, fa pu ti syin.

(Bow and reflect, silently)　（拜下，默念想云）

*I and all living beings, from beginningless time, have been
constantly obstructed by the grave offenses of the three
karmic actions and the six sense-faculties, not seeing any
Buddhas, not knowing the essentials of escape, merely
complying with birth and death and not knowing the wonderful principle. Now, although I know, I continue, along with
all other living beings, to be obstructed by all kinds of
grave offenses. Now, before Gwan Yin and the Buddhas of the
ten directions, for the sake of all living beings everywhere, I return my life in repentance and reform, praying
that there will be protection, and that offenses will be
caused to be eradicated.*

我及眾生,無始常為三業六根,重罪所障,
不見諸佛,不知出要,但順生死,不知妙理,我今雖知, 猶與眾生, 同為一切重罪所障.
今對觀音, 十方佛前, 普為眾生, 皈命懺悔,
「唯願加護」令障消滅。◎

(念已起立, 合掌唱云:)

(Stand with joined palms and say:)
EVERYWHERE, FOR THE SAKE OF THE FOUR SUPERIORS, FOR ALL IN
THE TRIPLE WORLD, FOR LIVING BEINGS OF THE DHARMA REALM,

「普為四恩三有」法界眾生,

Pu wei sz en san you, fa jye jung sheng,

I VOW THAT ALL CUT OFF THE THREE OBSTRUCTIONS, AS I RETURN
MY LIFE IN REPENTANCE AND REFORM.

悉願斷除三障,「歸命懺悔.

Syi ywan dwan chu san jang, gwei ming chan hwei.

(Bow and reflect silently:) (唱已, 五體投地, 心復念云:)
*Along with living beings, from beginningless time until the
present, because of love and views, I scheme for myself
within, and consort with bad friends outside. I do not rejoice compliantly in even a hair's breadth of the good of
others, but with the three karmic actions commit all manner
of offenses on a wide scale. Although what I do is not a
very great matter in itself, my evil mind pervades everything. It continues day and night without cease, covering
up its transgressions, errors, and mistakes, not wanting
people to know, not fearing evil ways, not ashamed, without
remorse, denying cause and effect.
Therefore, on this day, I have come to believe deeply in
cause and effect. I give birth to deep shame and great
fear and repent. I cut off that incessant mind, bring
forth the Bodhi-mind, cut off evil and cultivate good,
go diligently forward in the three karmic actions, reform
all my past errors, and rejoice compliantly in the slight-
est hair's breadth of the good of sages and ordinary people.
I recollect the Buddhas of the ten directions, who have great
blessings and wisdom which can rescue me and pull me, along
with all other living beings, out of the sea of the two
deaths, and can bring me straight to the shore of the three*

virtues. From beginningless time onward, I have not known that all dharmas are in their fundamental nature empty and still, and I have committed all manner of evil on a wide scale. Knowing now that all dharmas are empty and still, for the sake of seeking Bodhi and for the sake of living beings, I completely cut off every evil, and cultivate all good on a wide scale. I only pray that Gwan Yin will compassionately gather it in and receive it.

我與眾生無始來今，由愛見故，內計我人，
外加惡友，不隨喜他，一毫之善。唯徧三業，
廣造眾罪，事雖不廣，惡心徧布，晝夜相續，
無有間斷，覆諱過失，不欲人知。不畏惡道，
無慚無愧，撥無因果。故於今日，深信因果，
生重慚愧，生大怖畏，發露懺悔，斷相續心，
發菩提心，斷惡修善，勤策三業，翻昔重過，
隨喜凡聖，一毫之善，念十方佛，有大福慧，
能救拔我及諸眾生，從二死海，置三德岸，
從無始來，不知諸法，本性空寂，廣造眾惡，
今知空寂，為求菩提，為眾生故，廣修諸善，
徧斷眾惡。唯願觀音慈悲攝受。

(All kneel.) （觀已，眾跪唱云：）

WITH THE UTMOST SINCERITY OF MIND, I DISCIPLE (   ),
REPENT. THIS VERY MIND, SHARED BY ALL LIVING BEINGS OF THE
DHARMA REALM, IS FUNDAMENTALLY COMPLETE WITH THE THOUSAND
DHARMAS.

至心懺悔，弟子（某甲）等，與法界一切眾生，

現前一心，本具千法，

Jr syin chan hwei, di dz (   ) deng yu fa jye yi chye
jung sheng, syan chyan yi syin, ben jyu chyan fa,

IT HAS IN FULL ALL SPIRITUAL STRENGTH AND THE USE OF
BRIGHT WISDOM.

皆有神力，及以智明，

Jye you shen li, ji yi jr ming.

ABOVE, IT EQUALS THE BUDDHA-MIND; BELOW, IT IS IDENTICAL
TO ALL THAT LIVES.

上等佛心，下同含識，

Shang deng fwo syin, sya tung han shr.

BEGINNINGLESS DARK MOVEMENT BLOCKS THIS STILL BRIGHTNESS.

無始闇動，障此靜明，

Wu shr an dung, jang tsz jing ming.

CONTACT WITH THINGS DIMS AND CONFUSES IT, AND THOUGHTS
ARISE AND BIND IT IN ATTACHMENTS.

觸事昏迷，舉心縛著，

Chu shr hwun mi, jyu syin fu jau.

IN THE MIDST OF THE SAMENESS OF DHARMAS ARISE THE NOTIONS
OF SELF AND OTHER.

平等法中，起自他想，

Ping deng fa jung, chi dz ta syang.

IN ALL EXISTENCE, LOVE AND VIEWS ARE THE BASIS AND THE BODY
AND MOUTH ARE THE CONDITIONS: WITH THEM NO OFFENSE IS
NOT CREATED.

愛見為本，身口為緣，於諸有中，無罪不
造

Ai jyan wei ben, shen kou wei ywan, yu ju you jung, wu dzwei
bu dzau.

THE TEN EVILS, THE FIVE REBELLIOUS OFFENSES, SLANDERING
DHARMA, SLANDERING PEOPLE,

十惡五逆，謗法謗人，

Shr e wu ni, bang fa bang ren.

BREAKING THE PRECEPTS, BREAKING THE RULES OF PURE EATING,
DESTROYING STUPAS, RUINING TEMPLES,

破戒破齋，毀塔壞寺，

Pwo jye pwo jai, hwei ta hwai sz,

STEALING FROM THE SANGHA, DEFILING THE CONDUCT OF THE PURE,

偷僧祇物，污淨梵行，

Tou seng chi wu, wu jing fan heng,

DESTROYING PROPERTY OF THE SANGHA, EATING AND DRINKING THE
SANGHA'S FOOD,

侵損常住，飲食財物，

Chin swun chang ju, yin shr tsai wu,

AND FAILING TO KNOW REPENTANCE THOUGH A THOUSAND BUDDHAS
APPEAR IN THE WORLD --

千佛出世，不通懺悔，

Chyan fwo chu shr, bu tung chan hwei,

OFFENSES SUCH AS THESE ARE MEASURELESS AND BOUNDLESS;

如是等罪，無量無邊，

Ru shr deng dzwei, wu lyang wu byan,

WHEN THIS BODY IS CAST ASIDE, IT IS FITTING THAT I FALL INTO
THE THREE PATHS OF REBIRTH AND THERE BE ENTANGLED IN A MYRIAD
OF ILLS.

捨茲形命，合墮三途，備嬰萬苦，

She dz sying ming, he dwo san tu, bei ying wan ku.

MOREOVER, IN THIS PRESENT LIFE, BECAUSE A SWARM OF TROUBLES
EMBROILS ME, FOUL ILLNESSES WHICH BIND ME UP,

復於現世，眾惱交煎，或惡疾縈纏，

Fu yu syan shr, jung nau jyau jyan, hwei e ji ying chan,

AND OPPRESSIVE CONDITIONS BROUGHT ABOUT BY OTHERS, I AM OB-
STRUCTED IN THE DHARMAS OF THE PATH, AND DO NOT BECOME WELL-
SEASONED IN MY CULTIVATION.   NOW, HAVING MET *(Bow)*

他緣逼迫，障於道法，不得熏修，今遇

Ta ywan bi pwo, jang yu dau fa, bu de syun syou, Jin yu

229

THE PERFECT SPIRITUAL MANTRA OF GREAT COMPASSION, I AM ABLE
TO QUICKLY WIPE OUT THE OBSTACLES OF OFFENSES LIKE THESE.
(Rise, remain kneeling)

大悲圓滿神咒，速能滅除如是罪障，(起；持跪)

Da bei ywan man shen jou, su neng mye chu ru shr dzwei jang.

THEREFORE, ON THIS DAY, WITH UTTER SINCERITY, I RECITE AND
HOLD THIS MANTRA AND RETURN *(Bow)*

故於今日，至心誦持．歸向 (拜)

Gu yu jin r, jr syin sung chr, gwei syang

TO GWAN SHR YIN BODHISATTVA AND TO ALL THE GREAT MASTERS OF
THE TEN DIRECTIONS. *(Rise, remain kneeling)*

◎觀世音菩薩，及十方大師， (起；持跪．)

Gwan shr yin pu sa, ji shr fang da shr.

I BRING FORTH THE BODHI-MIND AND CULTIVATE THE PRACTICE OF
TRUE WORDS.

發菩提心，修真言行，

Fa pu ti syin, syou jen yan heng.

TOGETHER WITH ALL LIVING BEINGS I CONFESS MY MANY OFFENSES
AND SEEK REPENTANCE SO THAT THEY WILL BE EXTINGUISHED AT
LAST. I ONLY WISH *(Bow)*

與諸眾生，發露眾罪，求乞懺悔，畢竟消
除．唯願 (拜)

Yu ju jung sheng fa lou jung dzwei, chyou chi chan hwei, bi
jing syau chu. Wei ywan

THAT THE GREATLY COMPASSIONATE GWAN SHR YIN BODHISATTVA,
MAHASATTVA, WILL PROTECT AND UPHOLD US WITH HIS THOUSAND
HANDS *(Rise, remain kneeling)*

◎大悲觀世音菩薩摩訶薩，千手護持，(起跪)

Da bei gwan shr yin pu sa mwo he sa, chyan shou hu chr,

AND THAT WITH HIS THOUSAND EYES HE WILL ILLUMINE US AND
LOOK UPON US AND CAUSE OUR INNER AND OUTER CONDITIONS OF
OBSTRUCTION TO BECOME STILL AND EXTINGUISHED.

千眼照見，令我等內外障緣寂滅，

Chyan yan jau jyan, ling wo deng nei wai jang ywan ji mye.

I VOW THAT MY PRACTICE AND THE PRACTICE OF OTHERS WILL BE
COMPLETE IN ACCOMPLISHMENT. I VOW TO OPEN THE KNOWLEDGE OF
MY ORIGINAL SEEING AND TO HAVE CONTROL OVER DEMONS AND
EXTERNALIST PATHS.

自他行願圓成,開本見知,制諸魔外.

Dz ta heng ywan ywan cheng, kai ben jyan jr, jr ju mwo wai.

I VOW TO BE VIGOROUS IN THE THREE KARMIC ACTIONS AND TO CUL-
TIVATE THE PURE LAND CAUSE, SO THAT WHEN THIS BODY IS CAST
ASIDE, I WILL HAVE NO OTHER DESTINY BUT TO ATTAIN REBIRTH *(Bow)*

三業精進,修淨土因,至捨此身,更無他趣
決定得生,(拜)

San ye jing jin, syou jing du yin, jr she tsz shen , geng
wu ta chyu, jywe ding de sheng

IN AMITA BUDDHA'S LAND OF ULTIMATE BLISS, AND DRAW NEAR TO,
SERVE, AND MAKE OFFERINGS TO THE GREATLY COMPASSIONATE
GWAN YIN. *(Rise, remain kneeling)*

◎阿彌陀佛極樂世界,親承供養,大悲
觀音,(起;持跪.)

E mi two fwo ji le shr jye, chin cheng gung yang da bei
gwan yin.

I VOW TO BE COMPLETE IN ALL THE DHARANIS AND ON A WIDE
SCALE TO CROSS OVER THE MANY CLASSES OF BEINGS SO THAT THEY
ALL ESCAPE THE WHEEL OF SUFFERING AND REACH THE GROUND OF
WISDOM TOGETHER. NOW THAT THE VOWS OF REPENTANCE ARE MADE,
I RETURN MY LIFE IN WORSHIP TO THE TRIPLE JEWEL. *(Bow and
then stand.)*

具諸總持,廣度羣品,皆出苦輪,同到智
◎地.懺悔發願已,歸命禮三寶.(拜;起立;問訊)◎

Jyu ju dzung chr, gwang du chyun pin, jye chu ku lwun, tung
dau jr di. Chan hwei fa ywan yi, gwei ming li san bau.
*(For each name, each side of the Assembly bows once while
the other side recites:)* (兩边輪流一唱一拜)

NA MO THE BUDDHAS OF THE TEN DIRECTIONS. NA MO THE
DHARMA OF THE TEN DIRECTIONS. NA MO THE SANGHA OF THE TEN
DIRECTIONS

南無十方佛,南無十方法,南無十方僧.

Na mwo shr fang fwo, na mwo shr fang fa, na mwo shr fang
seng.

NA MO OUR ORIGINAL TEACHER SHAKYAMUNI BUDDHA.

南無本師釋迦牟尼佛

Na mwo ben shr shr jya mu ni fwo.

NA MO AMITA BUDDHA. NA MO KING OF A THOUSAND LIGHTS BUDDHA WHO ABIDES IN STILLNESS.

南無阿彌陀佛　南無千光王靜住佛

Na mwo e mi two fwo. Na mwo chyan gwang wang jing ju fwo.

NA MO THE GREAT DHARANI OF THE GREATLY COMPASSIONATE MIND, PERFECT, FULL, UNIMPEDED, VAST, AND GREAT.

南無廣大圓滿無礙大悲心大陀羅尼

Na mwo gwang da ywan man wu ai da bei syin da two lwo ni.

NA MO GWAN SHR YIN BODHISATTVA OF THE THOUSAND HANDS AND THOUSAND EYES.

南無千手千眼觀世音菩薩

Na mwo chyan shou chyan yan gwan shr yin pu sa.

NA MO BODHISATTVA WHO HAS ATTAINED GREAT STRENGTH. NA MO DHARANI-KING BODHISATTVA

南無大勢至菩薩　南無總持王菩薩

Na mwo da shr jr pu sa. Na mwo dzung chr wang pu sa.

TO THE BUDDHA I RETURN AND RELY, VOWING THAT ALL LIVING BEINGS UNDERSTAND THE GREAT WAY PROFOUNDLY, AND BRING FORTH THE BODHI MIND ◎•
(bow)

自皈依佛，當願眾生，體解大道，
發無上心

Dz gwei yi fwo, dang ywan jung sheng, ti jye da dau, fa wu shang syin.

TO THE DHARMA I RETURN AND RELY, VOWING THAT ALL LIVING BEINGS DEEPLY ENTER THE SUTRA TREASURY AND HAVE WISDOM LIKE THE SEA. ◎•
(bow)

自皈依法，當願眾生，深入經藏，
智慧如海。

Dz gwei yi fa, dang ywan jung sheng, shen ru jing dzang, jr hwei ru hai.

232

TO THE SANGHA I RETURN AND RELY, VOWING THAT ALL LIVING BEINGS, FORM TOGETHER A GREAT ASSEMBLY, ONE AND ALL IN HARMONY.

自皈依僧 當願眾生 統理大眾 一切無礙

Dz gwei yi seng, dang ywan jung sheng, tung li da jung, yi chye wu ai.

(On the word "sheng" of the final recitation, the side of the Assembly that is bowing stands; at the end, the entire Assembly makes one full bow, stands, and half-bows.)

和南聖眾

He nan sheng jung.

(誦至聖字,拜者起立,與大眾一起拜下;再起立;問訊.)

NA MO GWAN SHR YIN BODHISATTVA OF GREAT COMPASSION.

南無大悲觀世音菩薩   三稱

Na mwo da bei gwan shr yin pu sa.

VERSE FOR TRANSFERRING THE MERIT FROM BOWING REPENTANCE

禮懺功德回向

I DEDICATE THE MERIT AND VIRTUE FROM THE PROFOUND ACT OF BOWING REPENTANCE.

禮懺功德殊勝行

Li chan gung de shu sheng heng.

WITH ALL ITS SUPERIOR, LIMITLESS BLESSINGS,

無邊勝福皆回向

Wu byan sheng fu jye hwei syang

WITH THE UNIVERSAL VOW THAT ALL BEINGS SUNK IN DEFILEMENT,

普願沉溺諸眾生

Pu ywan chen ni ju jung sheng

WILL QUICKLY GO TO THE LAND OF THE BUDDHA OF LIMITLESS LIGHT (AMITABHA).

速往無量光佛剎

Shu wang wu lyang gwang fwo cha.

233

ALL BUDDHAS OF THE TEN DIRECTIONS AND THE THREE PERIODS OF
TIME.

十方三世一切佛.

Shr fang san shr yi chye fwo

ALL BODHISATTVAS, MAHASATTVAS. MAHA PRAJNA PARAMITA!

一切菩薩摩訶薩 , 摩訶般若波羅蜜.

Yi chye pu sa mwo he sa   Mwo he bwo re bwo lwo mi.

234

VOW TO BE REBORN IN THE WEST

淨土文

WITH ONE MIND I RETURN MY LIFE TO AMITABHA BUDDHA WHO IS IN
THE LAND OF ULTIMATE BLISS.

一心皈命　極樂世界　阿彌陀佛

Yi syin gwei ming,　ji le shr jye,　A Mi Two Fwo.

WISHING HIS PURE LIGHT ILLUMINES ME AND HIS KIND VOWS GATHER
ME IN.

願以淨光照我　慈誓攝我

Ywan yi jing gwang jau wo, tsz shr she wo.

NOW, WITH PROPER MINDFULNESS, I PRAISE THE THUS COME ONE'S
NAME,

我今正念　稱如來名

Wo jin jeng nyan,　cheng Ru Lai ming,

IN ORDER TO TAKE THE PATH OF BODHI AND TO SEEK REBIRTH IN
THE PURE LAND.

為菩提道　求生淨土

Wei pu ti dau,　chyou sheng jing du.

IN THE PAST, THE BUDDHA VOWED: "IF LIVING BEINGS WHO WISH
FOR REBIRTH IN MY LAND,

佛昔本誓若有眾生　欲生我國

Fwo syi ben shr,　rau you jung sheng,　yu sheng wo gwo,

AND WHO RESOLVE THEIR MINDS WITH FAITH AND JOY EVEN FOR
JUST TEN RECITATIONS, ARE NOT REBORN THERE,

志心信樂　乃至十念若不生者

Jr syin syin le,　nai jr shr nyan,　rau bu sheng je,

I WILL NOT ATTAIN THE PROPER ENLIGHTENMENT."

不取正覺

bu cheu jeng jyau.

THROUGH MINDFULNESS OF THE BUDDHA, I ENTER THE SEA OF THE
THUS COME ONE'S GREAT VOWS,

以此念佛因緣⊙ 得入如來大誓海中

Yi tse nyan Fwo yin ywan, de lu Ru Lai, da shr hai jung.

AND RECEIVE THE POWER OF THE BUDDHA'S KINDNESS. MY MULTITUDE OF OFFENSES IS ERADICATED AND MY GOOD ROOTS INCREASE AND GROW.

承佛慈力 眾罪消滅 善根增長

Cheng Fwo tse li, jung tzwei syau mye, shan gen tseng jang.

AS I APPROACH THE END OF LIFE, I MYSELF WILL KNOW THE TIME OF ITS COMING. MY BODY WILL BE FREE OF ILLNESS AND PAIN.

若臨命終 自知時至 身無病苦

Rau lin ming jung, dz jr shr jr, shen wu bing ku.

MY HEART WILL HAVE NO GREED OR FONDNESS, AND MY THOUGHT WILL NOT BE UPSIDE DOWN, JUST AS IN ENTERING CHAN SAMADHI.

心不貪戀 意不顛倒 如入禪定

Syin bu tan lyan, yi bu dyan dau, ru lu chan ding.

THE BUDDHA AND THE ASSEMBLY OF SAGES, LEADING ME BY THE HAND TO THE GOLDEN DIAS, WILL COME TO WELCOME ME.

佛及聖眾 手執金臺 來迎接我

Fwo ji sheng jung, shou jr jin tai, lai ying jye wo,

AND IN THE SPACE OF A THOUGHT I WILL BE REBORN IN THE LAND OF ULTIMATE BLISS.

於一念頃 生極樂國⊙

Yu yi nyan ching, sheng ji le gwo.

THE FLOWER WILL OPEN, AND I WILL SEE THE BUDDHA, STRAIGHT-WAY HEAR THE BUDDHA VEHICLE,

花開見佛 即聞佛乘

Hwa kai jyan Fwo, ji wen Fwo cheng,

AND IMMEDIATELY ATTAIN THE WISDOM OF A BUDDHA. I WILL CROSS OVER LIVING BEINGS ON A WIDE SCALE, FULFILLING MY BODHI VOWS.

頓開佛慧© 廣度眾生 滿菩提願

Dun kai Fwo hwei, gwang du jung sheng, man pu ti ywan.

ALL BUDDHAS OF THE TEN DIRECTIONS AND THE THREE PERIODS OF TIME!

十方三世一切佛
Shr fang san shr yi chye Fwo!

ALL BODHISATTVAS, MAHASATTVAS!
一切菩薩摩訶薩
Yi chye Pu Sa Mwo He Sa!

MAHA-PRAJNA-PARAMITA!
摩訶般若波羅蜜
Mwo He Bwo Re Bwo Lwo Mi!

****

信

AVATAMSAKA HYMN OF FAITH
--from Chapter Twelve, "Worthy Leader"--

FAITH IS THE SOURCE OF THE WAY;
FAITH IS THE MOTHER OF MERIT AND VIRTUE.
信為道元功德母,
AS THEY ARISE BY FAITH,
ALL WHOLESOME DHARMAS MUST BY FAITH BE NURTURED.
長養一切諸善法,
FAITH CUTS THE TANGLED WEB OF DOUBT,
ESCAPING LOVE'S DELUSIVE FLOW.
斷除疑網出愛流,
AND OPENS WIDE TO REVEAL THE TRUE AND UNSURPASSED NIRVANA'S
ROAD.
開示涅槃無上道.
FAITH HAS NO STAIN OR MAR,
BRINGING THE TURBID MIND PURIFICATION,
信無垢濁心清淨,

237

ERADICATING PRIDE,
OF ALL RESPECT AND REVERENCE THE FOUNDATION.

滅除憍慢恭敬本，

WITHIN THE DHARMA TREASURY
FAITH'S JEWEL OUTSHINES THE FAIREST GOLD;

亦為法藏第一財，

HENCE EVERY CONDUCT OUR HANDS BY FAITH MADE PURE RECEIVE
AND SURELY HOLD.

為清淨手受眾行．

FAITH IS THE HEALING SOURCE
BY WHICH OUR FACULTIES ARE CLEANSED AND QUICKENED.

信令諸根淨明利，

NOTHING CAN TURN ITS FORCE,
THE SOLID POWER OF FAITH CANNOT BE BROKEN.

信力堅固無能壞，

AND WHEN BY FAITH FOREVER
FROM ALL AFFLICTION WE DEPART,

信能永滅煩惱本，

THE BUDDHA'S MERIT WILL THUS BECOME THE SOLE DEVOTION OF
OUR HEARTS.

信能專向佛功德．

WITH FAITH THE MIND'S UNMOVED,
FREE FROM ATTACHMENT TO CONDITIONED ARISING;

信於境界無所著，

DISASTERS FAR REMOVED,
IN THE TRANQUILITY OF FAITH ABIDING.

遠離諸難得無難，

THE BLISS OF FAITH VICTORIOUS!

信樂最勝甚難得，

AMONG THE CONDUCTS OF ALL WORLDS,

譬如一切世間中，

THIS FAITH ALONE IS THE ONE MOST RARE AND PRECIOUS WISH-
FULFILLING PEARL.

而有隨意妙寶珠，

PROFOUNDLY WE BELIEVE:
TRUSTING THE BUDDHAS AND THE BUDDHAS' DHARMA,

深信於佛及佛法，

TREADING THE BODHI-PATH,
FOREVER FOLLOWED BY ALL TRUE DISCIPLES.

亦信佛子所行道，

AND TO THE GREAT ENLIGHTENMENT
OUR THOUGHTS ARE JOYFULLY INCLINED.

及信無上大菩提，

THE BODHISATTVAS WITH THIS DEEP HEART OF FAITH PRODUCE
THE BODHI-MIND!

菩薩以是初發心。

****

THE TRIPLE JEWEL SONG
三寶歌

First Verse:

LONG THE NIGHT OF TIME WE PASS THROUGH, BEING MEN AND GODS.

人天長夜，

Ren tyan chang ye.

IN THE DARKNESS OF THIS COSMOS, WHO WILL BRING FORTH LIGHT?

宇宙黮闇，誰啓以光明？

Yu jou tan an, shwei chi yi gwang ming?

WE HERE IN THE TRIPLE REALM ARE IN A BURNING HOUSE.

三界火宅，

San jye hwo jai.

SUFFERINGS OPPRESS AND VEX US, WHO CAN BRING US PEACE?

眾苦煎迫，誰濟以安寧？

Jung ku jyan pwo, shwei ji yi an ning?

239

KIND AND WISE HEROIC STRENGTH: NA MO BUDDHAS ALL!

大悲大智大雄力，南無佛陀耶！

Da bei da jr da syung li, Na Mwo Fwo Two Ye.

SHINE ON ALL TEN THOUSAND THINGS AND COMFORT ALL THAT LIVES.

照朗萬有，衽席群生，

Jau lang wan you, ren syi chyun sheng.

MERIT'S DEPTH AND VIRTUE'S SCOPE: THERE IS NO WAY TO TELL!

功德莫能名。

Gung de mwo neng ming.

Second Verse:

TWO TRUTHS MESH AND ARE UPHELD AS IN A DHARANI.

二諦總持，

Er di dzung chr,

STUDIES THREE INCREASE TO REACH THE DHARMA REALM IN SCOPE.

三學增上，恢恢法界身．

San shwe dzeng shang, hwei hwei fa jye shen.

WHEN AT LAST PURE VIRTUE'S FULL AND PERFECTLY COMPLETE,

淨德既圓，

Jin de ji ywan.

FILTH IS GONE, DISASTERS CEASE, NIRVANA: HOME SUPREME!

染患斯寂，蕩蕩湼槃城．

Ran hwan sz ji, dang dang nye pan cheng.

ALL IS EMPTY; FROM MIND ONLY: NA MO DHARMAS ALL!

眾緣性空唯識現，南無達摩耶！

Jung ywan sying kung wei shr syan, Na Mwo Da Mwo Ye.

PRINCIPLES REFLECTED, AS ALL COVERINGS DISSOLVE.

理無不彰，蔽無不解，

Li wu bu chang, bi wu bu jye

BRILLIANT IS THIS UNDERSTANDING, VAST AND CLEAR INDEED!

煥乎其大明．

Hwan hu chi da ming.

Third Verse:

PURE COMPORTMENT, PRECEPTS STERN: WE ALL RELY ON RULES.

依淨律儀，

Yi jing lyu yi.

WONDROUS HARMONY OF UNION, MAGIC MOUNTAIN'S TRUTH.

成妙和合，靈山遺芳型．

Cheng myau he he, ling shan yi fang sying.

CULTIVATE AND PRACTICE TO CERTIFY THE FRUITION.

修行證果，

Syou sying jeng gwo.

SPREAD THE DHARMA, HELP THE WORLD, KEEP BUDDHAS' LAMP ALIGHT!

弘法利世，燄續佛燈明．

Hung fa li shr, yan syu Fwo deng ming.

WORTHIES, SAGES--THREE VEHICLES FULL: NA MO SANGHA ALL!

三乘聖賢何濟濟，南無僧伽耶！

San cheng sheng syan syan he ji ji, Na Mwo sheng chye ye.

FORM TOGETHER A GREAT ASSEMBLY, ONE AND ALL IN HARMONY.

統理大象，一切無礙．

Tung li da jung, yi chye wu ai.

GARD AND HELP PROTECT THIS CITY: PROPER DHARMA DWELLS!

住持正法城．

Ju chr jeng fa cheng.

Chorus:

NOW I KNOW, THIS ALONE: THE TRUE REFUGE PLACE.

今乃知，唯此是，真正皈依處．

Jin nai jr, wei tsz shr, jen jeng gwei yi chu.

TO THE EXHAUSTION OF MY LIFE, I WILL CONTRIBUTE MY BODY AND LIFE.

盡形壽，獻身命，

Jin sying shou, syan shen ming,

TO RECEIVE IT WITH FAITH AND DILIGENTLY OFFER UP MY CONDUCT.

信受勤奉行．

Syin shou chin feng sying!

Triple Jewel Song 三 寶 歌

人天長夜， 宇宙諲闇， 誰啓以光 明；
ren tyan chang ye, yu jou tan an, shwei chi yi gwang ming!
二諦總持， 三學增上， 恢恢法界 身．
er di dzung chr, san shwe dzeng shang, hwei hwei fa jye shen.
依淨律儀， 成妙和合， 靈山遺芳 型．
yi jing lyu yi, cheng myau he he, ling shan yi tang sying

三界火宅， 衆苦煎迫， 誰濟以安 寧？
san jye hwo jai, jung ku jyan pai, shwei ji yi an ning?
淨德既圓， 染患斯寂， 蕩蕩涅槃 城．
jing de ji ywan, ran hwan sz ji, dang dang nye pan cheng.
修行證果， 弘法利世， 燄續佛燈 明．
syou sying jeng gwo, hung fa li shr, yan syu fwo deng ming.

大悲大智 大雄力， 南無佛陀 耶！（佛陀耶）
da bei da jr da syung li, na mwo fwo two ye! (fwo two ye)
衆緣性空 唯識現， 南無達摩 耶！（達摩耶）
jung ywan sying kung wei shr syan, na mwo da mwo ye! (da mwo ye)
三衆聖賢 何濟濟， 南無僧伽 耶！（僧伽耶）
san cheng sheng syan he ji ji, na mwo seng chye ye! (seng chye ye)

昭朗萬有 祇席群生， 功德莫能 名．
jau lang wan you, jen syi chyun sheng, gung de mwo neng ming.
理無不影， 蔽無不解， 煥乎其大 明．
li wu bu ying, bi wu bu jye, hwan hu chi da ming.
統理大衆， 一切無礙， 住持正法 城．
tung li da jung, yi chre wu ai, ju chr jeng fa cheng.

今 乃 知 唯此 是， 眞正歸依 處．
jin nai jr, wei tsz shr, jen jeng gwei yi chu.

盡形壽， 獻身命， 信受勤奉 行！
jin sying shou, syan shen ming, syin shou chin feng sying!

盡虛空 *(Jin Syu Kung)*
校 歌 *(School Song)*

法界佛教大學校歌

DHARMA REALM BUDDHIST UNIVERSITY SCHOOL SONG

THE BUDDHA-NATURE FILLS UP EVERYWHERE TO THE ENDS OF EMPTY
SPACE.

盡 虛 空 佛 性 充 滿 了
Jin syu kung Fwo sying tsung man lyau.

THE CONTINUAL GENERATIONS OF SENTIENT BEINGS PERVADE THE
DHARMA REALM.

徧 法 界 有 情 蘊 育 着
Byan fa jye you ching ywun yu jau.

LIVING BEINGS BECOME BUDDHAS; BUDDHAS IN TURN TRANSFORM
THEIR FELLOW BEINGS.

眾 生 成 佛 佛 化 同 胞
Jung sheng cheng Fwo; Fwo hwa tung bau.

THE TEN THOUSAND DHARMAS ARE MADE FROM THE MIND ALONE!
THE TEN THOUSAND DHARMAS ARE MADE FROM THE MIND ALONE!

萬 法 唯 心 造！萬 法 唯 心 造！
Wan fa wei syin dzau! Wan fa wei syin dzau!

UNITED IN OUR SINGLE GOAL, WE REVIVE THE SAGELY TEACHINGS.

團 結 一 致 復 興 聖 教
Twan jye yi jr fu sying sheng jyau.

SHARING BITTERNESS, COURAGEOUSLY STRIVING TOGETHER IN THE WAY,

齊 抖 擻 共 努 力 勇 猛 向 道
Chi dwo swo gung nu li yung meng syang dau.

WE WILL BE OPEN AND FAIR, UNSELFISH, AND ABOVE ALL,
STRAIGHT-MINDED.

要 大 公 除 自 私 直 心 最 好
Yau da gung chu dz sz, jr syin dzwei hau.

WASHING CLEAN THE DEFILING DUST IN THE POOL OF THE SEVEN
JEWELS.

七 寶 池 內 洗 滌 塵 埃
Chi bau shr nei syi di chen ai

244

UNTIL FINALLY, IN THE PURE, CLEAR LIGHT OF THE TEN THOUSAND
BUDDHAS--WONDERFUL ENLIGHTENMENT!

清　淨　光　明　萬　佛　妙　覺
Ching　jing　gwang　ming　wan　Fwo　Myau　Jyau!

THE TEN THOUSAND DHARMAS ARE MADE FROM THE MIND ALONE!
THE TEN THOUSAND DHARMAS ARE MADE FROM THE MIND ALONE!

萬　法　唯　心　造！萬　法　唯　心　造！
Wan　fa　wei　syin　dzau! Wan　fa　wei　syin　dzau!

****

轉法輪
TURNING THE DHARMA WHEEL

THE DHARMA WHEEL IS TURNING 'ROUND,

大　放　光　明　轉　法　輪
Da fang gwang ming jwang fa lwun,

THE LION ROARS HIS EXHORTATION.

師　子　吼　聲　萬　世　尊
Shr dze hou sheng wan shr dzwun.

AND LIVING BEINGS WHO HEAR THE SOUND,

六　道　眾　生　齊　聞　得
Lyou dau jung sheng chi wen de.

ATTAIN THE DOOR OF LIBERATION.

成　就　無　上　解　脫　門
Cheng jyou wu shang jye two meng.

THE DHARMA WHEEL IS TURNING 'ROUND,

大　放　光　明　轉　法　輪
Da fang gwang ming jwung fa lwun.

THE DHARMA WHEEL IS TURNING 'ROUND.

大　放　光　明　轉　法　輪
Da fang gwang ming jwung fa lwun.

****

Study Buddhism

go———— To per - fect———— en

light - en - ment,———————————— To——

per - fect   en - light-en - ment.———

THE DHARMA REALM VERSE:

WITH THE DHARMA REALM AS SUBSTANCE,
  WHAT COULD BE OUTSIDE?
WITH EMPTY SPACE AS FUNCTION
  NOTHING IS EXCLUDED.
THE MYRIAD THINGS ARE
  LEVEL AND EQUAL--
    APART FROM DISCRIMINATIONS.
WHEN NOT A SINGLE THOUGHT
  IS PRODUCED, THAT PUTS AN END
    TO WORDS AND DOCTRINES.

                    CHANCELLOR HUA

THE LUNAR CALENDAR OF THE HOLY ANNIVERSARIES
OF THE BUDDHAS AND BODHISATTVAS

	Lunar Month	Day
Birthday of Maitreya Bodhisattva	1	1
Birthday of Samadhi Light Buddha	1	6
Birthday of the Venerable God Shakra	1	9
Leaving Home Day of Shakyamuni Buddha	2	8
Birthday of the Sixth Patriarch, the Great Master Hui Neng	2	8
Nirvana of Shakyamuni Buddha	2	15
Birthday of Kuan Yin Bodhisattva	2	19
Birthday of Universal Worthy Bodhisattva	2	21
Birthday of the Great Master Ch'ang Ren	3	15
Birthday of Junti Bodhisattva	3	16
Leaving Home Day of the Great Master Ch'ang Chih	3	17
Birthday of Manjushri Bodhisattva	4	4
Birthday of Shakyamuni Buddha	4	8
Summer Retreat for Sangha begins	4	15
Birthday of Medicine King Buddha	4	28
Birthday of Ch'ieh Lan Bodhisattva	5	13
Birthday of Wei T'ou Bodhisattva	6	3
Enlightenment Day of Great Master Ch'ang Ren	6	15
Anniversay of Venerable Master Hua	6	16
Birthday of Great Master Ch'ang Chih	6	17
Day Kuan Yin Bodhisattva Accomplished the way	6	19
Birthday of Great Strength Bodhisattva	7	13
Buddha's Happy Day (Ullambana)	7	15
Birthday of the Patriarch P'u An Bodhisattva	7	21
Birthday of Dragon Tree Bodhisattva	7	24
Birthday of Earth Store Bodhisattva	7	30
Birthday of Elder Master Hsu Yun	7	30
Nirvana of the Sixth Patriarch, the great Master Hui Neng	8	3
Birthday of Burning Lamp Buddha of the Past	8	22
Nirvana of the Elder Master Hsu Yun	9	12
Leaving Home Day of the Great Master Ch'ang Ren	9	15
Leaving Home Day of the Venerable Master Hua	9	16
Enlightenment Day of the Great Master Ch'ang Jr.	9	17
Leaving Home Day of Kuan Yin Bodhisattva	9	19
Birthday of Medicine Master Buddha	9	30
Birthday of the First Patriarch Bodhidharma	10	5
Birthday of Amita Buddha	11	17
Shakyamuni Buddha Accomplished the Way	12	8
Birthday of Avatamsaka Bodhisattva	12	29

諸佛菩薩聖誕（農曆）

彌勒菩薩聖誕...1 月 1 日
定光佛聖誕...1 月 6 日
帝釋天尊聖誕...1 月 9 日
釋迦牟尼佛出家...2 月 8 日
六祖惠能大師聖誕...2 月 8 日
釋迦牟尼佛涅槃...2 月 15 日
觀音菩薩聖誕...2 月 19 日
普賢菩薩聖誕...2 月 21 日
準提菩薩聖誕...3 月 16 日
文殊菩薩聖誕...4 月 4 日
釋迦牟尼佛聖誕...4 月 8 日
藥王菩薩聖誕...4 月 28 日
伽藍菩薩聖誕...5 月 13 日
韋馱菩薩聖誕...6 月 3 日
觀音菩薩成道...6 月 19 日
大勢至菩薩聖誕...7 月 13 日
佛歡喜日...7 月 15 日
普庵祖師聖誕...7 月 21 日
龍樹菩薩聖誕...7 月 24 日
地藏王菩薩聖誕...7 月 30 日
虛雲老和尚誕辰...7 月 30 日
六祖惠能大師涅槃...8 月 3 日
然燈古佛聖誕...8 月 22 日
虛雲老和尚涅槃...9 月 12 日
觀音菩薩出家...9 月 19 日
藥師佛聖誕...9 月 30 日
達摩祖師聖誕...10 月 5 日
阿彌陀佛聖誕...11 月 17 日
釋迦牟尼佛成道...12 月 8 日
華嚴菩薩聖誕...12 月 29 日

觀音齋期表

1 月 8 日	2 月 7 日	2 月 9 日
2 月 19 日	3 月 3 日	3 月 6 日
3 月 13 日	4 月 22 日	5 月 3 日
5 月 17 日	6 月 16 日	6 月 18 日
6 月 19 日	6 月 23 日	7 月 13 日
8 月 16 日	9 月 19 日	9 月 23 日
10 月 2 日	11 月 19 日	11 月 24 日
12 月 25 日		

十齋期

【每月】	1 日	8 日	14 日	15 日
	18 日	23 日	24 日	28 日
	29 日	30 日	（月小 27 日起）	

六齋期

【每月】	8 日	14 日	15 日	23 日
	29 日	30 日	（月小 28 日起）	

南無護法韋陀菩薩
Namo Dharma Protector Weitou Bodhisattva

法界佛教總會簡介

The Dharma Realm Buddhist Association

法界佛教總會是上宣下化老和尚，於 1959 年在美國創立。本會是以法界為體；以將佛教的真實義理，傳播到世界各地為目的；以翻譯經典、弘揚正法、提倡道德教育、利樂一切有情為己任。本著上人所創的六大宗旨——不爭、不貪、不求、不自私、不自利、不妄語。奉行：凍死不攀緣，餓死不化緣，窮死不求緣，隨緣不變，不變隨緣，抱定我們三大宗旨。捨命為佛事，造命為本事，正命為僧事，即事明理，明理即事，推行祖師一脈心傳。數十年來，法總陸續成立了萬佛聖城、法界聖城等國際性道場多處。凡各國各教人士，願致力於仁義道德、明心見性者，皆歡迎前來共同研究、修持學習。

The Dharma Realm Buddhist Association (formerly the Sino-American Buddhist Association) was founded by the Venerable Master Hsuan Hua in the United States of America in 1959 to bring the genuine teachings of the Buddha to the entire world. Its goals are to translate the Buddhist canon, to propagate the Orthodox Dharma, and to promote ethical education. The members of the Association base themselves on Six Ideals established by the Venerable Master which are: no fighting, no greed, no seeking, no selfishness, no pursuing personal advantage, and no lying. Furthermore, they follow Three Great Principles: "Freezing to death, we do not scheme. Starving to death, we do not beg. Dying of poverty, we ask for nothing. According with conditions, we do not change. Not changing, we accord with conditions. We adhere firmly to our three great principles. We renounce our lives to do the Buddha's work. We take the responsibility to mold our own destinies. We rectify our lives as the Sangha's work. Encountering specific matters, we understand the principles. Understanding the principles, we apply them in specific matters. We carry on the single pulse of the patriarch's mind-transmission." Over the years, the Association has founded various international, spiritual communities open to every faith, such as the City of Ten Thousand Buddhas and the City of the Dharma Realm. Any person devoted to kindness, virtue, and truth, who wishes to understand his or her own mind, is welcome to study and cultivate in these communities.

宣化上人簡傳

Venerable Master Hsuan Hua

上人，名安慈，字度輪，接虛雲老和尚法，嗣溈仰，法號宣化。籍東北，誕於清末民初。年十九出家，廬墓守孝，修禪定，習教觀，日一食，夜不臥。1948 年抵香港，成立佛教講堂等道場。1962 年攜正法西來，在美開演大乘經典數十部。歷年來創辦法界佛教總會、萬佛聖城、法界聖城、金山聖寺、國際譯經學院、法界宗教研究院等正法道場二十多處，及法界佛教大學、僧伽居士訓練班、培德中學、育良小學等教育機構。1995 年示寂於美國。上人一生無私之精神，與慈悲智慧之教化，已令無數人改過自新，走向清淨高尚之菩提大道。

The Venerable Master Hua was also known as An Tse and To Lun. The name Hsuan Hua was bestowed upon him after he received the transmission of the Weiyang Lineage of the Chan School from Elder Master Hsu Yun. He was born in Manchuria near the turn of the century and left the home-life at the age of nineteen. After the death of his mother, he lived in a tiny hut by her graveside as an act of filial respect. During that time, he meditated and studied the Buddha's teachings. He ate only one meal a day before noon and never laid down to sleep. In 1948 the Master arrived in Hong Kong, where he founded the Buddhist Lecture Hall and other monasteries. In 1962 he brought the proper Dharma to America and the West, where he lectured extensively on the major works of the Mahayana Buddhist canon and established the Dharma Realm Buddhist Association and over twenty Way-places of the Proper Dharma including the City of Ten Thousand Buddhas, Gold Mountain Monastery, the International Translation Institute, and the Institute of World Religions. He also founded various educational centers, such as the Dharma Realm Buddhist University, Developing Virtue Secondary School, and Instilling Goodness Elementary School. The Master manifested the stillness in America in 1995. His selfless spirit and wise, compassionate teachings inspired many people to correct their faults and to begin to walk upon the pure and lofty path to Bodhi.

法界佛教總會 · 萬佛聖城
Dharma Realm Buddhist Association & The City of Ten Thousand Buddhas
4951 Bodhi Way, Ukiah, CA 95482 U.S.A.
Tel: (707) 462-0939 Fax: (707) 462-0949

國際譯經學院 The International Translation Institute
1777 Murchison Drive, Burlingame, CA 94010-4504 U.S.A.
Tel: (650) 692-5912   Fax: (650) 692-5056

法界宗教研究院（柏克萊寺）
Institute for World Religions (at Berkeley Buddhist Monastery)
2304 McKinley Avenue, Berkeley, CA 94703 U.S.A.
Tel: (510) 848-3440   Fax: (510) 548-4551

金山聖寺 Gold Mountain Monastery
800 Sacramento Street, San Francisco, CA 94108 U.S.A.
Tel: (415) 421-6117   Fax: (415) 788-6001

金聖寺 Gold Sage Monastery
11455 Clayton Road, San Jose, CA 95127 U.S.A.
Tel: (408) 923-7243   Fax: (408) 923-1064

法界聖城 The City of the Dharma Realm
1029 West Capitol Avenue, West Sacramento, CA 95691 U.S.A.
Tel/Fax: (916) 374-8268

金輪聖寺 Gold Wheel Monastery
235 North Avenue 58, Los Angeles, CA 90042 U.S.A.
Tel/Fax: (323) 258-6668

長堤聖寺 Long Beach Monastery
3361 East Ocean Boulevard, Long Beach, CA 90803 U.S.A.
Tel/Fax: (562) 438-8902

華嚴精舍 Avatamsaka Vihara
9601 Seven Locks Road, Bethesda, MD 20817-9997 U.S.A.
Tel/Fax: (301) 469-8300

金峰聖寺 Gold Summit Monastery
233 First Avenue West, Seattle, WA 98119 U.S.A.
Tel: (206) 284-6690   Fax: (206) 284-6918

金佛聖寺 Gold Buddha Monastery
248 E. 11th Avenue, Vancouver, B.C. V5T 2C3 Canada
Tel:(604)709-0248　Fax:(604)684-3754

華嚴聖寺 Avatamsaka Monastery
1009 Fourth Avenue S.W., Calgary, AB T2P 0K8 Canada
Tel/Fax: (403) 234-0644

法界佛教印經會
Dharma Realm Buddhist Books Distribution Society
臺灣省臺北市忠孝東路六段 85 號 11 樓
11th Floor, 85 Chung-Hsiao E. Road, Sec. 6, Taipei, R.O.C.
Tel: (02) 2786-3022, 2786-2474　Fax: (02) 2786-2674

法界聖寺 Dharma Realm Sage Monastery
臺灣省高雄縣六龜鄉興龍村東溪山莊 20 號
20, Tung-hsi Shan-chuang, Hsing-lung Village, Liu-Kuei,
Kaohsiung County, Taiwan, R.O.C.
Tel: (07) 689-3713　Fax: (07) 689-3870

彌陀聖寺 Amitabha Monastery
臺灣省花蓮縣壽豐鄉池南村四健會 7 號
7, Su-chien-hui, Chih-nan Village, Shou-Feng, Hualien County, Taiwan, R.O.C.
Tel: (03) 865-1956　Fax:(03) 865-3426

般若觀音聖寺(紫雲洞觀音寺)
Prajna Guanyin Sagely Monastery(formerly Tze Yun Tung Temple)
Batu 5 1/2, Jalan Sungai Besi, Salak Selatan, 57100 Kuala Lumpur, Malaysia
Tel: (03)7982-6560　Fax: (03) 7980-1272

登彼岸觀音堂 Deng Bi An Temple
161, Jalan Ampang, 50450 Kuala Lumpur, Malaysia
Tel: (03) 2164-8055　Fax: (03) 2163-7118

蓮華精舍 Lotus Vihara
136, Jalan Sekolah, 45600 Batang Berjuntai, Selangor Darul Ehsan, Malaysia
Tel: (03) 3271-9439

佛教講堂 Buddhist Lecture Hall
香港跑馬地黃泥涌道 31 號 11 樓
31 Wong Nei Chong Road, Top Floor, Happy Valley, Hong Kong, China
Tel:(2)2572-7644　Fax:(2)2572-2850

萬佛聖城日誦儀規

西曆二〇〇三年五月八日 · 七版
佛曆三〇三〇年四月初八 · 釋迦牟尼佛聖誕

發行人　法界佛教總會

出　版　法界佛教總會 · 佛經翻譯委員會 · 法界佛教大學

地　址　Dharma Realm Buddhist Association &

　　　　The City of Ten Thousand Buddhas

　　　　4951 Bodhi Way, Ukiah, CA 95482 U.S.A.

　　　　電話: (707) 462-0939　傳真: (707) 462-0949

　　　　The International Translation Institute

　　　　1777 Murchison Drive Burlingame, CA 94010-4504 U.S.A.

　　　　電話: (650) 692-5912　傳真: (650) 692-5056

倡　印　美國法界佛教總會駐華辦事處 (法界佛教印經會)

　　　　臺灣省臺北市忠孝東路六段 85 號 11 樓

　　　　電話: (02) 2786-3022, 2786-2474　傳真: (02) 2786-2674

　　　　劃撥帳號:1321798-5　帳戶: 張淑彤

　　　　法界文教基金會

　　　　臺灣省高雄縣六龜鄉興龍村東溪山莊 20 號

　　　　電話: (07) 689-3713

ISBN 0-88139-857-8

● 佛典所在，即佛所在，請恭敬尊重，廣為流通。